Richard Baxter

The Cure of Church Divisions

Or, directions for weak Christians, to keep them from being dividers, or troublers of the church: with some directions to the pastors, how to deal with such Christians

Richard Baxter

The Cure of Church Divisions
Or, directions for weak Christians, to keep them from being dividers, or troublers of the church: with some directions to the pastors, how to deal with such Christians

ISBN/EAN: 9783337042264

Printed in Europe, USA, Canada, Australia, Japan

Cover: Foto ©Lupo / pixelio.de

More available books at **www.hansebooks.com**

THE CURE
OF
CHURCH-DIVISIONS:

OR
Directions for weak Christians, to keep them from being Dividers, or Troublers of the Church.
With some Directions to the Pastors, how to deal with such Christians.

The Third Edition.

By RICHARD BAXTER.

Joh. 17. 21. *That they all may be one, as thou, Father art in me and I in thee: that they also may be one in us, that the World may believe that thou hast sent me.* 22. *And the glory which thou gavest me, I have given them, that they may be One, even as We are One.* 23. *I in them, and thou in me, that they may be made Perfect in One; and that the world may know that thou hast sent me, and hast Loved them, as thou hast Loved me.*

1 Cor. 1. 10. *Now I beseech you, brethren, by the name of our Lord Jesus Christ, that ye all speak the same thing, and that there be no divisions among you: but that ye be perfectly joyned together in the same mind, and in the same judgement.*

1 Cor. 3. 3. *For ye are yet carnal: for whereas there is among you envying and strife and divisions, are ye not carnal, and walk as men?*

London, Printed for *Nevil Symmons* at the three Crowns over against *Holborn Conduit*. 1670.

III. *Prognosticks of this Book.*

1. IT is none of the business of this book to single out any one Party in the world, and to tell you by Application how farr they are under the guilt of Schism: I meddle with the *Cause*, & leave each person to make application to himself. It is SIMPLE CATHOLICK CHRISTIANITY which I plead for, and the *Love* and *Unity* and *Concord* which are its Ligaments and Essentiall parts. And it is a SECT as a SECT, and a FACTION as a faction, and not this or that *Sect* or Faction, which I detect and blame. Yet I doubt not but as in the same City there are the *wise* and the *foolish*, the *sound* and the *sick*, and in the same Army there are *valiant* men, and Cowards, so in the same Churches there are Christians of various degrees of *wisdom Integrity* and *strength*: And all men should earnestly desire to be of the *wisest*, the *Holiest* and the most *fruitful* sort, and not of

the more *erronious*, *impure*, or *scandalous* and unprofitable. And if the *sick* will make themselves a *Party*, and call the *sound*, the *Adverse Party*, I will endeavour to be one of a *Party* in that sence; and to *obey* God as exactly as I am able, and to *worship* him as *spiritually* and *holily* as I can, and to Love him with all my *mind*, and *heart*, and *strength*, and lament that I can reach no higher, and do no more: and if any will call this by the name of Heresie or Schism, they shall see that I can avoid Heresie and Schism at as dear a rate, as enduring the Name and Imputation of that which I avoid. It is not the Name of a Schismatick that I am writing against, but the *Thing*, by what ever *Name* it is called. It is UNITY, LOVE and PEACE which I am pleading for: and it is DIVISIONS, HATRED, and CONTENTION which I plead against: and it is the *Hypocrisie* of men which I detect, who betray *Love*, *Unity*, and *Peace* by a *Judas* kiss; and will not, or dare not openly renounce them, and defie them, but kill them with dissembling kindness: who cry them up, while they tread them down and *follow peace* with all men, that are not of their *party*, as the Dog followeth the Hare, to tear it in pieces and destroy it: Who fight for LOVE by making o-
thers

thers seem *odious* and *unlovely*; By evil surmisings, proud undervaluing the worth of others, busie and groundless censuring of men, whose case they knew not; aggravating frailties; stigmatizing the persons, the actions, the worship and religious performances of dissenters, with such odious terrible names, and Characters, as their pride and faction do suggest; and all this to strengthen the interest of their *side* and *party*, and to make themselves and their consenters to seem *wise* and *good*, by makeing others seem *foolish* and *bad*: Though they thereby proclaim themselves to be so much the worst, by how much they are most void of *Love*. They are all for *Concord*, but it is only on their narrow factious terms; They are for *Peace*; but it is not of the whole *street*, but of *their house* alone; or not of the whole *City*, but of their *street* alone; or not of the whole *Kingdome*, but of their *City* alone. O what a blessed thing were *peace*, if all would derive it from *their wills*, and terminate it in their *interest*, and they might be the *Center* of *Unity* to the world! that is, that they might be *Gods* or *Christs*! such excellent Architects are they that they can build *Christs* house by pulling it in Peices; and such excellent Chirurgeons, that they will heal Christs body by

A 3   separating

separating the members, and can make as many *Bodies* as there are separated parts.

2. Nor is it any or much of the business of this book, to speak to those that I think are deepliest guilty of the Schisms of the Christian world: For they are out of hearing, & will not read or regard my writings. It is the *Roman* Head and Center of Unity which hath done most to divide the Church. And it is the contending of *Rome* and *Constantinople* for the Supremacy which hath made the greatest Schisms that the Christian world hath known: And the *Regiment* of such Lords must be answerable to their *Power* and Greatness, and the simple terms of Christian Unity left us by Christ and his Apostles, must be turned into a Religion large as the Decrees of all the Councels, and (say half of them) and the Popes Decretals also. And that there may be no way out of this wilderness, but the *Confessors present will*, you must not in all these so much as distinguish *fundamentals* from the rest; but so much *material belief* is *necessary to Salvation*, as each mans opportunities and helps obliged him to receive; that is, The faith which is necessary to Salvation (materially or objectively) is as various as the number of persons in the world; To one more is necessary, to ano-

ther less, to some none at all of the Christian faith). And you must suppose that the Priest is well acquainted with the internal capacity of every mans Soul, and with all the instructions, opportunities, and suggestions of his whole life, and can tell what measure of belief he hath, and whether it be proportionable to his helps; and so can tell him whether he be capable of Salvation, though neither Pope nor Councel have given any standard by which to judge. And though no man can be assured of his own Salvation; and though another man could not be saved by the faith that saveth *him*. So much are we mistaken to think that it is the *Pope* that hath the Keys of Heaven, when it is every Priest, who is the only judge of the measures of the persons faith. These new made multiplied Articles of Religion, these Additions to Christianity, this proud Church-tyranny, I doubt not is the great cause of Schism in the world: And when I have had opportunity to write against it, I have born my testimony against it, as is yet legible. But it is not that sort of men that I am here most to speak to; but to them that profess to be more teachable and willing to know the truth.

3. And yet I add, though this Book be written principally to save the darker sort of honest Christians, from the sin and misery of Church-divisions, I write it not principally for them to read; For I know their prejudice, weakness and incapacity, after-mentioned: But I write it to remember the Teachers of the *Churches*, what principles they have to preach and strengthen, and what Principles to confute and to destroy, if ever they mean to save the people from this state of sin, and the Churches from the sad effects. And if Ministers neglect the faithful discharge of so great and necessary a duty, let them remember that they were warned, if they find themselves overwhelmed in the ruines.

II. The *Reasons* moveing me to this work are these.

First, It is my calling to help to save people from their sins; and Church-division is a heap of sins.

2. The more I love them that I hope are Tender-conscienced, and dare not sin, when they are convinced of it, the more I am bound to endeavour their conviction, remembring who hath said, *Thou shalt not hate thy Brother in thy heart, thou shalt in any wise rebuke thy Neighbour, and not suffer sin upon him*, Lev. 19. 17. 3. LOVE

3. LOVE is not an appertinance of my Religion, but my Religion it self. *God is Love, and he that dwelleth in Love, dwelleth in God, and God in him*: (who can speak a higher word of any thing in all the world?) Love is the end of faith, and faith is but the Bellows to kindle Love: Love is the fulfilling of all the Law; the end of the Gospel; the nature and mark of Chrifts Difciples; the divine nature; the fum of holinefs to the Lord; the proper note by which to know, what is the man, and what his ftate, and how far any of his other acts are acceptable unto God: without which, if we had all knowledge and belief, all gifts of utterance and higheft profeffion, we were but as founding Brafs; and as a tinkling Cymbal. And if all our goods were given to the poor, and our bodies to the fire, it would profit nothing. Love is our foretaft of Heaven, and the perfection of it is Heaven it felf, even the ftate and work of Angels and of Saints in glory. And he that is angry with me, for calling men to Love, is angry for calling them to *Holinefs* to God and *Heaven*. *Holinefs* which is againft *Love* is a contradiction: it is a deceitful *Name*, which Satan putteth upon *unholinefs*. All Church principles which are againft Univerfal *Love*, are againft *God*, and *Holinefs*.

and the Churches *life*. And he that saith, he loveth God, and hateth his Brother is a Lyar. To be *holy* without *Love*, is to *see* without *light*, to *live* without *life*. He that said, *The wisdom from above is first pure, then peaceable, gentle*, &c. did no more dream of separating them, then of dividing the *head* of a man from his *heart*, to save his life: *Jam.* 3. 17. Nor no more than he that said, *Follow peace with all men, and Holiness*: *Heb.* 12. 14. No necessity can justifie such a division: *Holiness* and *Love* to God, are but two names for one thing. *Love to God* and to *man*, are like *Soul* and *Body*, that are separated no way but by death. *Love* and *Peaceableness*, differ but as *Reason* and *Reasoning*: Love may be without *Passive Peace* (from others to us,) but never without *Active Peace* (from us to others)

4. I have had so great opportunity in my time, to see the working of the mystery of iniquity, against Christian Love, and to see in what manner Chrifts House and Kingdome is edified by divisions, that if I be ignorant after such sad experience, I must be utterly unexcusable, and of a seared Conscience, and a heart that seemeth hardened to perdition. God knoweth how hardly sin is known in its secret root, till men have tasted the bitterness of the fruit:
Therefore

Therefore he hath permitted the *two Extreams* to shew themselves openly to the world in the effects: And *one* must be noted and hated and avoided, as well as the *other*. I thought once that all that talk against *Schism* and *Sects*, did but vent their malice against the best Christians, under those names: But since then I have seen what Love-killing principles have done! I have long stood by while Churches have been divided and sub-divided; one Congregation of the division labouring to make the other contemptible and odious; and this called, the *Preaching of truth, and the purer worshiping of God*: I have seen this grow up to the height of *Ranters* in horrid Blasphemies, and then of *Quakers*, in disdainful pride and surliness; and into the way of *Seekers*, that were to seek for a Ministry, a Church, a Scripture, and consequently a Christ. I have many a time heard it break out into more horrid revilings of the best Ministry and Godliest people, than ever I heard from the most malignant Drunkard: I have lived to see it put to the Question in that which they called, the *little Parliament*, whether all the Ministers of the Parishes of *England* should be put down at once. When *Love* was first killed in their own breasts, by these

fame

same principles, which I here detect, I have seen how confidently the killing of the King, the Rebellious demolishing of the Government of the Land, the killing of many Thousands of their Bretheren, the turnings and overturnings of all kinds of Rule, even that which they themselves set up, have been committed, and justified, and prophanely fathered upon God. These with much more such fruits of Love-killing principles, and divisions I have seen. And I have seen what fierce, censurors, proud, unchristian tempers they have caused or signified; In a word, I have long seen that *envious wisdom* (whatever it pretend) *is not from above, but is earthly sensual and devilish*; and that *where envy and strife is* upon pretence of Religious precedency of wisdom, there is *confusion and every evil work*, Jam. 3. 15,16. And if after so long, so sad, so notorious experience, you would have me still to be tender of the brood of Hell, I mean these *Love-destroying wayes*, and to shew any countenance to that which really hath done all this, you would have me as blind as the *Sodomites*, and as obdurate as *Pharaoh* and his *Egyptians*, and utterly resolved never to learn the will of God, or to regard either good or evil in the world.

5. The same sins are continued in without repentance. The same *pride* and *ignorance* is still keeping open our divisions: and if after such warnings, as the world scarce ever had the like, we shall be still impenitent; if we shall sin our selves into suffering, and sin in our suffering as we did before, even the very same sin of *Divisions* which brought us to it; how heinous is our Crime, and how dreadful the Prognostick of our greater ruine; and how guilty are those Ministers of the blood of Souls, that will not tell men of the sin and danger.

6. I know that *Dividing Principles* and *Dispositions*, do tend directly to the ruine and damnation of those in whom they do prevail. That which killeth *Love*, killeth all grace and holiness, and killeth Souls: That which quencheth Love, quencheth the Spirit (a thousand fold more then the restraining of our gifts of utterance doth:) That which banisheth Love, banisheth God. That which is against *Love*, is against the design of Christ in our Redemption, and therefore may well be called Antichristian: and if the *Roman Kingdom* (for so it is rather to be called than a *Church*) had not such *Moral* marks of Antichristianity, (which Dr. *More* hath notably opened

in

in his *Myſtery of iniquity*;) if they were not the Engineers for the *Diviſion* of the Chriſtian world; by a falſe *Center*, and by impoſſible terms of Unity, and by the engine of *tearing dividing impoſitions*; if among them were not found the blood of the Saints and the Martyrs of Jeſus, I ſhould in charity, fear to ſuſpect them of Antichriſtianity, notwithſtanding all the Prophetical paſſages which ſeem otherwiſe to point them out; becauſe I ſhould ſtill ſuſpect my underſtanding of thoſe prophecies, when the law of *Loving my neighbour as my ſelf*, is plain to all.

They are dangerouſly miſtaken that think that Satan hath but one way to mens damnation. There are as many wayes to Hell, as there be to the extinguiſhing of *Love*. And all tendeth unto this, which tendeth to hide or deny the *Lovelineſs*, that is, the *Goodneſs*, of them whom I muſt Love: much more that which repreſenteth them as *odious*. And there are many pretenſes and wayes to make my neighbour ſeem unlovely to me: One doth it as effectually by unjuſt or unproved accuſations of *ungodlineſs*, or ſaying, Their worſhip is Antichriſtian, formal, ridiculous, vain; as another doth by unjuſt and unproved accuſations of Schiſm, Diſobedience

or

or Sedition. And they that love Godliness, may be tempted to cast off their love of their Neighbours, yea of the truly Godly, when they once believe that they are ungodly. And the white Devil is a Love-killer as well as the black. He is as mortal an enemy to Love, who backbiteth another, and saith, he is Prophane, or he is an empty formalist, or he is a lukewarm temporizing complying man-pleaser] as he that saith [He is a pievish factious Hypocrite.] I am sure he was no Malignant, nor intended to gird at Godliness, nor to grieve good men, who told us that it is Satans way to transform himself into an Angel of Light (that is, one that pretendeth to make higher motions for Light & for Religious strictness, than Christ himself doth;) and that his Ministers are sent forth by him as *Ministers of Righteousness*, 2 Cor. 11. 14, 15, 16. who will seem more righteous, than the Preachers of truth. Satan will pretend to any sort of strictness, by which he can but mortifie Love. If you can devise any such strictness of opinions, or exactness in Church orders, or strictness in worship, as will but help to *kill mens love*, and set the Churches in divisions, Satan will be your helper, and will be the strictest and exactest of you all: he will reprove
Christ

Christ as a Sabbath-breaker, and as a gluttenous person, and a Wine-bibber, and a friend (or Companion) of Publicans and Sinners, and as an enemy to *Cæsar* too. We are not altogether *ignorant of his wiles*, as young unexperienced Christians are. You think when a wrathful envious heat is kindled in you against men for their faults, that it is certainly a zeal of Gods exciting: But mark whether it have not more *wrath* than *Love* in it: and whether it tend not more to *disgrace* your brother than to *cure* him, or to *make parties* and *divisions*, than to *heal* them: If it be so, if St. *James* be not deceived, you are deceived as to the author of your zeal, *Jam.* 3. 15, 16. and it hath a worse Original than you suspect. It is one of the greatest reasons which maketh me hate Romish Church tyranny, and Religious cruelties against dissenters, because as they come from want of Love, so I am sure that they tend to destroy the Love of those on whom they are inflicted, and to do more hurt to their Souls than to their Bodies. The Devil is not so silly an Angler as to fish with the bare Hook; nor such a Fool as when he would damn men, to intreat them openly to be damned; nor when he would kill mens Love, to intreat them plainly, not to Love but hate their neighbours:

neighbours: But he doth it by making you believe that there is juft and neceſſary cauſe for it; and that it is your duty, and that you ſhould be lukewarm in the cauſe of God, of truth, of Godlineſs, if you did not do it: that ſo you may go on without ſcruple, and do ſo again, and not repent. Even they that killed *Chriſts Apoſtles*, did it as a *duty*, and a part of the ſervice of God, *Joh.* 16. 2. And *Paul* himſelf did once think *verily that he ought to do many things* which he did, againſt the *Name* and Cauſe and Servants of Jeſus, *Act.* 26. 9. And as he did, ſo he was done by; and as he meaſured to others, it was meaſured to him again; For they that *bound themſelves in an Oath* to *kill him*, did deeply intereſs God and Conſcience in the cruelty. But believe it, it is *Apoſtacy* to fall from Love: your Souls dye, when Love dieth. The opinions, the Church Principles, the ſideings, the Practiſes, which deſtroy your *love*, deſtroy your *graces* and your *ſouls*. You *die* while you have a name to *live*, and think that you grow apace in Religion. Therefore better underſtand the Tempter; and when backbiters are deriding or vilifying your neighbours, take it to ſignifie in plain Engliſh [I pray you love not theſe men, but hate them.] And I have told you

you in this treatife, that when one faith unjuftly [*kill them, banifh them*] and another faith [*Have no Communion with them*] it is too often the fame inward affection which both exprefs, but in various wayes: They are agreed in the affumption, that their neighbour is *unlovely*.

And when Love is dead, and yet religion feemeth to fervive and to be increafed by it, it is lamentable to think what a degenerate, fcandalous, hypocritical Religon that will be, and how odious and difhonourable to God. To preach without Love, and to hear without Love, and to pray without Love, and to communicate without Love, to any that differ from your Sect, O what a loathfome facrifice is it, to the God of Love? If we muft leave our gift at the *Altar*, till we are reconciled to one offended brother, what a gift is theirs, who are unreconciled to almoft all the Churches of Chrift? or to multitudes of their Bretheren, becaufe they are not of their way? yea, that make their communion the very badge and means of their uncharitablenefs and divifions? Sirs, thefe are not matters of indifferency, nor to be indulged by any faithful Paftor of the Church.

7. And I know that thefe principles are as mortal to the *Churches*, as they are to

Souls. And that if ever the Churches have peace, prosperity or healing, it must be by the means of *Love* and *Concord*, and by destroying the *principles* which would destroy them. One thinketh that it must be by a *Spanish* Inquisition, and by forcing or killing the dissenters; And another thinketh it must be by Excommunicating them all, and making them odious, and making their own party seem thereby to be better than theirs. But I *know* that it must be by revived *Love*, or it will never be. I *know it*, and whoever is angry with me for it, I cannot choose but know it. When the Papists had murdered so many hundred thousands of the *Albigenses* and *Waldenses*, who would have thought, but they had done their work? When the *French* Massacre had murdered 30000 or 40000, and dispatcht the Leaders of the *Protestant* party, who would have thought that they had but strengthened them? When the Duke *D'Alva* had done so much to drown the *Belgick* Protestants in Blood, he little thought that he was but fortifying them. Queen *Maries* Bishops little thought that their English Bonfires were but to light men to see the mischief of their cause; and like the firing of a *Beacon* to call all the Land to take them for the Enemies of man-kind

kind; and that the cafe would have been fo quickly altered. When the Irifh had murdered two hundred thoufand, they little thought that they had but excited the Survivers to a terrible revenge. I will come no nearer, but you may eafily do it your felves. *If we bite and devour one another, we shall be devoured one of another,* Gal. 5.15. The queftion is, but who fhall be *devoured first*, and who referved for the fecond courfe. *If any man have an ear to hear let him hear*: *He that leadeth into captivity shall go into captivitie*: *He that killeth with the Sword, must be killed with the Sword*: *Here is the Patience and Faith of the Saints*. Rev. 13. 9, 10. God Ruleth the world ftill when he worketh not miracles! Have we not feen a proud Victorious Army diffolved without a drop of blood? and have we not feen that God approveth not of proud felf-exaltation, and violating the Sacred power of our Governours, and ufurping their places of Authority: Hath not the drunken world had yet experience enough to teach them, that the Church of God is not to be built up or repaired, by their tumultuous quarrellings and frayes.

How long Lord, muft thy Church and Caufe, be in the hands of unexperienced furious fools, who know not what Holinefs

or

or Healing is, but think that victory over mens Bodies, must be the cure of their Souls, and that hurting them is the way to win their Love! or that a Church is constituted of *Bodies* alone while *Souls* are absent, or no parts! who will make themselves the Rulers of thy Flock in despite of thee and of thy Cause and Servants, without thy call or approbation, and think that the work of a Soldier, is the work of a *Father* and a *Physician*! whose cures are all by amputation; and whose piety consisteth in flying from each other, and esteeming and using their Brethren as their foes; who scatter thy flocks on all the mountains, when Christ hath prayed that they may all be one!

Perhaps, Reader, thou art one of them that thinketh, that the settlement and happiness of the Church, must be won like a game at foot-ball; and therefore scruplest not to toss it in the dirt, and tumultuously to strive with and strike up the heels of all that are against thee, (so that peaceable passengers cannot safely come near your game or pass the streets.) But when you have got the Ball, have you done the work? Are you still so ignorant as not to know, how uncertain still you are to keep it, and that one spurn can take it from you? and suppose you could secure all your conquests, are the Churches healed ever the more? Mens *hearts* must be conquered before this healing work is done. And therefore the Apostle saith that *we are more than Conquerours*, when we are killed all the *day long* and *accounted* as Sheep to the *slaughter*, Rom. 8. 34, 35. that is, it is more gain and honour to our selves, to suffer in faith and patience by our enemies, than to conquer them in the field; and it is more profitable also unto them, and tendeth to a more desirable conquest of them: Because when Conquerors do but exasperate them; and if we hurt their bodies, we harden them the more against our cause, and against the means of their own Salvation, our patient Martyrdom and suffering by them, may tend at last to open their eyes, and turn their hearts, and save their souls, by shewing them the *Truth*, the *Goodness* and the *Power* of Christ, and of his Word and Spirit. This is the meaning of being more than Conquerours. The *Irish* are conquered by us, but not converted: The *Scots* and *English* were conquered by *Cromwell*, but their *hearts* were not conquered, nor their Religion changed by him. They that think that they could get and keep the upper ground, and have Dissenters bodies and estates

estates at their will, they could soon settle the Church in Unity and Concord, do tell all the world, how ignorant they are of the nature of Christianity, and of the fear of God, and of the *means* of the *peace* and *Concord* of the Church: Either *you* would give up your *own judgments* and *Consciences*, or *practice* your selves to the will of men, if you were in their power, or not. If *you would not*, why should you think that *others* will? If you would, you do but tell the world, that you are Atheists, and have neither a God, nor Cnscience, nor Religion. But it is not evidence enough of your folly, to say in your hearts there is no God, and to fear them that can but kill the body, more than him that can punish both body and soul in hell; but you must also shew that you know neither God nor Man, by thinking that all others are Atheists also, and judging of them by your selves; as if they set their *Souls* and their everlasting hopes, at as base a price as you do yours. I tell you again that a battel or a foot-ball skuffle will not settle, the discomposed and divided Churches; unless you think that a heap of Carkasses slain in the field, possess the quietness, and concord which you desire: The *Soul* is the man, and *Love* is the Christian Life, and the true Cement of the Churches unity; and Love muſt cauſe Love, as Fire cauſeth Fire; and hurtful wrath doth moſt powerfully quench it, and hath theſe fifteen hundred years, (but eſpecially theſe thirteen hundred) been the wolviſh Scatterer of the flocks of Chriſt: And muſt that be now the way to build it, which hath ſo long been the way to pull it down. It is *Love* that muſt be our Union, and Love that muſt cauſe it, or we ſhall never have the Union of a Chriſtian Church. By this ſhall all men know that you are Chriſts Diſciples, if you have Love one to another. If you believe not this, pretend not to believe in Jeſus Chriſt, who doth affirm it.

I confeſs I am ſo far guilty of ſuperſtition my ſelf, that if I had been one of the *Changers* of our *ancient Government*, I ſhould have been ſomewhat the more backward for his *Nameſake*, to the beheading of *Chriſtopher Love*, leſt it ſhould be an ill *Omen* both to Church and State, but eſpecially to the *Actors* of it.

8. Another of the Motives of this Diſcourſe is, becauſe I know that times of moſt temptation, are times of greateſt danger, and commonly of greateſt ſin. And all faithful Paſtors muſt know what are the ſpecial Temptations of the Time and

and Place where they live in. When had we ever greater Temptations to Love-killing principles and practices than now, except in the times of the miserable Wars? I need not name them to you. The harder it is for men to Love them that hate them, that censure them unjustly, that revile them, and reproach them, and make them odious, or that hurt them, the more cause have Ministers and all Christians to set a double watch upon their love; Lest before they are aware, a *flaming* and consuming zeal, do tell others that *they know not what manner of Spirit they are of*, Luk. 9. 55.

9. Yea it is not only a time of great Temptation to this sin, but of *common guilt*: They are multitudes that are overtaken already with this sin. Is not the Land in a continual *heart war*? Are there not parties against parties, and cause against cause, and heart-risings, and passion, and censurings of Dissenters, to say no worse? And is it not time to bring water when we see the flames?

10. And I perceive *few know* so heinous a sin to be any *sin at all*; But all factions and parties are still justifying their Love-killing wayes; and reproaching those whom they have wronged; As if when they have sinfully withdrawn their Love from them, it were

were no crime to take away next, their good names, and all that they have but power to take away. And when they have cast their bretheren out of their *estimation* and *affection*, they think it a piece of commendable zeal or justice, to cast them out of Christian communion, and if they could out of the land and of the world. And shall Ministers stand by, and see men take such *sin* for *duty*, and *serve God* by abusing his *Servants*, and look for a *reward* for *dividing* and *pulling down* his Church, and never tell them what they are a doing?

11. And the old *Non*-conformists who wrote so much against separation, were neither *blind* nor *temporizers*. They saw the danger on that side. Even Brightman on *Rev.* that writeth against the Prelacy and Ceremonies, severely reprehendeth the separatists. Read but the writings of Mr. *John Paget*, Mr. *John Ball*, Mr. *Hildersham*, Mr. *Bradshaw*, Mr. *Baine*, Mr. *Rathban*, and many such others against the separarists of those times, and you may learn that our Light is not *greater* but *less* than theirs, and that we see not further into that cause than they did; and that change of times doth not change the truth; nor will warrant us to change our Religion, unless we will make our Religion subject to the wills and inte-

rests of men, and change it as oft as the times shall change.

12. Lastly, if your *friends* tell you not of your *faults* and *errors* in *Love*, those whom you account your *enemies* will do it in *wrath*. And though all sober Christians should learn by the keenest rebukes of their Adversaries, yet passion and prejudice maketh it so difficult, that it usually hardeneth men more in their sin: And this is another thing, which causeth me the more to abhor division, and to long for the reconciling of the minds of all dissenting Christians; Because while they take each other for adversaries, nothing that is written or said by any is like to do the Adversaries any good. Nay I must confess when I see an adversary tell men of their sin, especially with furious spleen and wrath, mixing together words and swords, I am greatly afraid, lest by that temptation, Satan will draw the reproved to impenitency, and greatly harden them in their sin, and make them glory in that as a virtue, which such a person doth so reprove.

But if you will neither hear of your sin nor duty by adversaries nor friends, by fair speeches nor by foul, you fasten the guilt upon your selves. Remember I pray you, that I am not kindling fires, nor drawing
Swords

Swords against you, nor stirring up any to do you hurt, but only perswading all dissenters to love one another, and to forbear but all that is contrary to love. And if such an exhortation and advice seem injurious or intollerable to you, the Lord have mercy on your Souls.

III. And now without a spirit of Prophecy; I will foretell what entertainment this Paper must expect.

1. Some on the one side will say, It is sharper and rounder dealing than all this, that must cure the Schismes in the Church: And if you would heal our Divisions, why do you not conform your self, but stand out as one of the party that divideth?

2. Some on the other side will say, that it is an unseasonable time, when so much anger is breaking forth against those that we account *Dividers*, to mention their faults, and so to stir up more. I will give these men no other answer, than to bid them read the last part of this Book; or else do not talk till they know of what.

3. And some will say that I am doing that which will prove a hurt to my self and others. For if I should draw the People to Communion with the Conformists, there would little compassion be shewed to the Ministers that cannot conform. But selfish

fish wisdome must be shut out of the Council when we are consulting about the healing of the Churches, and the good of Souls. And indeed there is little danger of this consequence, as long as the people are far more averse to Communion or Concord with the parish-churches, than the Nonconforming Ministers are. But suppose it prove true, should wee not doe good to Souls, and save men from sin, and heal divisions, at the dearest rate? what though it cost us more than is here mentioned? The reviving of decayed Love, and the closure of any of the Churches wounds, is a recompence worth our liberties and lives.

4. And those that are most guilty of the Love-killing principles here detected, and are most eminent in *self-conceited ignorance,* will do by me and by this book, according to their principles, and as they use to do by others. Before they have soberly read it over, they will carry about the Sectarian reports of it from hand to hand; And when one hath said it, the rest will affirm it, that [I have clawed with one party, & have girded at the other, and have sought to make them odious by bringing them under the reproach of Separation, and of censuring and avoiding the ungodly; and that being lukewarm my selfe, and a complyer with sin, I
would

would have all others do so too: And that these Reconcilers are neither flesh nor fish, and attempt impossibilities, even to reconcile light and darkness, Christ and Belial; and that for the sake of Peace we would sell the Truth, and would let in Church-corruptions out of an over-eager desire of agreement: And when they have all done, neither party will regard them, but they shall fare worse than any others; and will lose both sides, whilst they are for neither.] I know it is the nature of the disease which I am curing, to send forth such breath and scents as these; and I intend not to bestow a word to answer them.

5. And some of the wise and sober Ministers, who mark more the inconveniences of one side, than of the other, and look more to *outward occurences,* than to the *Rule,* and to the inward state of Souls; especially such as have not seen the times and things that I have seen, will think that though all this be true, it is unseasonable, and may give advantage to such as love not Reformation. And to them I shall return this answer. 1. That if we stay seven years more for a seasonable time, to oppose the radical sin of uncharitableness, we may be in our graves, and the sinners in their graves, and the sin may be multiplyed and rooted past all hope

of remedy. And why may you not as well stay seven years more, for a seasonable time, to Preach down all other sins as well as this? Is this the least malignant, or least dangerous sin? 2. There was never a more seasonable time to tell men of their sin, than when the temptation to it is the greatest; when it is most growing and multiplying among us; When God hath been so heinously dishonoured by it; when the world doth ring of it; when many Volumes reproach them for it; And when the sensual and ungodly are hardened by it in their scorn of godliness, to the apparent peril of their damnation: Yea more, to turn our complaints from our Law-givers upon our selves. It is *want* of *Love*, and it is *Dividing* principles and practices, that have silenced so many Ministers, and brought us into all the confusions and calamities which we see and undergo.

6. But there are many sincere and considerate Ministers, who knowing this which I say to be true, will be the more excited by it to lead the younger and passionate sort of Religious people, into the wayes of Love and peace, and to save them from the dangers here detected, and, perswade them to the practise of these Directions. And for the use of these I write this Book.

And

And yet, to end as I began, I muſt add theſe notices, for your right underſtanding of it.

1. That this is not my firſt attempt upon this work; but the progreſs of what I have been upon this three and twenty years. About fifteen or ſixteen years ago, I preacht on the third Chapter of Saint *James*, in a larger and a cloſer manner on this Subject, than here I write: becaſue the times then called me to it.

2. I perſwade no Chriſtian to juſtifie or own the ſins or the leaſt defects of any Church, Miniſter or People, in their worſhip or in their lives, though I perſwade you to communion with the Churches, perſons and worſhip-actions, which have many faults: (for on earth there is no perſon, Church, or Worſhip faultleſs, and without corruption.) I juſtifie not the faults of my own daily Prayers, and yet I never pray without them.

3. I am not perſwading Miniſters to any unwiſe and unſeaſonable preaching, againſt the dividing Principles of the weak, when the neceſſities of the Auditory more require other doctrine; (much leſs to exaſperating railings and invectives; And leaſt of all to wrathfull violence). But only with prudence, in ſeaſon and with prudence, in ſeaſon and with Love and gentleneſs;

d men into the truth; If even
and Hereticks, *the Servant of*
st strive, but be gentle to all
teach; patient, in meekness in-
e that oppose themselves, if God,
will give them repentance to the
g of the truth, 2 Tim. 2. 24, 25.
more must the Children of
be used with Love and tender-
he fierceness of any contradict
only add, that it is not an un-
person that speaketh it, but
rough the mercy of God, hath
numerous flock in Love and
ace by such like means; and
lamentable effects of the con-

I say so much in this Treatise
ash censuring of others, I give
rule for mens censuring of
They know more by them-
y may search into the depth of
nd intentions, which we can-
ey are allowed to be more
l censorious of themselves, than
: It more concerneth them:
ave more to do with them-
nay be bolder with themselves.
ers in order to visible Church-
by visible and publick evi-
C   dence:

dence. But in order to their preparation for the judgement of God, we must direct them to judge themselves according to the truth in the inward parts.

5. While I draw you to peace and moderation towards others, I desire not to quench the least degree of Christian zeal. Nay I endeavour to kill that which would kill it. The *purified peculiar people of the Redeemer are Zealus*, but *of what?* not to consume and destroy one another, nor to hate and flye from one another; nor to vilifie and backbite one another; but they are *zealous of good works*: And *Paul* will tell you what are *good works*, Gal. 5.22, 23. *Love, joy, peace, long-suffering, gentleness, goodness, faith, meekness, temperance*: Be zealous in loving all Christians as Christians, and all men as men: Be zealous for *Peace, if it be possible, as much as in you lyeth, live peaceably with all men*, Rom. 12. 18. Be zealously patient, gentle, good, meek, temperate. And the works of the flesh are--*hatred, variance, emulation, wrath, strife, sedition, heresies*: A zeal for these is *earthly sensual* and *devilish*, as *James* telleth you. And remember that the word which is translated there [*Envy*] is [*Zeal*] in the Original: But our translators were afraid, lest the prophane would have mistaken it, if

if they had translated it [*Zeal*] ver. 16. *where zeal and strife is* (that is, a *striving contentious zeal*) *there is confusion and every evil work.*] If you believe this, how dare you blame me for writing to save you from *confusion and every evil work*?

6. I will conclude with the repetition of one thing delivered in this Treatise; that among all the rest, two separating dividing principles will never give peace to the Church where they prevail. The one is the confounding mens *Title* to *visible Church Membership* and *Communion*, with their Title to Justification and Salvation. The other is, the *Imposing of new terms and titles* of Visible membership and Communion; and rejecting the sufficiency of the *terms* and *title* of *Christs appointment.* Christ hath solemnly and purposely made the *Baptismal Covenanting with him*, to be the *terms* and *title* to Church membership and Communion; And the *owning* of this *same Covenant* is the sufficient Title of the adult. And the imposers that come after, and require another kind of evidence of Conversion, or Sanctification than this, do confound the Church, and enslave the people, and leave no certain way of tryal, but make as various *terms* and *titles*, as there are various degrees of wisdome and Cha-

rity, and various opinions, in the Pastors (yea in all the People to whom they allow the judgement of such Causes) in the several Churches. In this Point, the sober Anabaptists seem to come nearer the truth than they.

I add no more, but Christs conclusion, that a' house or Kingdom divided against it selfe cannot stand; The book it self was written near two years ago; put this preface, *Feb.* 2. 1669.

AN

AN ABSTRACT OF THE DIRECTIONS.

1. Forget not the difference between the younger sort of Christians, and the Elder. The peril of the Church from young Christians.

2. Observe the secret workings of spiritual pride, and how deep rooted and odious a sin it is, and what special temptations to it, the younger and emptier sort of Christians have.

3. Overvalue not the Common gift of utterance, nor a high profession, as if grace were appropriated to such alone, who are called Professors.

4. Affect not to be made eminent and conspicuous in holiness, by standing at a farther distance from common Christians, than God would have you.

5. Understand the true difference between the church as Visible and as Regenerate or mystical; and the several qualifications of the Members. What Scandals were in the primitive Churches in Scripture-times.

6. Understand well the different Conditions and terms of Communion with the Church as mystical and as visible, and the different privileges of the members: that you may not presume to impose any Conditions which

which God hath not imposed, nor unjustly grudge at the presence of those that are not sincere.

7. Get true and deep apprehensions of the necessity and reasons of Christian Unity and Concord; and of the sin and misery of divisions and discord: what Scripture saith herein.

8. When any thing needeth amendment in the Church, the best Christians must be the forwardest to Reform, and the backwardest to divide on that pretence.

9. Forget not the great difference between the Churches casting out the impenitent; and the Godlyes separating from the Church it self, because the wicked are not cast out. The first is a great duty: the second usually a great sin. Luthers case.

10. Expect not that any one lawfully received into the Church by Baptism, should be cast out of it, or denyed the priviledges of the Church, but according to the rules of Christian discipline, by the power of the Keys; that is, for obstinate impenitency in a gross or scandalous sin, upon proof, and after sufficient private and publick admonition.

11. Understand what the power of the Keys is, and what the Pastors office is; as they are the Governours of the Church, entrusted by Christ with the power of admission and rejection: that so you may know how far you are to rest in the Pastors judgment, and may not usurp any part of their office to your selves.

12. Study well Christs gracious nature and office; and his great readiness to receive the weakest that com to him; that so you may desire a Church discipline agreeable to the Gospel.

13. Yet lest you run into the worse extream, remember still that the destroying of sin, and the sanctifying

of

of men to God, was the work of our Redeemer: And that Holiness and Peace must go together: And that our outward Church-order and discipline, must be subservient to the inward spirituality and prosperity of the Church regenerate. And no such favour must be shewed to sinners as favoureth sin, and hindereth Holiness.

14. Though your Governours are the Judges, what persons shall be of your publick-Church Communion; yet it is you that must judge who are fit or unfit for your private familiarity.

15. Understand how much it hath pleased God to lay all mens happiness or misery upon their own choice: And seek not to alter this order of God.

16. Though the profession of Christianity which entitleth men to Church-Communion, must be credible; yet remember that there are various degrees of Credibility: And that every profession which is not proved false, is credible in such a degree as must be accepted by the Church.

17. Know how far it is that either Grace or Gifts are necessary to a Minister, that you may give to both their due.

18. Understand well the necessity of your Communion with all the Universal Church, and wherein it consisteth; and how far it is to be preferred before your Communion with any particular Church.

19. Engage not your selves too far in any divided Sect, and espouse not the interest of any party of Christians, to the neglect and injury of the universal Church, and the Christian Cause.

20. Be very suspicious of your Religious passions, and carefully distinguish between a sound and sinful zeal; least you father your sin on the Spirit of God, and

think you please him more when you most offend him.

21. Lend not a patient ear to backbiters; nor hastily believe the most religious people, when they speak ill of others.

22. Make not your selves judges of other mens actions; much less of their state before you have a Call; or before you have sufficient knowledge of the person and of the case.

23. Mistake not the nature of the sin of Scandal, as if it were the bare displeasing of another: when it is the laying of a stumbling-block or occasion of sinning before another.

24. Make Conscience of Scandalizing one party as well as another: and those most, who are most in danger by your offence.

25. Be not over tender of your reputation with any sort of men on earth: nor too impatient of their displeasure, censures or contempt. But live above them.

26. Use not your selves (needlesly) to the familar company of that sort of Christians, who use to censure them that are more sober, Chatholick & charitable than themselves: Unless you be as much or more, with the soberer sort, who will shew you the sin and mischief of Love-killing principles and divisions.

27. Take heed of misjudging of the answers of your prayers, and of taking those things to be from God, which are but the effects of your prejudice, passion or weakness of understanding.

28. Do not too much reverence the revelations, impulses or most confident opinions of any others upon the account of their sincerity or holiness; but try all judiciously and soberly by the word of God.

29. Take

29. Take heed lest the trouble of your own disquieted doubting minds, do become a snare, to draw you, to some uncouth way of Cure; and so make the fancy of some new opinion, sect or practice, to seem your remedy, and give you ease; and so perswade you that it is the certain truth.

30. Keep in the rank of a humble disciple or Learner in Christs Church, till you are fit and called to be Teachers your selves.

31. Grow up in the great substantial practical truths and duties; and grow downwards in the roots of a clearer belief of the Word of God, and the life to come: And neither begin too soon with doubtful opinions, nor ever lay too much upon them.

32. Lay not a greater stress upon your different words and manner of prayer, than God hath laid: And take heed of scorning, reproaching or slighting, the words and manner of other mens worship, when it is such as God accepteth from the sincere. Where the Case about forms of prayer is handled.

33. When you are sure that other mens way of worship is sinful; yet make it not any other, or greater sin, than indeed it is; and speak not evil of so much in it as is good. And slander not God as a hater or rejecter of all mens Services, which are mixt with infirmities; or as a partial hater of the infirmities of others, and not yours.

34. Think not that all is unlawfully obeyed which is unlawfully commanded.

35. Think not that you are guilty of all the faults of other mens worship with whom you joyn; no not of the Ministers or Congregations: Nor that you are bound to separate from all the worship which is faultily performed; For then there must be no Church-Communion

upon

upon Earth. Where is more about extemporary prayer and imposed forms.

36. Yet know what Pastors and Church-Communion you may joyn with, and what not: And think not that I am perswading you to make no difference.

37. In your judging of Discipline, reformation, and any means of the Churches good; be sure your eye be upon the true End; and upon the Particular Rule; and not on either of them alone. Take not that for a means which is either contrary to the word of God; or is in its nature destructive of the end.

38. Neglect not any truth of God; much less renounce it, or deny it. But yet do not take it for your duty to publish all, which you judge to be truth; nor a sin to silence many lesser truths, when the Churches peace and welfare doth require it.

39. Know which are the Great dutyes of a Christian life, and wherein the nature of true Religion doth consist: And then pretend not any lesser duty, against these greater; though the least when it is indeed a duty, is not to be denyed or neglected.

40. Labour for a sound judgement to know good from evil, least you trouble your selves and others by mistakes: Forsake not the guidance of a judicious Teacher, nor the Company of the agreeing generality of the godly.

41. Let not the bare fervour of a Preacher, or the loudness of his voice, or affectionate utterance, draw you too far to admire or follow him, without a proportion of solid understanding and judiciousness.

42. Your belief of the necessary Articles of faith, must be made your own, and not taken meerly on the Authority of any. And in all points of belief or practice, which are necessary to Salvation, you must ever

keep

keep company with the Universal Church: For it were not the Church, if it erred in those. And in matters of Peace and Concord the major vote must be your guide. In matters of humane obedience your Governours must be your guides. And in matters of high and difficult speculation, the judgment of one man of extraordinary understanding, is to be preferred before the Rulers, and the major Vote.

43. Reject not a good cause, because it is owned by some bad men: And own not a bad cause for the goodness of the Patrons of it. Judge not of the Cause by the persons, when you should judg of the persons by the Cause

44. Yea, take the bad examples of religious men, to be one of your most perillous temptations. And therefore labour to discover what are the special sins of professours in the age you live in, that you may be specially fortified against them.

45. Desire the highest degree of holiness, and to be free from the Corruptions of the times: but affect not to be odd & singular from ordinary Christians in lawfull things

46. When you have to do only with stigmatized scandalous ones, to vindicate the honour of Christianity from their Scandal, go as far from them as lawfully you can: But with the Common sort of Sinners, whose Conversion you are bound to seek, go not as far from them as you can; but purposely study to come as near them as lawfully you may, that you may have the better advantage to win them to the truth.

47. Whenever you are avoiding any error forget not that there is a contrary extream to be avoided, of which you are not out of danger.

48 Think more, and talk more of your faults and failings against others; especialy against Princes. Magistrates and Pastors, than of their faults and failings against you.   49 Take

49. Take notice of all the good in others which appeareth; and talk rather of that behind their backs, than of their faults.

50. Study the duty of instructing and exhorting, more than of reproof and finding fault.

51. The more you suffer by Rulers or any men, the more be watchful, lest you be tempted to dishonour them or to withdraw or abate the Love which is their due.

52. Make Conscience of heart-revenge, and tongue-revenge, as well as of hand-revenge.

53. When you are exasperated by the hurt which you feel from Magistrates, remember also the Good which the Church receiveth by them.

54. Learn to suffer by good people, and by Ministers; and not only by ungodly people, or by Magistrates.

55. When you complain of violence and persecution in others; take heed lest the same inward vice work in you, by Church cruelties and damning censures, against them or others. Persecution and separation often have the same Cause.

56. Keep still in your eye, the state of all Christs Churches upon earth; that you may know what a people they are through the world whom Christ hath Communion with: & may not ignorantly separate from almost all the Church of Christ, while you think that you separate but from those about you. *Queres about separation*

57. Yet let not any here cheat you by the bare names and titles of Unity, to the papal usurping head of the Church: nor must you dream of any Head & Center of Unity to the universal Church but Christ himself.

58. Take heed of superstition; indiscreet zeal hath been the usual beginner of superstition: Malignity in this age the sharpest opposer for the Authors sake: Formality in the next age hath made a Religion of it.

And

And then the zealous, who first invented it, have turned most against it, for the sake of the last owners; And thus the world hath turned round. Instances lay'd down of the superstition of Religious people in this age.

59. If through the fault of either side, or both, you cannot meet together in the same assemblies; yet keep that Unity in faith, love and practice, which all neighbour Churches should maintain; And use not your different assemblies to reviling, and destroying Love and Peace.

60. When the Love-killing spirit, either cruel or dividing, is abroad among Christians; be not idle, nor discouraged Spectators, nor betray the Churches peace by lazy wishes; But make it a great part of your labour and Religion, to revive Love and Peace, and to destroy their contraries. And let no censures or contempt of any party take you off: But account it as comfortable to be a Martyr for Love and Peace by blind Zealots or proud Usurpers, as for the faith by Infidels or Heathens: And take the pleasing of God (whoever is displeased) for your full reward.

The Additional Directions to the Pastors.

1. Let it be our first care to know and do our own duty: And when we see the peoples weakness and divisions, let us first examine and judge our selves, and lament and reform our own neglects. Ministers are the Cause of most divisions.

2. It is needful to the peoples Edification and Concord, that their Pastors much excel them, in knowledge and utterance, and also in prudence, holiness, and heavenly mindedness: that the reverence of their callings and persons may be preserved; and the people taught by their Examples.

3. Inculcate still the necessary conjunction of Holiness and Peace; and of the Love of God and Man: And that Love is their Holiness it self, and the sum of their Religion; the End of faith, and the fulfilling of the Law. And that as Love to God uniteth us to Him; so Love to man must unite us to each other. And that all doctrine and practices which are against Love and Unity, are against God, against Christ, against the Spirit, against the Church, and against Mankind.

4. If others shew their weakness by unwarrantable singularities or divisions, shew not your greater weakness, by impatience, and uncharitable censures or usage of them: especially when self-interest provoketh you.

5. Distinguish between them that separate from the Universal Church, or from all the Orthodox and Reformed parts of it; and those who only turn from the Ministery of some one person or sort of persons, without refusing Communion with the rest.

6. Distinguish between them who deny the being of the Ministry and Church from which they separate: and those who remove only for their own Edification, as from a worse or weaker Ministry, & a Church less pure.

7. Distinguish between those who hold it simply unlawful to have Communion with you: and those who only hold it unlawful to prefer your assemblies before such as they think to be more pure.

8. Remember Christs interest in the weakest of his Servants; and do nothing against them which Christ will not take well.

9. Distinguish between weakness of Gifts and of Graces: and remember that many who are weaker in the understanding of Church orders, may yet be stronger in grace than you.

10. Think on the Common Calamity of mankind:

what strange disparity there is in mens understandings, and will be: And how the Church here is a Hospital of diseased souls; of whom none are perfectly healed in this life.

11. *Distinguish still between those truths and duties, which are or are not of* necessity: *and between the* tolerable *and the* intolerable *errors. And never think of a* Common Unity *and* Concord, *but upon the terms of* necessary points; *and of the* primitive simplicity; *and the forbearance of* dissenters *in tolerable differences.*

12. *Remember that the Pastoral Government is a work of* Light *and* Love: *And what* these *cannot do, we cannot do. Our great study therefore must be first to* know *more and to* Love *more than the* people; *and then to convince them by cogent evidence of truth; and to cause the warmth of our* Love *to be felt by them, in all the parts of our ministration and converse: As the warmth of the Mothers milk is needful to the good nutrition of the Child. The History of Martin.*

13. *When you see many evils which* Love *and* evidence *will leave uncured; yet do not reject this way, till you have found one that will better do the work, and with fewer inconveniences.*

14. *When you reprove those weak* Christians, *who are subject to errors, disorders and divisions; reflect not any disgrace upon* piety it self: *but be the more careful to proclaim the honour of* Godliness, *and true* Consciencious strictness, *lest the ungodly take occasion to despise it, by hearing of the faults of such as are accounted the zealousest professors of it.*

15. *Discourage not the people from so much of* Religious exercises, *in their families, and with one another, as is meet for them in their private stations.*

16. Be

16. *Be not wanting in abilities, watchfulness and diligence, to resist Seducers by the evidence of truth; that there may be no need of other weapons: And quench the sparks among the people, before they break out into flames.*

17. *Be not strange to the poor ones of your flocks; but impartial to all; and the servants of all: Mind not high things, but condescend to men of low estate.*

18. *Spend and be spent for your peoples good, Do all the good that you are able for their bodies, as well as for their souls. And think nothing that you have too dear to win them, that they may see that you are truely fathers to them; & that their welfare is your chiefest care.*

19. *Keep up the reverence of the ancient and experienced sort of Christians; and teach the younger what honor they owe to them that are their Elders in age & grace: For whilest the Elder who are usually sober and peaceable, are duly reverenced, the heat of rash and giddy youth, will be the better kept in order.*

20. *Neither neglect your interest in the Religious persons of your charge, lest you lose your power to do them good; Nor yet be so tender of it, as to depart from sober principles or wayes to please them: Make them not your Rulers; nor follow them into any exorbitancies, to get their love, or to escape any of their censures.*

21. *Let not the Pastors contend among themselves: especially through envy against any whom the people most esteem. A reproof of ignorant, pievish, backbiting, quarrelsome Ministers.*

22. *Study our great pattern of Love and tenderness, meekness and patience: and all those texts which commend these virtues; till they are digested into a nature in you; that healing virtue may go from you, as wasting fire proceedeth from the incendiaries. The Texts recited.*

DIRECTIONS

DIRECTIONS
FOR
WEAK CHRISTIANS,

How they may escape the troubling, dividing, and endangering of the Church by their Errours in Doctrine, Worship, and Church-Communion.

IF we had never been warned by the History of the Sacred Scripture, or of the former Ages of the Church, yet our experience in this present Age is enough to tell both us and our Posterity, how great perturbations, and calamities may come to the Church of Christ, by the miscarriages of the more zealous Professors of Religion; and how great a hindrance such may prove to the prosperity of the Gospel; to the Love and Unity of Christians; to the Reformation, and holy order of the Congregations, and to all those good ends which are desired by themselves. How great a dishonour they may prove to the *Christian name*, and what occasions of hardening the wicked in their contempt of *Godliness*, to their everlasting ruine, and the sufferings of Believers.

There

Therefore seeing the peace and welfare of the Church, is much more valuable, than the peace and welfare of an individual soul, as I have Directed you how to escape your *own disturbance* and *undoing*, so I think it as necessary to direct you, how to escape being the Plagues and disturbers of the Church and the instruments of Satan in resisting the Gospel, and destroying others. And you should be the more willing to hear me in this also, because by hurting others you hurt your selves, and by wronging the Church of God, you cross your own desires and ends (if you are Christians indeed;) and by doing good to others, and furthering the cause of Godliness and Christianity, you do good to your selves and further your own Consolation and Salvation.

DIRECT. I.

First, observe this General direction; see that *you forget not the great difference between Novices and experienced Christians; between the babes and those at full age; between the weak and the strong in grace:* Level them not in your estimation. It is not for nothing that the Spirit of God in Scripture maketh so great a difference between them, as you may read in *Heb.* 5. 11, 12, 13, 14. and 6. 1, 2. 1 *Tim.* 3. 6. 1 *John.* 2. 12, 13, 14. There are *babes*, *strong men*, and *fathers* among Christians. There are some that are *dull of hearing*, and have *need* of *milk*, and *are unskilfull* in the *word of righteousness*, and must be *taught the principles*; and there are others who can digest *strong meat, who b reason of Use*, *have their senses exercised to discern both good* and *evil*. Novice must not be made Pastors of the Church. It is not for nothing that the *Younger* are so often commanded reverence and submission to the *Elder*; and that the Pastors and Governours of the Church, are usually called by the name of *Elders*; because it was supposed that the *elder sort* were the most experienced and wise, and therefore Pastors and Rulers were to be chosen out of them. And why is it that children must so much honour their fathers and mothers, and must be governed by them? It is not meerly because generation giveth the Parents a propriety in their children: For God would not have *folly* to be the governour of *wisdom*, upon pretense of such propriety: But it is also because that it must ordinarily be supposed that Infants are ignorant, and Parents have understanding, and are fit to be their Teachers, as having had *longer time and helps to learn*, and more *experience* to make their knowledge clear and firm. If the young and unexperienced were ordinarily as wise as the aged or mature, why are not children made governours of their Parents, or at least commanded to instruct and teach them, as ordinarily as Parents must do their children? The Lord Jesus himself would be subject to his mother and reputed father in his Child-hood, *Luk*. 2. 51. Can there be a livelier conviction of the arrogancy of those novices, who proudly slight the judgments of their elders, is presuming groundlesly that they are wiser than they? Yea Christ would not enter upon his publick Ministry or Office, till he was *about thirty years* of age. *Luk*. 3. 23. He is blind that per-

ceiveth

ceiveth not in this example, a most r
demnation of the pride of those th
shell on their head into the Minist
sten to be teachers of others, befor
time or meanes to *learn*; and that
the judgements of the aged, who d
conceits, before they understand
which they are so confident. It was
answer, in *John* 9. 21. [*He is of*
But they that are *under age* now th
to be the wisest, because they are
the fiercest. The *old* were wont to
and now the young deride the old
ractor of a truculent people *Deut.*
regard not the person of the old: th
verence not their age. How many
mands are there in *Solomons*
younger sort, to hearken to the
Parents? The contrary was the
sons; and the shame of *Samuels*,
Was *Rehoboam* unwise in forsakin
the aged, and hearkning to the y
And are those people wise that in t
Salvation, will prefer the veheme
novice, before the well-setled judge
perienced aged Ministers? I know
too oft ignorant, and that wisdo
wayes increase with age: But I kn
Children are never fit to be the
Church; And that old men *may b*
young men are never wise enou
work. We are not now consideri
fall out rarely as a wonder, but wh
to be expected.

Most of the Churches confusions and divisions have been caused by the younger sort of Christians: Who are in the heat of their zeal, and the infancy of understanding: Who have *affection* enough to make them drive on, but have not *judgement* enough to know the way. None are so fierce and rash in condemning the things and persons which they understand not, and in raising clamours against all that are wiser and soberer than they. If they once take a thing to be a sin which is no sin, or a duty which is no duty, there is no person, no Minister, no Magistrate, who hath age, or wisdom, or piety enough, to save them from the injuries of juvenile temerity, if they do not think and speak and do according to their green and raw conceits.

Remember therefore to be alwayes sensible of the great disadvantages of youth, and to preserve that reverence for experienced age, which God in *nature* as well as in *Scripture* hath made their due. If *time* and *labour* were not necessary to maturity of knowledge, why do you not trust another with your health, as well as a studied experienced Physician, and with your Estates, as well as a studied Lawyer? And why do not Sea-men trust any other, to govern the ship, as well as an experienced Pilot? Do you not see that all men ordinarily are best, at that which by long study they have made their profession.

I know those that I have now to do with, will say, that *Divinity is not learnt by labour and mens teaching, as other Sciences and Arts are; but by the teaching of the spirit of God: and therefore the youngest may have as much of it as the eldest.*

Answ.

Answ. There is some *truth*, and some *falshood*, and much *confusion*, in this objection. It is *true*, that the saving knowledge of Divinity, must be taught by the Spirit of God: But it is false, that *labour* and *humane teaching* are not the means which must be used by them, who will have the teaching of the spirit. And the objection confoundeth, 1. The *spirits teaching* us by *inditing the Scripture*, with the *spirits teaching* us the *meaning of the* Scripture. 2. And it confoundeth the *common knowledge* of Divinity, with the *saving knowledge* of it. No man cometh to a *common knowledge*, fit for a Teacher of others, without the *spirits* teaching us by the *Scripture:* For that was the first part of the *spirits* teaching us, to inspire the Prophets and Apostles to deliver a *teaching Word* to the Church, by which we might *all be taught of God* through all generations. But many men have excellent *common knowledge*, by this word, and by the *common* help of the spirit, without that *special* help which begetteth saving knowledge. Many prophesied and workt miracles in Christs name, who had no *saving* knowledge of him, *Mat.*7. 22, 23. And *Paul rejoyced* that *Christ was preached*, even by them that did it *of strife* & *envy, to add affliction to his bonds:* Phil.1.15,16,17,18. *saving* knowledge must have a *special* help of grace; And they which had but *common* knowledge, may by the spirit *have saving* knowledge in a *little time,* by bringing it to the heart, and making it clear, and lively and effectual. But that may be a means of saving others, which saveth not the man that hath it. And all knowledge requireth *time* and *labour*, to obtain it, though the Spirit giveth it, and though

it

it may be sanctified to us in a little time.

1. Consider, I pray you, why else it is, that God hath so multiplied commands, to dig for it as for Silver, amd search for it as a hidden treasure: to cry for knowledge and to lift up our voice for understanding: to wait at the posts of wisdoms doors: to search the Scriptures and meditate in them day and night: Is not this such study and labour as men use, to get understanding in other kind of professions? Are not these the plain commands of God? and are they not their deceivers who contradict them?

2. Is it not a blaspheming of Gods spirit, to make it the Patron of mens sloth and idleness, under pretence of magnifying grace? When so many Texts command us diligence, and slothfulness is so great a sin? And none are so forward to preach as these same men that cry down mens teaching.

3. Why hath God setled a Teaching Office in his Church, and commandeth all to attend and hear and learn; if we are taught by the Spirit without mans help? Why were the Apostles sent out into all the world? And why are they commanded to teach all Nations, and to teach the Church all that Christ commanded them? and why doth he promise to be with them to the end of the world? but that this is the way of the Spirits teaching, to teach those first who are our outward teachers, and then to help us to understand them? And those are taught of God, who are taught by those who are sent of God to be their teachers, and have the inward concurrence of his grace.

4. Advise with the experience of all the world who was the man that ever you knew able to expound one Chapter in the Bible, by the inward teaching of the Spirit alone without any labour of his own, or help from others, by voice or writing? Where dwelleth that man who by meer inspiration, can turn one Chapter out of Hebrew or Greek into the vulgar tongue? The first part of our preaching or publishing the Scriptures is by Translating them into a language which is understood. When *Ezra* in his Pulpit of wood, did read the law, and give the sence, the meaning is, that he read it in the ancient Hebrew Tongue, in which it was written, and turned it into the language which the Jews then used (who were grown much strangers to their ancient speech.) Where is the man that can solidly unfold any Doctrine of Divinity, which he never read or heard of, or can teach that truth, and defend that Religion, which he was never taught by man? He is a stranger in the world, who seeth not, that as in Law and Physick and other professions, though some are ignorant even when they are old, yet commonly all men are wisest and ablest in their own profession, and those know most, who having natural capacities have had best help, and longest time, and hardest studies, the Spirit assisting them by his *common help*, to make it *Knowledge*, and by his *special grace* to make it a *sanctifying knowledg*. Therefore remember to give due respect to them that have been *longer* in Christ than you, and to them that have *longer studied* the Scriptures, and to them that have had greater helps and experience: And do not too easily imagine, that those who are below

low them in all these advantages, are yet above them in sound understanding: Though such a wonder may sometime come to pass.

DIRECT. II.

Observe well the secret and subtil workings of spiritual pride, and how deep-rooted and dangerous a sin it is, and what special temptations to this odious sin, the younger and empty-headed Christians have; that the resistance of them may be your daily care.

PRide is the self-idolizing sin: the great rebel against God: the chief part of the Devils image: that one sin which breaketh every commandment: the Heart of the old man: the root and Parent and summary of all other sin: the Antichristian vice, which is most directly contrary to the life of Christ: the principal object of Gods hatred and disdain, and the mark of those whom he delighteth to tread down: and the certain Prognostick of dejection and abasement, either by humbling repentance, or damnation.

It is called [*Spiritual Pride*] from the Object, when men are proud of *spiritual excellencies*, real or supposed. And this is so much worse than Pride of Beauty, apparel, riches, high places, or high birth, as the abuse of great and excellent things, is worse then the abuse of vanities and trifles: and as things spiritual are in themselves

more

more contrary to the nature of pride, and therefore the sin hath the greater enormity.

The common exercise of this Religious or spiritual pride, is first about our *Knowledge*, and secondly about our *Godliness* or *Goodness*.

1. *Pride* of our *understandings*, worketh thus: First, a man that was formerly in darkness, is much affected with the new-come light, and perceiveth that he knoweth much more then he did before: And then he groweth to a carnal and corrupt estimation of it, valuing it more as *Nature* is *pleased* with it, then as it is sanctified by it: Delighting in *knowledge* for it self, more than for the purity, love and heavenliness which it should effect. Then he looketh about him on the ignorant sort of people, who know not what he knoweth, and seeth how far they are below him: And he thinketh with himself, what a difference hath God made between *Me* and *Them*: And because *Thankfulness* is a duty, he observeth not how *Pride* doth twist it self with it, and creep in under the protection of its name: And how *Thankfulness* and *Pride* have the same expressions, and both of them say, *I thank thee, O Father, that thou hast hid these things from the wise and prudent, and hast revealed them to babes: I thank thee, O God, that I am not as other men are, extortioners, unjust, adulterers, or even as this Publican*, *Luk*. 18. 11. And then he is so taken up with the things which he knoweth, that he perceiveth not what knowledge yet he wanteth. And the deep *affection* which his knowledge worketh in him, or the tickling *pleasure* which he hath in knowing, joyned with this *ignorance* of his

his *ignorance* in other things, doth make him over-confident of all his apprehensions, as if every thing which he imagineth were an absolute certainty: And so he wanteth that humble suspicion of his own understanding, which a true acquaintance with his ignorance would have caused in him: And thus he groweth to *overvalue* all his own conceivings, and to under-value all the opinions and reasonings of others, which are contrary to his own: And thence he proceeds to corrupt his Religion with such mis-apprehensions; and his rash unsuspected understanding entertains one error first, and then *that* lets in many more; till he have espoused a *self-chosen frame* of doctrine, instead of the sacred truths of God, and method of the Gospel: And from hence he proceedeth to choose his Religious exercises also, according to these mis-apprehensions: These make him *Duties* which are no *Duties*; and *sins* which are no *sins*: And thus he calleth *evil, good, and good, evil*; and *putteth darkness for light, and light for darkness, bitter for sweet, and sweet for bitter*. And having made him a Religion of his own, he confidently thinketh that it is of God: And next he valueth all men that he hath to do with according as they are *nearer* or *farther off*, from this which he accounteth the way of God: he chooseth his *Church* or *party* whom he will joyn with, by the test of this Religion which his pride hath chosen: He zealously declaimeth against the opposers of his way, as against the adversaries of truth and Godliness, and consequently of God himself. He prayeth up his opinions, and preacheth them up, and contendeth for them; and pray-

Prayeth and preacheth and disputeth down all that is against them. He laboureth to strengthen the party that is for them, and to weaken that which is against them: And thus he divideth the kingdom and family of Christ; He destroyeth first, the Love of his brother and neighbour in himself, and then laboureth to destroy it in all others, by speaking against those that are not of his way, with contempt and obloquy to represent them as an *unlovely* sort of men: And if the interest of his cause and party do require it, perhaps we will next destroy their persons: And yet all this is done in zeal of God, and as an acceptable service to him: And they think all are Neuters and Lukewarm, who prosecute not the Schism as fervently as they, and fight not against Love with as much vehemency: Yea and in all this, they are still confident, that they *Love the Brethren* with a *special Love,* and make it the mark that they are Christs disciples, and that they are passed from death to life, because they love the party and persons, who are of their own opinion and way. And thus PRIDE insensibly, while they perceive it not at all, doth choke their opinions, their Religions, their parties, and make their Duties and their sins, and rule their judgements, affections and their actions, which is all but the same thing, which the Scripture in one word calleth HERESY. And all that I have said, you may find said in other words in the third Chapter of *James.*

And there are two things which greatly promote this sin: The one is a conceit that all their apprehensions are the *Spirit's dictates,* or the effect
of

of its illumination. And the works and teachings of the spirit, are not to be contradicted, or suspected, but to be honoured. Therefore they think that it is a resisting of the Spirit, to resist their judgement: And they are perswaded that their apprehensions are caused by the spirit, partly because they had no such thing whilest they lived in wickedness, but it came in either with their change or shortly after: And therefore they think that the same light which shewed them their sinful state, doth shew them also all these principles: And partly because they find themselves as deeply *affected* with these misapprehensions, as with other which are sound and right; therefore they are confident that they come from the same spirit: and specially when these thoughts come in upon the reading of the Scripture, or in meditation, or after earnest prayer to God, to teach them by his spirit and lead them into the truth, and not suffer them to err; and when they find that they have good ends and meanings, and a desire to know the truth; all this perswadeth them that it is the spirit from whom their thoughts proceed; when yet it may be no such thing.

And another much greater and commoner cause of this *self-conceitedness* is this: All mens understandings are naturally imperfect: Our knowledge about *Natural* things is small and dark, much more about things supernatural: The wisest must say, *we know but in part*: And the variety of mens degrees of knowledge, joyned with the difference of their educations, and advantages and fore-going thoughts, doth make as
great

great a diversity of understanding
ons: And yet it is very hard to an
a sufficient diffidence and suspici
king mind. For what a man *know*
that he *knoweth*. But no man th
know that he erreth: For that
on. If I knew that I erred in jud
know that the thing is otherwise
to be: which is impossible to t
standing at the same time: For th
no *judging*, as being contrary
When I see such a difficulty about
pass *no judgment* at all, but rem
pence, then I can easily perceive
rant of it: But when I pass any jud
not perceive that my judgment i
it be in the cure of it, and by the sa
changeth it: when I erre, I can n
I erre, but *in sensu diviso*, when I
when I know that I erred, I so
And because every thing which a
doth appear in some kind of light
appeareth in some form, and as clo
qualities, the understanding ther
hath some thought or other of it:
notice of it, we shall have some ki
on and opinion of it: And fev
world do appear to us in such
shapes, as to leave the understand
bious, whether it be this or tha
that which hath *no appearance* at all
ignorant, and have no conceptio
one part of a thing is seen, and m
of it are unseen, we are all apt

the whole according to the part which we see, and not allow a just suspension or suspicion for all the parts which are unseen. That which I see, affecteth me as a thing seen: But that which *I see not*, is *nothing* to me, and therefore affecteth me not at all. That part which I know, I know *that it is*, and so far, *what it is*: It is in my mind and memory: But that part which I know not, I know not *that it is*, or know not *what it is*: so that seeing *one part* of things, and not seeing *another*, (yea perhaps *many* others) doth not only cause our error in judging of them, but also maketh it very hard, to question or distrust our judgements: For we must not be *Scepticks* and doubt of *all things*; nor must we deny belief to so much as is revealed to us: And therefore however at the present we apprehend things, just such we are usually confident that they are. And in this difficulty all error and the lamentable consequences of it do come in.

But what shall a man do in so hard a streight? Why this every humble man must do. He must tread safely, and proceed warily, and try the spirits, and try the doctrines offered him throughly, and this by all the means which God hath appointed him for that use. He must not strive against the light; but he must take heed of taking darkness for light, or harkening to the deceiver, when he transformeth himself into an angel of light, (which is not unusual;) what cometh with evidence of truth, must be received as truth, and held fast, and not again let go; however sometimes it may have a second and third tryal. And when you see any truth, remember that it is still with a defective sight, and that you see

but

but in part: And therefore allow a freedom in your understandings, to receive the rest. You are *certain* that you see *not all* that is to be seen, of any Doctrine or Science, any more than of any creature: And you are uncertain what influence the unknown parts, would have upon that part which you know, or what alteration it would make upon your apprehension, if you saw them altogether in their connexion. Therefore be sure that in your most confident apprehensions, you never forget that there is still much more *unknown* to you than you yet know. And this will preserve a humility and modesty in your understandings, and a capacity and fitness to receive more knowledge: When the forgetting of this, will make you proud and arrogant and presumptuous, and like the *fool* that *rageth* and *is confident*, even in your ignorance and shame; and will shut up your minds against that knowledge which you want.

But especially if you know that your advantages for knowledge have been less than other mens: that you are young, or that it is but a few years since you entred upon the study of the Scriptures, or that you have not any stronger naturall parts than other men; or that you have not had that measure of learning which might further your knowledge of the holy Scriptures; but that others that differ from you have had much more of all these helps and means than you; common reason here commandeth you to be modest, and not over-confident in your own opinion, nor too much to slight the judgements of such others.

Especially if those that differ from you, be not only more learned, but as truly conscionable as you,

r own understandings. 17

like to be unfeigned lovers of truth,
:d more, and meditated more, and
re religious experiences than your
et more, if they are the *greater num-*
y that differ from you, and you are
ur conceits; in this case rash confi-
wn opinions, is too palpable a sign
ride.

he *Learnedst men are not always the*
utters of Religion. Answ. Many men
the Languages and Sciences, who
ed in the Scriptures; because they
heir studies that way. And many
ed in the Scriptures, and the Sacred
yet live in sin, though they are able
ruth for others. But those that well
Scriptures, without Learning the
ch they are written in, and the Cu-
times and Countreys, or without
and long study both of the Scrip-
es, and the writings of them that
nd them, are so few, so very few, if
at if you will pretend to be one of
need of some miracle or something
, to make your selves or others be-
are not deceived. See what I have
large, in my *Unreasonableness of In-*

reater number are not always in the
re why should my singularity discou-
w. The greater number through the
n the right about Christianity; for
hristians. And the greater number
istians be not in the right perhaps

E

in many points of Learning, and Scholaſtick controverſies, becauſe they are not Learned in ſuch controverſies. But all Godly men and Chriſtians are in the right in all points *eſſential* to *Godlineſs* and *Chriſtanity*: and therefore they are in the certain way of life. And if in any *integral* or *accidental* point, you think that you are wiſer than the greater part of men, as Learned and as Godly as your ſelf, you muſt give very good proof of it to your ſelf and others, before it is to be believed, I know that in all ages, God giveth ſome few men more excellent *natural* parts, than others: and he engageth ſome in deeper and more laborious ſtudies than others: and he bleſſeth ſome mens ſtudies more than others: and therefore there are will *ſome few* who know more, than the reſt of the Countrey or of mankind: and it were well for the reſt, if they knew theſe, and would learn of them: But theſe are ſuch as come to their knowledge by *hard and laborious ſtudies and meditation*, though alſo by the *ſpirit* bleſſing their endeavours: And they are ſuch as *give proof* of the knowledge which they pretend to: And they are ſuch as *employ* their knowledge to preſerve the *peace* and *concord* of believers, and do not proudly make a ſtir with it, to ſet up their own names, though thereby they ſet the world on fire.

Make therefore no more of theſe vain defences of your Pride, Let no man think of himſelf and his own underſtanding above what is meet. I perſwade you not to deny any truth which indeed you know, nor to doubt of any thing which is made truly *certain* to you. But value not your underſtanding above their worth; and fix not too rashly upon your first apprehensions; and go not away with a passionate confidence, in your poor, raw, untryed and defective conceptions. But remember that you know but little, and must have time and labour to grow up to the rest. *Be not wise in your own conceits.* Rom. 12.16. and 11. 25. Prov. 26. 5. and 28. 11. And this is commonly the sin of the *slothful*, that never were at that pains for knowledge, by which it must be attained. The *sluggard is wiser in his own conceit, than seven men that can render a reason*, Prov. 26. 16. You little think when you are conceited of your knowledge, that you are farther from wisdom than a fool. Prov. 26. 12. *Seest thou a man wise in his own conceit? There is more hope of a fool, than of him. Be not wise in thy own eyes*, Prov. 3. 3. *Wo to them that are wise in their own eyes, and prudent in their own sight*, Isa. 5. 21. *Be not righteous overmuch, neither make thy self over-wise: why shouldest thou destroy thy self?* The self-conceited must become *fools* in their own esteem, if ever they will be wise, as the worldly wise must own that which is folly in the judgement of the world, if ever *they* will be wise: 1 Cor. 3. 18.

2. And there is a *Religious Pride* of *Goodness*, as well as of *Knowledge*, which must yet more carefully be avoided, as being yet worse than the former, as the thing abused is much better. And this worketh as subtilly and secretly as the former. It may not only consist with *many complaints* and *confessions of sinfulness, weakness* and *unworthiness*, but even with *doubts of sincerity* and so much dejectedness as seemeth to draw near to desperation. It is an ordinary thing to hear the same persons

talk in a complaining, doubting and almost despairing manner of speech, and yet to have *high expectations* of respect from others, and to be most *proudly impatient* of the least *undervaluing* or *neglect*. Yea *Pride* will make an *advantage to it self*, of all these *humble confessions and complaints:* And it is an old observation, that many are proud of their *humility*: For though it be true that *Austin* saith, that *Grace is a thing which no man can use amiss*; the meaning is only, that Grace *efficiently* can do nothing amiss: (For if it do amiss so far it is not grace:) Yet *objectively* all Grace may be abused, that is, a man may make it the object of his pride, and the occasion of many other sins.

And this *Religious Pride* of *Goodness*, doth ordinarily work under the pretext of *Thankfulness* to God for his grace, and *Zeal* for *Holyness*: But it may be known by this, that it always tendeth to lift us up, and to the diminishing of Love to others, and the contempt of the weak, and the censuring of our brethren, and the division and disturbance of the Church of God. They are lamentable effects which this Pride produceth, in the Church and all Societies where it cometh. It maketh all mens Goodness seem little, except our own: It causeth the people to undervalue their Pastors, and turneth compassion of mens weakness into a sowr contempt: it setteth a man in his own conceit, so near to God, that he looketh down on other men, as earthly animals in comparison of himself. It maketh new terms of Church-Communion, and teacheth men to make narrower the door of the Church, than God hath made

worketh, and appeareth, and is aggravated. 21

made it: It causeth men to deny and vilifie Gods grace, in those that answer not their expectations: And to think that the Church is not worthy of their Communion: And to think that none are so fit as they, to be the Reformers of the Church and of the word.

I intreat those who are in danger of this pernicious sin, to think with themselves. 1. What a heynous crime and folly it is for one that but lately was a child of the Devil, and a sink of sin, to be proud so quickly of their goodness: And for one that so lately was groaning and weeping with a broken heart for a sinful life, to be already puffed up with the conceits of godliness. And for one who daily maketh confession to God, of a sinful heart, and a faulty life, and of great unworthiness, to contradict all this by an over-valuing of his own piety; And how incongruous it is for one, who professeth to hope for justification by free grace and mercy only, and to have nothing of his own but what's defiled, and who abhorreth the Doctrine of merit, and talketh so much of our emptiness and insufficiency, to be yet puffed up with the conceit of his spirituality and worth. And what an odious self-contradiction it is, to make your self like the Devil in pride, because you think you are like God in holiness.

2. And consider, that the more you are proud of your *Goodness*, the less you have to be proud of: If this sin be predominant, it is certain that you have no saving grace at all: And what an odious thing and miserable case is it, to be proud of Holiness, when you are unholy; and to be damned both for *want* of it, and for being *proud* of it:

That a man should be proud of that, for want of which we must suffer the fire of Hell! But if your pride be not predominant, yet it is certain that in what measure soever you have that vice, in that measure you are destitute of grace: For true grace and pride are as contrary as life and death.

3. And study well the meaning of all these Scriptures (For you shall not say that I mis-interpret them to you.) Why was it that Christ mentioneth the Parable of the Pharisee, and the Publican? one thanking God that he was not so bad as others, and the other thinking himself unworthy to look up to heaven. *Luke* 18. 10, 11, &c. Why did he give us the parable of the prodigal who confesseth that he was unworthy to be called a Son; and of his elder brother who swelled with envy at his entertainment? Why was it that Christ seemed not strict enough to the Pharisees, in keeping the Sabbaths, nor in his Diet, nor in his Company, but they called him a gluttonous person and a wine-bibber, and a friend of Publicans and Sinners? Was it not because their *Pride* and Superstition made them think too highly of their own religiousness? and to make sins and duties which God never made, and then to condemn the innocent for want of this humane religiousness? What was the sin condemned in *Isa.* 65. 5. [Which *say, Stand by thy self; come not near to me; for I am holier than thou*] What meaneth that command in Phil. 2. 3. *Let nothing be done through strife or vain glory, but in lowliness of mind, let each esteem others better than themselves,*] Read this verse over upon your knees, and beg of God

to

to write it on your hearts: And I would wish all Assemblies of dividers and unwarrantable Separatists, to write it over the doors of their meeting places. And joyn with it, *Rom.* 12. 10. *Be kindly affectioned one to another with brotherly love, in honour preferring one another* (that is, *before your selves.*) But specially read and study, *Jam.* 3.

In a word, if God would cure the Church of *Religious pride*, the pride of *wisdom*, and the *pride* of *Piety* and *Goodness*, the Church would have fewer *Heresies* and *contentions*, and have much more peace, and much more *true wisdom* and *goodness* it self.

DIRECT. III.

Overvalue not the common gift of utterance, nor a high profession, as if the presence or absence of either of them, did prove the presence or absence of true saving grace.

YET I shall anon tell you, that neither of these must be *undervalued*, nor accounted needless, useless things. But the *overvaluing* them hath caused great distempers in the minds and affections, and communion and practise, of many very well meaning Christians. When God had first brought me from among the more ignorant sort of people, and when I first heard religious persons pray without forms, and speak affectionately and seriously of spiritual and heavenly things, I thought verily that they were all

undoubted

undoubted Saints; and the sudden apprehension of the difference of their gifts and speech from others, made me think confidently that the one sort had the mark of God upon them, and the other had nothing almost of God at all: Till ere long of those whom I so much honoured, one fell off to *sensuality* and to *persecuting formality*, and another fell to the foulest *heresie*; and another to disturb the Churches peace by turbulent animosities and divisions. But the experiences of this Kingdom these twenty six years, hath done so much to convince the world what crimes may stand with high professions, that I know not that I ever met with the man, that would deny it: seeing every sect casteth it upon all the rest, however some of them would justifie themselves. But I greatly fear lest the generation which is now springing up and knew not those men, nor their miscarriages, will lose the benefit of these dreadful warnings, and scarce believe what high professors did turn the proudest overturners of all Government; and resisters and despisers of ministry and holy order in the Churches and the most railing Quakers, and the most filthy and blaspheming Ranters: to warn all the world to take heed of being *Proud of superficial gifts and high profession*; and that he that standeth in his own conceit, should take heed lest he fall.

When gifts, of utterance in prayer or talking are thus overvalued, and high professions are taken to have more in them than they have, men presently model their *affections*, and then the Church according to these mis-conceivings: And a talkative person who by company and use hat got

got more of these gifts, than better Christians; shall be extolled and admired, when many a humble upright soul, that wanteth such utterance, shall be said to be *no professor*, and so to be unworthy of the Communion of Saints.

Mistake me not: I know that though profession may be without sincerity, yet sincerity cannot be without some profession, when there is opportunity to make it: And I know that Grace is a vital principle, and like fire which will work and seek a vent if you would restrain it: And that Gifts of utterance are great mercies of God for the Edification of the Church. But here lyeth your unhappy errour in this case. 1. You take the *common profession* of *Christianity* to be *no profession* at all, because there is wanting a profession of *greater zeal* and forwardness. When as the *common sort* of people in this Land, do profess to stand to their baptismal Covenant, in which they own the essential parts of Godliness and Christianity, and all that is of absolute necessity to Salvation. He that truly understandeth the baptismal Covenant and Consenteth to it, doth perform all which is necessary to a state of grace: If he profess this, he professeth, both true faith and repentance, and sanctification, and mortification, and all that is necessary to make a man a Christian. How then can you say that these are no *Professors*? I tell you (except a few Apostates) the common sort of people in this Land or Professors of true faith and godliness! Whether they are *true Professors* without dissembling is another question; but they are *professors* of the *truth*.

If you say, that their ignorance and ungodly lives doth shew that they either understand not the baptismal Covenant, or Consent not to it. I answer, Mark well what you say your selves: For this doth but shew that they are *Hypocrites*: You cannot say then that they are *no Professors*, but that they are *dissembling professors*. They profess the truth, they doe not truly and uprightly profess it. I tell you, all the common sort of the people in *England*, are either Saints or Hypocrites: see how I have proved this to them in my Treatise called *The formal Hypocrite*. They all profess enough to save them if they sincerely professed it. He that is baptized and professeth himself a Christian, and yet is a drunkard, a swearer, a fornicator, or such like, is certainly an Hypocrite as going against his own profession: The very Creed, Lords Prayer and Ten Commandments have enough to condemn him as an hypocrite. And will you now come in, and justifie these men from their *hypocrisie*, by saying that they are no *Professors*? If they were no Professors, they could be no *Hypocrites*, but meer Atheists or Infidels. I know that those are the *highest* sort of *Hypocrites*, who counterfeit the *highest* zeal and piety, by the highest profession: But this is but a difference in *degree*. Who ever professeth to be a Christian, professeth true Repentance, faith and holiness, and is an Hypocrite if he be not a Saint.

And then Consider, that if you would exclude any of these from the Communion of the Church, it must not be because they are *no professors*, but because they are hypocrites, ignorant or scandalous? And if so, then no man must be shut out, but

but upon *sufficient proof*: An unproved hypocrite or sinner, is no *hypocrite* or *sinner* in the judgement of the Church: and therefore Hypocrites are alwayes a great part of the visible Church. Otherwise Church-Communion would be founded on meer injustice and tyranny, if men shall be called Ignorant, Scandalous and Hypocrites without proof. And therefore to exclude baptized professors, by whole Parishes or Multitudes, without bringing proof against each person one by one, is quite to over-turn Chrifts rules and order, and Church Constitutions and all Church justice. I confess it is the thing which I have long lamented (and often written of especially in my Treatise of *Confirmation*) that those who are baptized in Infancy, are not called to a more explicite understanding profession of the Covenant then made, and have not a more solemn transition into the number of adult Communicants: And we are not out of hope that this may at last be brought to pass. But in the mean time, the *same persons* though *less regularly* do make *profession* of the same thing both at the *Lords Table*, and in their *publick worship*, and in their common *claim* to the faith and honour of Christianity, so that all such must be rejected as hypocrites upon accusation and *proof* of *Impenitency in some gross sin*, and not in the *lump*, as if they were *no professors*. For *professors* certainly they are.

And though I abhor their malignity who would vilifie Religion, by over-hasty accusing of higher Professors; and would flatter the wicked and ignorant, by making an indifferency and tepidity seem sufficient in the things of God; yet God
would

would have me bear witness to this truth to cure some mens contrary extream: that as this age as is said, doth need no proof, how heniously *high professors* may miscarry? so in the place where I exercised my Ministry, I found some give me a satisfying evidence in their last sickness, that they had long lived a truly godly life, who were never noted by their Neighbours, for any extraordinary zeal at all. If you ask me, How can it stand with grace to be so much hid? I answer, They made the *common profession* of *Christianity*: they usually attended the publick worship: they lived blamelesly in their places: but they were of silent retired dispositions, and were inferiours who by their superiours were restrained from *private meetings* and some converse with more zealous persons which they desired. And for ought you know there may be very many such; who must not be rejected as *no professors*, nor without a particular accusation and proof: unless you would be used in the like kind your selves.

DIRECT. IV.

Affect not to be made eminent and Conspicuous in Holiness, by standing at a farther distance from these lower Professors, than God would have you.

IT is the loathsome scab of the Romish Church that they who will be taken for *Religious*, must go into a Monastery of Fryers and Nuns, and separate

Affect not more conspicuous distance. 2

parate themselves from the rest of Christians, as worldly secular people: that so their *Religion* may be a *noted thing*; and they may be set up in their singularity, as publick spectacles, for the world to admire: Though perhaps they come thither but under the gripes of Conscience, to expiate the guilt of whoredome, murder, or some notorious sins, which the contemned seculars never committed. And it is somewhat easie to proud corrupted nature to enter into a life of greater self-denial, than most Monasticks are put upon, when by it they shall be thus separated from the rest of mankind, as a people of more admired holiness. To set our selves up in a separated society, as persons whom the world must account more Religious than the common sort of Christians, hath so much ostentation in it, as is a great allurement to Pride. For many a one who perceiveth how childish a thing it is, to set out ones self to be observed for *fine clothes*, or for bodily *comeliness*, or for *high entertainments*, *curiosities* houses, lands or such vanities, doth yet think that it is an excellent thing, to be honoured by men, especially by the wisest and the best, as a person of *Wisdome*, and *Piety*, and *Goodness*. And indeed it is the truest and the highest honour to be *Wise* and *Good*: And it is exceeding natural to man to desire honour: And it is lawful to have a due and moderate sense and regard to our honour: And all this being so, how easie is it for Pride to take this advantage, and to go a little farther, while we think that we go but this far, and keeep within our bounds.

And the root of the errour lyeth in *Atheism*,

Self-

Self-fishness, and *Carnality*. By the
lect the *Honouring* of *God*, which
utmost aim, and to which all o
should be purely referred, as a mea
cond, we *Idolize* our *selves*, and ar
centered in our *selves*, and seek
our *selves*, which we should wholl
alone. And by the third, we ov
and his esteem, and live upon the
breath of mortals, and seek the h
given by one to another more t
which is of God: Whereas we sho
grand care and study, to be pleasin
which is the highest honour, and
cessary to be sought; and should b
rent as to the esteem and thoughts o
ing no further regardable, than it co
divine and ultimate end.

And when Pride hath thus turned
soul, from God, to our *selves*, an
ture, it is a *working sin*, and will be
ing to fetch in fewel for its self to f
find out wayes to make our selves c
observed in the world: And to sep
into distinct Societies, that the wo
are *above Communion* with the cold
Christians, is one of the most not
this self-exalting end.

And many Christians that are m
yet so much mis-understand the
ciples of Communion, that th
should corrupt the Church, and si
if they stood not in a *separated state*
the colder sort. And this is cau

Saporation, how caused, 31

taking those Scriptures to speak of all cold and carnal Christians, which speak only of the Heathen and Infidel world. And this cometh to pass by the happiness of their *birth* and *breeding*: because they are born and bred where there are almost none, but professed Christians, and they see not the swarms of Heathens that worship idols and creatures, or of the Infidels who scorn and persecute the Christian name, therefore they live as if there were no such persons. They know that the World and the Church comprehend all mankind; and that the Church is gathered out of the World: And because they see the Church, but see not the World, out of which it is gathered, therefore they are looking for the World in the Church, and think that the commoner sort of Christians are the World; and the better and more zealous sort only are the Church, which therefore must be gathered out of the world. And so they gather the Church out of the Church, while they think that they gather it out of the World. And all this is because they know no more than they see, or at least are affected with no more; but live as if *England* or *Europe* were all the World. One years abode in *Asia* or *Africa* might cure this errour.

In 2 Cor. 6. 12, 13. &c. the Apostle forbiddeth the Christians to marry with Infidels; because *light hath no communion with darkness, nor righteousness with unrighteousness, nor Christ with Belial.* And therefore inferreth, that he that *believeth hath no part with an Infidel, nor the Temple of God any agreement with Idols.* And for this he citeth the words of the Prophet. *Come out from among them, and be ye separate, and touch not the unclean thing.* All these words which the Apostle so plainly speaketh only against marrying with Infidels and Idolaters, and having communion with them, either *intimately* or in their *sin*, are by abundance of ignorant Professors abused, as if they had commanded us to separate from the colder and common sort of Christians, and to *come out* of the Church whereof they are members. What profaning of Gods word is this? and how gross and palpable a contradicting of its plain expressions? It was a Church of such mixed Christians as our Churches do consist of, to which the Apostle wrote those words; and because he commandeth them to separate from intimacy with *Heathens* and *Infidels* (yet so as when they are once married to them, to continue in it;) therefore these men say, that one part of the Church is called to come forth and separate from the rest.

And with the like abuse they apply the command [*Come out of Babylon*] to them that have no communion with *Babylon*; And when *ignorance*, *uncharitableness*, and *passion*, have taught them to call Christs Churches *Babylon*, they add sin to sin, the sin of separation to the sin of slander and reproach; and abuse the Text according to their false exposition of it.

DIRECT.

DIRECT. V.

Understand rightly the true difference between the Mystical and the Visible Church, and the qualification of their Members; and do not confound them, as if it were the same persons only, that must be Members of both.

THE Mystical Church indeed hath none but true Saints. But the *Visible Church* containeth multitudes of *Hypocrites*; who profess themselves to be what they are not: They profess to believe in God, while they neglect him; and to be ruled by God, while they disobey him, and are ruled by their lusts: They profess to Love God and forsake the world, whilest they love the world, and God is not in all their thoughts: They profess to love the holy Scriptures, whilest they neglect them and love not the holiness of their precepts. They profess to believe in Jesus Christ, whilest their hearts neglect his grace and government. They profess to believe in the holy spirit, and to hold the communion of Saints in the Catholick Church; whilest they resist the Spirit, and love not Saints. All his sheweth that they are *Hypocrites*. But abundance of Hypocrites are in the Visible Church. Nay, God would have no Hypocrites cast out, but those who bewray their hypocrisie by impenitency in proved Heresie or gross sin.

We must not model the Church of Christ according

cording to our private fancies: We are not the Lords of it, nor are we fit or worthy to dispose of it! Look into the Scripture, and take it for the Rule, and see there of what manner of persons the Visible Church hath been constituted in all ages of the world till now. In the first Church in *Adams* family, a *Cain*, was the first born member, and so continued, till he was excommunicated for the murder of his brother. In a Church of eight persons who were saved out of all the world, the Father and Pastor was overtaken with gross drunkenness, and one of his sons was a cursed *Cham*. In a Church of six persons saved from the wickedness of *Sodom*, two of them (*Lot*'s sons in law) perished in the flame, among the unbelievers: a third was turned into a pillar of salt: the Father and Pastor was drunk two nights together, after the sight of such a terrible miracle, and after so strange a deliverance to himself: and committed incest twice in his drunkenness: The two that remained (his daughters) caused his drunkenness purposely and committed incest with him. In the Church in *Abrahams* family, there was an *Ishmael*: And in the Church in *Isaacs* family there was an *Esau*: and even *Rebekah* and *Jacob* guilty of deceitful equivocation: And *Abraham* and *Isaac* denied their wives to save themselves in their unbelief. In *Jacob*'s family was a *Simeon* and *Levi*, who murdered multitudes under a pretense of Religion, and under the cover of false deceit: And almost all his sons moved with envy, sold their brother *Joseph* for a slave: and some were hardly kept from murdering him: And his daughter *Dinah* was defiled

iled by desiring to see the company and fashions of the world. In the Church of the *Israelites* in the Wilderness, after all the miracles which they had seen, and the mercies they had received, so great were their sins of unbelief and murmuring, and lust, and whoredomes, and idolatry, and disobedience, that but two of them that came out of *Egypt*, were permitted to enter the promised Land: In the times of the Judges they so oft renewed their idolatry, besides all their other sins, that they spent a great part of all those ages in captivity for it. And when the villanies of *Gibeah* had imitated the *Sodomites*, and ravished a woman to death, the Tribe of the *Benjamites* defended it by a war; and that in three battels, till fourty thousand of the innocent *Israelites* were slain, and twenty five thousand of the *Benjamites*. Look through all the Books of *Samuel*, the *Kings*, and *Chronicles*, and the *Prophets*; from the sad story of the sons of *Eli* and of *Samuel*, to all the wicked Kings that followed, who kept up odious idolatry (even *Solomon* himself) and scarce two or three of the best did put down the high places. And when *Hezekiah* was zealous to reform, the hearts of the subjects were not prepared, but derided or abused the Messengers whom he sent about, to call the people home to God: *Manasseh*'s wickedness is scarcely to be parallel'd: And when God sent his Prophets to call them to repentance, they mocked his Messengers, and despised and abused his Prophets, till the wrath of the Lord arose, and there was no remedy: 2 *Chron.* 36. 15, 16. Read over the Prophets, and see there what a people this Church

of G:d was. The ten Tribes were c
roboam to sin, by setting up Calves
Bethel, and making Priests of the
people, and forsaking the Temple
worship of God, and the lawful l
these lawful Priests at *Jerusalem*, v
Wolves, and greedy dogs, and carel
Shepherds: The false Prophets v
the people were most accepted: T
accused of cruelty, oppression, who
kenness, Idolatry, and hatred of thos
reform them. They were grievous
Which of the Prophets did not your fa
persecute? saith Christ, *Matt.* 2
was the Church of God, and many
ly visible Church: And all these tv
were not so big as *England*, and we
ness of all the Earth, no more than
large Wood or Forrest.

But doubtless the Gospel Chu
more large and pure. Let us ther
view of it: And I beseech you rem
what I say is not to make sin less odi
Church or Godly less esteemed,
you the frame of the *visible Church* i
tions, and how it differeth from the
you should take on you to be wiser th
to build his house after a better rule
pel, and the primitive pattern, an
being wise in your own conceits,
righteous overmuch. *Eccles.* 7. A
forget not, that the *Primitive Ch*
most pure, and the *pattern* of those fo
had *inspired Apostles* to be its *Guides*

Prophets to be its *Helpers*, and abundance of *Miracles* and extraordinary gifts, to *gather* and *edifie* it; to silence its enemies, and to terrifie and restrain offenders, and to bring up the Church to the highest degree of holiness that could be well expected. And withall, the Members were not *driven in by force* by Magistrates, nor *allured* by any *worldly commodities*, but were a *few Volunteers*, who in a time of persecution, professed Christ, to their hazard or suffering in the world. Yet see what they were.

The faultiness of the Teachers.

The Apostles before the death of Christ, though they had so long heard his doctrine, and seen his miracles, understood not that he must die for our sins, and be buried, and rise again, and ascend into Heaven, and there intercede for us, and rule the Church. *Joh.* 12. 16. and 10. 6. *Luk.* 18. 34. and 9. 45. and 24. 43, 44, 45 *Peter* so much perswaded Christ from that suffering by which the world was to be redeemed, that Christ speaketh to him as he did to the Devil. *Matth.* 4. *Get thee behind me Satan; for thou savourest not the things that be of God, but those that be of men.* *Matth.* 16. 22, 23. *James* and his beloved disciple *John* (called sons of thunder, perhaps for this or such like zeal) would have called *for fire from heaven* to destroy the unbelieving adversaries of the Gospel, and knew not of what spirit they were. *Judas* was one that was sent out to preach the Gospel by Christ himself, (who knew his heart.) Many that preached and prophesied and cast out Devils in his name, were workers of iniquity, whom he never knew with special approbation. *Matth.* 7. 22, 23. When he came to his sufferings, they all slept when they should have watched and prayed with him one hour in his agony; and this after his admonition. When they should have confessed him in suffering they all *forsook him and fled, Matth.* 26. 56. And *Peter* that seemed to stick closer to him, did with forswearing thrice deny him, after he had promised to die with him, and not to forsake him, though all forsook him: And when he was dead they said, *Luk.* 24. *We trusted this was he that should have delivered Israel*, as if their faith had been extinct. And when he rose and appeared to them they hardly believed what they saw: and *Thomas*, one of them, resolved that he would not believe, unless he might put his fingers into his side.

And when they spake with him before his *Ascension*, they dreamed still of an earthly grandure, and askt him, *Whether now he would restore the Kingdome unto* Israel? *Act.* 1. And they understood not the descent of the Holy Ghost.

And when the Holy Ghost was come upon them, one of their first Deacons *Nicholas* was the original of a Sect whose doctrine Christ did hate. *Paul* and *Barnabas* contended even to parting, *Peter* dissembled by a sinful separation, walking not uprightly, and drew away *Barnabas* into the dissimulation: *Gal.* 2. *Phil.* 1. 15, 16. [*Some preach Christ even of envy, and strife, and some of good will. The one preach, Christ of contentions not sincerely, supposing to add affliction to my bonds.*] Many were made like the heads of Sects; and some were of *Paul*, and some of *Apollo's*, and some of *Cephas* (as the Papists be now.) And some
built

of the Primative Churches.

built hay and stubble, which must be consumed, 1 *Cor.* 3. 12. Of *Timothy* and the rest *Paul* saith, [*I have no man like minded ; for all seek their own, and not the things which are Jesus Christs.* 3 Joh. 9. 10. *Diotrephes who loveth to have the preeminence among them receiveth us not, prating against us with malicious words: and not content therewith, neither doth he himself receive the Brethren, and forbideth them that would, & casteth them out of the Church.*] As the Apostles themselves before Christs death, were striving which of them should be the greatest; so this vice still followed many of the Pastors; so that *Peter* is fain to exhort them, *not to Lord it over Gods heritage, nor to rule them by constraint, but willingly.* 1 *Pet.* 5. And what abundance of Sect-masters did arise from among the Ministers of the Gospel in the Apostles own times? Insomuch as *Paul* forewarneth the famous Church of *Ephesus,* not only that *greivous Wolves* (that is, Hereticks) *should enter, that spared not the flocks,* but also that, *of their own selves men should arise, speaking perverse things to draw away disciples after them. Act.* 20. 30. And in the Apostles dayes, while *one had a Prophesie and another a Psalm, &c.* they brought confusion into the Church-worship, even by abuse of extraordinary gifts: And they so abused the *Love-feasts* at the Lords Supper, that *Paul* was fain to perswade them rather to eat at home. 1 *Cor.* 14. and 1 *Cor.* 11. so much of the true state of the Primitive Teachers and Pastors of the Church.

The faults of the Church of *Rome.*

What Heretical Judaizers were among them, is intimated in *c.* 1. *&* 3. to the *Romans.* And how

F 4 little

little they underſtood the doctrine of Juſtification is intimated in *chap*. 3, & 4, & 5, & 6, & 7, & 8. What diſſentions there were about meats, and drinks, and days, the weak judgeing the ſtrong, and the ſtrong deſpiſing the weak, appeareth, *chap*. 14, & 15. And ſome cauſed *diviſions and offences contrary to the Doctrine which they had learned, ſerving not the Lord Jeſus but their own bellies, and by good words and fair ſpeeches deceiving the hearts of the ſimple*, Rom. 16. 16, 17.

The faults of the Church of *Corinth*.

1 Cor. 1. 11, 12. [*There are contentions among you---Every one of you ſaith, I am of* Paul, *and I of* Apollo's, *and I of* Cephas, *and I of* Chriſt. Mark the extent of the ſin (*every one of you*) that is, very many among you, 1 Cor. 3. 13. *I could not ſpeak to you as ſpiritual, but as carnal--- For ye are yet carnal---* v. 12. *If any build on this foundation, wood, hay, ſtubble,* -- v. 15. *he ſhall ſuffer loſs*. chap. 4. 18, 21. *Some are puffed up--- Shall I come to you with a rod or in love?* --- chap. 6. 5, 6, 7, & *I ſpeak to your ſhame, Is there not a wiſe man among you? Becauſe ye go to Law one with another (before Heathens,) Nay you do wrong and defraud, and that your bretheren. Know ye not that the unrighteous ſhall not inherit the Kingdom of God?* -- chap. 11. 17, 18, 19, 20, 21. *I praiſe you not that you come together, but for the better but for the worſe. For firſt of all, when you come together in the Church. I hear that there be diviſions among you-- For there muſt be alſo Hereſies among you, that they which are approved may be made manifeſt among you --- When you come together into one place, this is not to eat the Lords Supper: For in eating every one taketh before other,*

his

of Rome and Corinth. 41

his own supper, and one is hungry, and another is drunken. Vers. 23 30. *He that eateth and drinketh unworthily, eateth and drinketh damnation to himself, not discerning the Lords body* --- *For this cause many are weak and sick among you, and many sleep.* Chap. 14. Reproveth their abuse of unknown tongues, and their disorder in Gods publike worship --- Chap. 15. 12, 13, 14, 15. [*If Christ be preached that he rose from the dead, how say some among you, that there is no resurrection. But if there be no resurrection of the dead, then Christ is not risen ; And if Christ be not risen, then is our preaching vain, and your faith is vain; yea and we are found false witnesses of God* --- v. 17. *and ye are yet in your sins.* 2 Cor. 12. 20, 21. *I fear lest when I come, I shall not find you such as I would, and that I shall be found to you such as ye would not. Lest there be debates, envyings, wraths, strifes, back-bitings, whisperings, swellings, tumults ; and lest my God will humble me among you, and that I shall bewail many that have sinned already, and have not repented of the uncleanness and fornication and lasciviousness which they have committed.*] Besides that *Paul* and his Ministry was slandered and much slighted among them, as by his large and vehement apologies and expostulations doth appear; These were the faults of the Church of the Corinthians.

The corruptions of the Churches of *Galatia*.

Gal. 1. 6,7,8,9. *I marvel that you are so soon removed, from him that called you, to the grace of Christ, to another Gospel ; which is not another ; but there are some that trouble you, and would pervert the Gospel of Christ : But though we or an Angel from*
heaven

heaven, preach any other Gospel to you, than that which we have preached to you, let him be accursed-- Chap. 3. 1, 2, 3. O foolish Galathians! who hath bewitched you, that you should not obey the truth? before whose eyes--- Are ye so foolish? Having begun in the spirit, are ye now made perfect by the flesh?. Have ye suffered so many things in vain-- chap. 4. 9. How turn ye again to weak and beggarly elements, whereto ye desire again to be in bondage. verf. 10. 11. Ye observe dayes; and months, and times, and years; I am afraid of you, lest I have bestowed on you labour in vain---v. 16. Am I therefore become your enemy because I tell you the truth? Tell me, ye that desire to be under the Law --- v. 29. As then, he that was born after the flesh persecuted him that was born after the spirit, even so it is now (The Legalists persecuting the Apostles) Chap. 5. 2. Behold I Paul say unto you that if ye be circumsised Christ shall profit you nothing. v. 3, 4. For I testifie again to every man that is circumcised, that he is a debtor to do the whole Law: Christ is become of no effect to you. Who ever of you are justified by the Law, ye are fallen from grace: v. 9. A little leaven leaveneth the whole lump. 12. I would they were even cut off which trouble you. Chap. 6. 12. As many as desire to make fair shew in the flesh, they constrain you to be circumcised.

The corruptions of the Church of Colosse.

Col. 2. 20, 21, 22, 23. If ye be dead with Christ from the rudiments of the world, why as though living in the world, are ye subject to ordinances? Touch not, tast not, handle not (which all are to perish with the using) after the Commandements and Doctrines of men? Which things have indeed a shew of wisdoms in will-worship. The

Galatia, Colosse, and Ephesus, &c. 43.

The corruptions of the Church of *Ephesus*.

Rev. 2. 4, 5. *Nevertheless I have somewhat against thee, because thou hast left thy first love--Remember from whence thou art fallen, and do thy first works, or else I will come unto thee quickly, and will remove thy Candlestick.* Act. 20. 30. *Of your own selves shall men arise, speaking perverse things, &c.* as aforesaid.

The corruptions of the Church of *Pergamus*.

Rev. 2. 14, 15, 16. *I have a few things against thee, because thou hast there them that hold the doctrine of Balaam, who taught Balac to cast a stumbling block before the children of Israel; to eat things sacrificed to Idols, and to commit fornication: so hast thou also them that hold the doctrine of the Nicolaitans, which thing I hate--Repent, or else I will---*

The faults of the Church of *Thyatira*.

Rev. 2. 20, 21, 22. *I have a few things against thee, because thou sufferedst the woman* Jezebel, *which calleth her self a Prophetess, to teach and to seduce my servants to commit fornication, and to eat things sacrificed to Idols.*

The faults of the Church of *Sardis*.

Rev. 3. 1. *Thou hast a name that thou livest and art dead--I have not found thy works perfect before God.* 4. *Thou hast a few names even in* Sardis *which have not defiled their garments.*

The faults of the Church of *Laodicia*.

Rev. 3. 15, 16, 17 *Thou art neither cold nor hot--I will spue thee out of my mouth--and knowest not that thou art wretched and miserable and poor and blind and naked.*

I have been thus large in citing the words of the Text, to make it plain to you, of what kind

of

of Members the Visible Churches were then made up. And to affect their hearts with the sense of their partiality, who can plead for many things as duties, and plead against many things as sin, without one plain word of Scripture on their side; and yet can read all these without either sense or notice.

Yet mark, I pray you, that I am far from saying that God *alloweth* any of these sins, or that any should make light of them: For all must abhor them: Nor do I say, that none of the *Churches ought* to have excommunicated any of these offenders for these sins. Some of them I doubt not, should have been cast out. But these are the uses which I desire you to make of all these Texts.

- First, before you judge any Church to be *no Church*, be able to prove it hath worse crimes to nullifie it than any of these had. For none of these were for these faults pronounced *no Churches of Jesus Christ*.

Secondly, observe that no one Member, is in all these Scriptures, or any other, commanded *to come out and separate* from any one of all these Churches, as if their communion in worship were unlawful. And therefore before you *separate* from any as judging communion with them unlawful, be sure that you bring greater reasons for it, than any of these recited were.

DIRECT.

DIRECT. VI.

Understand well the different conditions and terms of Communion with the Church as invisible and as visible; and the different priviledges of the Members; that so you may not presume to impose any conditions which God hath not imposed; nor yet to grudge at the reception of those that are not sanctified and sincere.

ALL Christians are agreed that it belongeth to God only to make the conditons of Church-communion; and therefore it belongeth not to us to invent them, nor to our wit to censure what God hath done, but to search the Scripture till we find it out, and then obey it. This is the great controversie which hath troubled the Church: When men know not who should be Members of the Church and who not, and when they have no certain rule or charecter to know whom they must receive, it is no wonder if confusion and contention be the complexion and practice of such Churches. And here the Pastors have torn the Church, by running into contrary extreams. Some have thought that the Visible Church must be constituted only of such persons as satisfie the Pastors and the people of the truth of their sanctification, by some special account of their conversion or the work of grace upon their hearts, in a distincter manner

than

than the ancient Church required of the baptized: Wherein being agreed of no certain terms, to know anothers sanctification by, their Churches are diversified according to the measure of the strictness or largeness, censoriousness or charity of the Pastors & the People; while on thinks that person to have true grace, whom another thinks to have none. And so they that will be *most uncharitable*, do pretend to the reputation of being the *most pure*, because they are most *strict:* And multitudes are shut out whom Christ would have to be received, & his *children* are numbred with the *dogs*.

On the other side there is one or two of late among us, who think that the Church is but *Christs School*, where he *teacheth the way* to true Regeneration; and not a *Society of professed Regenerate ones* or *Saints:* And that all who own Christ as the *Teacher* of the Church, and submit to the *Government of the Pastors*, and are willing to learn how to be regenerate, should be baptized, though they profess not any *special saving faith of repentance*. And their reasons are, because first, else all that doubt of their sincerity must *lie*, or be kept out. Secondly, because that in the Church of the Jews, the multitude were such as were *openly ungodly*. And some of the Papists talk also at this rate, though indeed they are themselves yet utterly unresolved in this point.

What Church soever is constituted according to either of these *two opinions*, will not be constituted according to the mind of Christ: But yet with this difference: The first opinion introduceth Church-*tyranny*, and *injustice*, and is founded in the want of *Christian charity*, and *knowledge hedge*, and tendeth to endless separation and confusions. But the second opinion inferreth all these greater mischiefs.

First, It confoundeth the *Catechumens* with the *Christians*, and maketh all *Christans* who are but willing to learn to be Christans. Secondly, it maketh the Christian Church to consist of such as *are no christians:* As that person certainly is not, who consenteth not that Christ be his Teacher, Priest and King: For to such a one, he is *no Christ*; seeing these are the essential parts of his *Mediatory office*. And the new device of distinguishing *Christs Apostolike* and *Mediatory offices*, and so the *Church congregate* and the *Church regenerate* accordingly, will not serve to defend this conceit. For as Christ is not *divided*, so his office for which he is called *Christ* is but *One*, which entirely is called the office of a *Saviour*, or *Redeemer*, or *Mediator*, which are all one: And the essential parts of it are, first his Priestly, second Teaching and Ruling offices or works: And this which is called his *Apostleship*, is but the same which is called his *Teaching* or *Prophetical Office*, and is a part of his *Mediatory* or *saving Office*. And he is no *Christian*, nor is that any *Congregated Christian Church*, which professeth not to take Christ for his *Mediator* his *Priest* and *King*, as well as for an *Apostle* a *Prophet* or *Teacher*. Thirdly, they therefore who hold the aforesaid doctrine, do introduce a new sort of Christianity. Fourthly, and a new sort of Baptism, which the Church of Christ never knew to this day. And therefore they do ingenuously profess their dissent from our form or words in Baptism, because we put the baptized to renounce
the

the flesh the world, and the devil, and to use such covenanting words as must signifie special grace. But through the great mercy of God, Baptism is still the same thing in all the Christian Churches in the world, the Reformed, the *Roman*, the *Greek*, the *Armenian*, yea and the *Ethiopian* too, for all their seeming reiteration of it. And Baptism among them all, is the same now as it hath been in all Generations, from Christs institution of it. So that we fully maintain as well as the *Romans*, that Christianity hath by *this sacred Tradition* been safely delivered down to us to this day. What a Christian is, and what Christianity is, may be most certainly known, by this which is commonly called our *Christening*; In which the profession and Covenant which maketh men Christians is so express and unchanged from age to age. Therefore these men who would have our Baptism changed, do speak plainly, but impudently; as if they were raised in the end of the world, to reform the Baptism and Christianity of all ages, and were not only wiser than the universal Church from Christ till now, but also at last must make the Church another thing. I intreat the Reader who would know the judgement of all antiquity about Baptism, as supposing saving grace, to read those numerous citations of Mr. *Gataker* in the Margin of his book against *Davenant*, of Baptism. Fifthly, and by this new doctrine they destroy all that *special Love* which Church-members or visible Christians as such, should bear to one another. For if no *faith* or *consent* must necessarily be professed at Baptism, but that which is *common* to the *ungodly*

and

False terms of Communion.

and children of the devil, then *all Church members as only such*, must be taken to be but ungodly, and no man must love a Church-member as such, with a special love, as a visible Saint; but only as one of the hopefuller sort of the ungodly. Sixthly, and hence it will follow, that either *none* must make *any profession of saving Faith* and *Repentance* (and so all appearance of holiness must be driven out of the world) or else the Church must be constituted of two sorts of professions and professours; *tota specie* distinct from one another; yea more distinct than Infidels are from their new sort of Christians. And consequently it must needs be indeed *two Churches* and not one, *viz.* One Church of those who take Christ for their *Teacher only*, and another of those that take him *entirely as Christ*. Seventhly, and by this rule the *Socinians* and *Mahometans*, who confess Christ to be a *great Teacher*, but deny him to be the *Priest* and *sacrifice* for sin, may be *baptized*, and taken for *Christians*. These and many more absurdities follow upon this new conceit. But I must desire the Reader who would see more of it, to peruse my Disputations about *Right to Sacraments*, where it is handled at large.

As to their Objections I answer. First; no man is called to *lye*, nor yet are the *fearful* to be shut out: For as no man is perfectly acquainted with his own heart, so no man is to profess a perfect knowledge of it: But if a man speak as he thinketh upon faithful endeavours to avoid self-deceit, no more can be expected of him. He that can say [Though I am not certain that there is no secret fraud in my heart, yet as far as I can

G   discern

discern it, I am willing to be a Christian upon the terms of Gods Covenant, and to take Christ for my Teacher, Priest, and King] must offer himself, and must be received into the Church.

Secondly, and as to the Jews case, I have proved in the fore-mentioned Disputations, First, that it was no less than a profession of saving faith, which was made in the Covenant of Circumcision. Secondly, that men were then to be put to death, for almost all those enormous crimes which we now excommunicate men for: And the dead are not members of the Church on earth. Thirdly, that all that in *matter of fact* was found among them contrary to this, was contrary to Gods Law: And to argue against the Law from mans breach of the Law, *a facto contra jus*, is very bad arguing. Fourthly, that it is far surer and clearer reasoning about the Evangelical state and order of the Church, from the *Gospel*, than from the *Law* of *Moses*, much more than from the *violations* of that law. Fifthly, but yet all the corruptions of the Churches, as I have cited and proved them before, do shew us the difference between the Church, *as visibly Congregate*, and as *Regenerate*; and shew us that the presence of *scandalous sinners*, will not warrant us to *separate* or to un-church the Church. And this may suffice against that errour.

The true conditions of admittance into the Church and state of Christianity are these.

First, *A true belief in God the Father, Son, and Holy-Ghost, and a Devoting our selves sincerely to Him, as our reconciled Father, our Saviour, and our Sanctifier, in a resolved Covenant, or Consent, renouncing*

nouncing the Devil, the world, and the flesh, (ex-preſly or impliedly) is the whole and the only condition of our Communion with the Church myſtical, or the living body of Chriſt (which is called *The Church*, in the firſt and moſt famous ſenſe.)

Obj. If this muſt be wrought in us before we are in the myſtical Church, then a ſtate of holineſs may be found in ſuch, as are yet out of the body of Chriſt in the world: But if this be after our entrance into the Church, then leſs may ſufficiently qualifie us for admittance.

Anſw. It is neither *before* nor *after*: but it is our *change and entrance it ſelf.* To be a *member* of the Church *myſtical*, and to be a *Chriſtian* is all one: and this is *Chriſtianity*. If I ſhould ſay that the *making a man a Rational free agent, is the making him a member of the Rational world*; would you think that this muſt be either anteceedent or conſequent to his change, which is nothing elſe but the change it ſelf?

Secondly, *That which maketh a man a member of the Univerſal Church, as Viſible, is his Baptiſm.* Which is, *his profeſſion of the ſame true Faith aforeſaid, and conſent to the Covenant; or his viſible dedication to God the Father, Son, and Holy Ghoſt, as his Reconciled Father, his Saviour and Sanctifier, by a Vow and Covenant in Baptiſm.*

Where note that Baptiſm hath two parts: The *Covenant* there made, and openly declared between God and Man: And the *Sacramental, obſigning and inveſting ſign*; which is the *waſhing in water.* The *Profeſſion it ſelf,* or *open covenanting with God,* is the thing ſtatedly neceſſary to the *being of Vi-*

sible Christianity: And the *washing with water*, is *necessary* as a duty where it may be had, and as a *means* to the *orderly* and *regular* entrance; by which the *Church* is commonly to judge who are its admitted members and who not. As *inward consent*, and *outward profession* of *consent*, and *publick solemnization*, are the necessaries to a state of marriage; the first being as the *soul*, the second as the *body*, and the third as the *wedding garments*; so is it in this case. So that in short, if you take *Baptism* aright for the *Covenant* and the *Sign*, there is no other entrance into the Visible Church, nor any other condition necessary to a title to its communion. But if you take Baptism improperly, for the *washing* alone, there is no *title* to such *washing* necessary but *Professed faith* and *covenanting*. So that if you require more, or invent and impose any further conditions, and deny *baptized professors* of *Christianity* to be *visible members* of the Church, you are superstitious devisers of a way of your own, and makers of *will worship*, and not obedient submitters to the way of God.

Profession then of *Belief* and *consent to the Covenant*, is our *title-condition* to communion with the Universal Visible Church. This profession must be solemn, and solemnized under the hand of a Minister of Christ, who hath the Keyes of the Church, or Kingdom of heaven; that it may be satisfactory to the Church, and valid at its barr. Those that are baptized at age, have present Right to communion with the adult. Those that are baptized in infancy (upon good right) are admitted to such *Infant-communion* as they are capable of. And at years of discretion, they themselves

must

must own the Covenant, which their Parents entered them into. The more solemnly this is done (as it was in baptism) the better it is: But if it be done but by a professing themselves to be Christians, and attending Christs ordinances with his Church, it is valid; unless they forfeit the credit of their profession, by proved Heresies or crimes in which they live impenitently.

But then it must be here observed, what a *Profession of Christianity* is, which intitleth to Baptism and Church communion. And *objectively*, it must be the *whole Baptismal Covenant that must* be professed: No less, is to be taken as a *profession of Christianity*: And as *to the Act*, it must be first, *A signification* of the mind, by *word* or *writing*, or some intelligible *sign*. Secondly, it must *seem* to be *understood*: For no man consenteth to that which he *understandeth not*. But herein any intelligible sign of a *tollerable understanding* must be accepted, though we find that the persons conceptions are raw and not so distinct and clear as they ought, nor the expressions ready, orderly or compt. Thirdly, it must seem to be *serious*: For that which is apparently dissembled or ludicrous is null: Fourthly; It must be *de presenti*, a present giving up our selves to Christ, and not *only* a promise *de futuro*, that we will heareafter take him for our *Saviour* and *Lord*, and not at present. Fifthly, it must *seem* to be *voluntary*, and not constrained: for then it is not serious. Sixthly, It must *seem* to be *deliberate*, and *resolute* and *setled*, and not only the effect of a mutable passion. This goeth to make it a real *Profession* in the common sense of all mankind.

G 3 Obj.

Obj. *But how few among us do so much as seem to be understanding, serious, and resolved in covenanting with Christ?*

Ans. In the *Degree* of these, we all fall short of that which is our *duty:* But if you accuse any of the want of so much as is necessary to an *acceptable Profession*; First, you must be sure that you speak not by *uncharitable surmise* and *hear-say*, but upon certain *proof* or *knowledge.* Secondly, and that therefore you speak it not at a venture, of *whole Parishes* or *families*, but only of *those persons* by *name*, whom you know to be guilty. Thirdly, and that you remember that it is the *Pastors office to judge*, and that you expect not that every one must give an account of their knowledge *to you:* and if there be a mis-judging, it is the fault of the *Pastor*, and not *yours* (of which more anon.) Fourthly, that persons *Baptized* are *already* admitted into the Church, and therefore if they make profession of Christianity, they must not be put to bring any other proof of their title; but it lies on you to *disprove* it, if you will have it questioned. And to reject them from communion without a proved accusation, is *Tyranny* and *Lording* it over the Church of God. These are Gods terms of Church-communion; and if you will needs have stricter, you must have none of his making, but your own.

Obj. *But all visible Christians and Churches, are visible Saints and Regenerate; and so are not ours.*

Answ. To be a *Visible Saint*, is to profess to be a *Saint:* And whosoever doth profess the *Baptismal Covenant* professeth to be a *Saint*. Conversion, Regeneration, Faith and Repentance, are all contain-

contained, into taking *God the Father, Son, and Holy Ghost, for our Father, Saviour, and Sanctifier.*

Obj. But *you may teach a Parrot to speak those words.*

Answ. It's true: And perhaps to speak any words which you use your selves: But if you will thence conclude, that words must not be taken as a *Profession*, you grosly err, or abusively wrangle; or if you in'err thence, that your neighbour understandeth himself no more than a Parrot doth, you must prove what you say to the *Pastor* of the Church: For God hath not allowed him to *excommunicate* baptized persons, because you say that they are ignorant. And if they are willing to learn, it is fitter to teach them than *to excommunicate them.*

And here I must lament it, that I have met with many censorious Professors, who would not communicate with the Parish Churches, because the *people are ignorant*, who, when I have examined *themselves*, have proved *ignorant* of the *very substance of Christianity*, so that I have been much in doubt whether I ought to admit them to the Lords Table or not. They knew not whether Christ was *Eternal*, or whether he was *God when he was on earth*, or whether he be *Man now he is in heaven*; nor what *Faith* is, or what *Justification* or *Sanctification* is, nor what the *Covenant* of grace is; nor what *Baptism* or the *Lords Supper* are; nor could prove the Scripture to be the word of God; or prove mans soul to be immortal; but gave false or impertinent answers about all these: and yet could not joyn with the *ignorant Churches.*

And next I desire you here to observe the *different*

Priviledges, as well as the different Conditions of *Visible* and *Invisible* Church-membership.

The members of the Church mystical or Regenerate, have the pardon of all sin, and acceptance with God, and comunion with him, and with his Church in the spirit, and are the adopted children of God, and heirs of everlasting life, and shall live in heaven with Christ for ever.

The meer *Visible* Members of the Church, that are not regenerate by the *spirit*, as well as sacramentally by *water*, have only an *outward Communion* with the Saints, and have only the *Bread and Wine* in the Sacrament, and only a *name to live* when they are dead. And are these such great matters, that we should envy them to poor sinners that must have no more? Have we the *Kernel*, and do we envy them the *Shell*? Have we the *Spirit* and do we envy them the *flesh*, or *outward signs* alone?

Yea, consider further, that it is more for the sake of the truly faithful, than for their own, that all Hypocrites have their station and priviledges in the Church: God maketh use of their *Gifts* and *Profession* for his elect; to many great services of the Church: and is it not then a foolish ingratitude in us, to murmur at their presence?

Understand well the conditions and reasons of this visible state of membership, and how far it is below the state of the Regenerate, and it will turn your separating murmuring into a thankful acknowledgment of the wisdom of God.

DIRECT.

DIRECT. VII.

Get right and deep apprehensions of the Necessity and Reasons of Christian Unity and Concord: and of the Sin and Misery of Divisions and Discord.

WHen we have but *slight apprehensions* of a duty we easily neglect it, & scarce reprove our selves for it, or repent of our omission. And when we have but slight apprehensions of the evil of any sin, a little temptation draweth us to it; and we are hardly brought to through repentance for it: And there is in many Christians, a strange inequality and partiality in their apprehensions of good and evil. Some duties they dare not omit, and they judge all ungodly who omit them: when some others as great are past by, as if they were no part of Religion. And some sins they fear with very great tenderness, when we can scarce make their consciences take any notice of others as great.

And usually they let out all their zeal on one side only, while they over-look the other. The Papist seemeth so sensible of the good of *Unity*, and the evil of *Divisions*, that he thinketh usurpation of an Universal Church-Monarchy, and Tyranny, and horrid bloud-shed, to be not only lawful, but necessary for the prevention and the cure. But to make him as sensible of the wickedness of these *unlawfull means*, and of the good of a *serious spiritual Religiousness*, and of *Christian*
Love

Love and tenderness and forbearance, here is the great difficulty.

And on the other side, many are very sensible of the need of spirituality and seriousness in Religion, and of the evil of hypocritical formality and imagery, and of usurpation of the prerogatives of Christ, and of the plague of persecuting Pride and cruelty, who yet have little sense at all, of the good of Unity, and of the mischiefs of divisions in the Church. Yea many are so careful to be found exact in their obedience to God, that they build very much for *duties* and against *sins*, upon dark and very far-fetcht consequences, and upon a few obscure and doubtful passages in Scripture, when there is no express words, or clear text at all, to bear them out: And doubtless the darkest intimations of the will of God, must not be disregarded. But on the other side, we cannot bring them to lay to heart, some duties and sins, which are over and over, an hundred times, and that with vehemenncy, exprest and urged in the plainest words.

And because all Christians pretend to submit to the word of God, I will try whether it be not thus with you in the present case, and will cite many plain expressions of Scripture, for Christian *Unity* and *Concord*, that you may either better perceive your duty, or plainly shew your great partiality.

Zech. 14. 9. *In that day there shall be One Lord and his name One.* Ezek. 34. 23. *And I will set up One Shepheard over them.* Ezek. 37. 23. *I will make them One Nation—& One King shall be King to them all, and they shall be no more two Nations, nor divided*

Scriptures against Division.

divided into two Kingdoms any more. 24. *And David my servant shall be King over them, and they shall have one shepherd.* Jer. 32. 39. *I will give them one heart and one way.* So Ezek. 11. 19. Joh. 21. 22. *That they all may be One; as thou Father art in me, and I in thee; that they also may be One in us, that the world may believe that thou hast sent me. And the glory which thou gavest me, I have given them, that they may be one, even as we are one; I in them, and Thou in me, that they may be made perfect in one, and that the world may know that thou hast sent me; and hast loved them as thou hast loved me.* Joh. 11.52. *That he should gather together in One, the children of God that are scattered abroad.* Act. 1. 14. *These all continued with one accord, in prayer and supplication. And* Chap. 2. 1. *They were all with one accord in one place.* Act. 4. 24, 32, *They lift up their voice to God with one accord, and said, Lord thou art God.--And the multitude of them that believed, were of one heart, and of one soul.* Act. 5. 12. *They were all with one accord in* Solomons *Porch.* Act. 15. 25. *It seemed good to us, being assembled with one accord--* 2 Cor. 11. 2. *I have espoused you to one husband--* Eph. 4. 1, &c. *I the prisoner of the Lord beseech you that ye walk worthy of your vocation wherewith ye are called with all lowliness and meekness; with long-suffering forbearing one another in love: endeavouring to keep the unity of the spirit in the bond of peace. There is One body, and One spirit, Even as ye are called in One hope of your calling. One Lord, One Faith, One Baptism, One God and Father of all, who is above all, and through all, and in you all.* ---v. 12. 13. *For the perfecting of the Saints, for the work of the Ministry, for the edifying of of the body of Chrift. Till we all come in the Unity of the faith, and of the knowledge of the Son of God, unto a perfect Man: that we henceforth be no more children, toffed to and fro, and carried about with every wind of doctrine, by the flight of men, and cunning craftinefs whereby they lye in wait to deceive: But fpeaking the truth in love, may grow up into him in all things who is the Head, Chrift: From whom the whole body fitly joyned together, and compacted by that which every joynt fupplyeth, according to the effectual working in the meafure of every part, maketh increafe of the body, to the edifying of it felf in love.*

1 Cor. 12. 3, 12, 13. *No man can fay that Jefus is the Lord, but by the Holy Ghoft--As the Body is One, and hath many Members, and all the members of that One body, being many are One body, fo alfo is Chrift. For by one Spirit, we are all baptized into One body.--v. 22.23. Nay much more thofe members of the body, which feem to be more feeble are neceffary: And thofe members of the body which we think to be lefs honourable, upon thefe we beftow more abundant honour, & our uncomely parts have more abundant comelinefs. For our comely parts have no need; but God hath tempered the body together, having given more abundant honour to that part that lacked: that there fhould be no Schifm in the body, but that the members fhould have the fame care one for another. And whether one member fuffer all fuffer with it, & if one be honoured, all rejoyce--*v.15. *If the foot fay, Becaufe I am not the hand, I am not of the body, is it therefore not of the body--* (By all this you may fee, that even the *loweft, difhonoured, weak and uncomely* members, muft not be denied to

And against Divisions. 61

be of the Church (or body of Christ.)

1 Cor. 13. 4, 5. *Charity suffereth long, is not easily provoked, thinketh no evil-----The greatest is charity. v. 13.*

1 Cor. 1. 10. *Now I beseech you brethren, by the name of our Lord Jesus Christ, that ye all speak the same thing, and that there be no divisions among you: but that ye be perfectly joyned together in the same mind and in the same judgement.* v. 12, 13. *Every one saith, I am of Paul and I of Apollo--Is Christ divided? was Paul crucified for you? or were ye baptized into the name of Paul.* Ch. 3. 15. *If any mans work be burnt, ye shall suffer loss; yet he himself shall be saved, yet so as by fire----* Ch. 3. 3, 4. *For ye are yet carnal: For whereas there is among you envying and and strife and divisions, are ye not carnal, and walk as men? while one saith, I am of Paul &c.*

Rom. 14. 1. *Him that is weak in the faith receive, but not to doubtful disputations.* v. 3. *Let not him that eateth, despise him that eateth not: and let not him which eateth not judge him which eateth: for God hath received him: who art thou that judgest another mans servant? to his own Master he standeth or falleth. One man esteemeth one day above another; Another esteemeth every day alike. Let every man be fully perswaded in his own mind: He that regardeth a day, regardeth it to the Lord!* v. 10. *But why dost thou judge thy brother? or why dost thou set at nought thy brother? we shall all stand before the judgment seat of Christ. Let us not therefore judge one another any more* v. 13, 14. *I know and am perswaded by the Lord Jesus, that there is nothing unclean of it self; but to him that esteemeth any thing unclean, to him it is unclean.* v. 17. *For the Kingdom of God is,* not meat and drink, but righteousness and peace and joy in the Holy Ghost: For he that in these things serveth Christ, is acceptable to God and approved of men: Let us therefore follow after the things that make for peace. v. 22. Hast thou faith? Have it to thy self before God. Ch. 15. 1, 2. We that are strong ought to bear the infirmities of the weak, and not to please our selves. Let us every one please his neighbour for his good, to edification. For even Christ pleased not himself.---v. 5, 6. Now the God of patience and consolation, grant you to be like minded one towards another, according to Christ Jesus: that ye may with ONE MIND, and ONE MOUTH, glorifie God.----Wherefore receive ye one another, as Christ received us, to the glory of God.

Ch. 16. 17, 18. Now I beseech you brethren, mark them which cause divisions and offences contrary to the doctrine which ye have learned and avoid them. For they that are such serve not our Lord Jesus, but their own belly, and by good words and fair speeches deceive the hearts of the simple.

Act. 20. 30. Also of your own selves shall men arise, speaking perverse things, to draw away Disciples after them.

Joh. 13. 35. By this shall all men know that ye are my Disciples, if ye have love one to another.

1 Cor. 11. 17, 18. I hear there are divisions among you: For there must be also heresies among you, that they which are approved may be made manifest.

Matth. 13. 29, 30. Nay, lest while ye gather up the tares, ye root up also the wheat with them: Let both grow together till the harvest----41. The Angels shall gather out of his Kingdom, all things that offend, and them which do iniquity, and shall cast them into a fur-

Divisions and Separation. 63

a *furnace of fire---* Then *shall the righteous shine forth as the Sun, in the Kingdom of their Father.*

V. 47. *The Kingdom of heaven is like a net, cast into the Sea; which gathered of every kind: which when it was full, they drew to the shore; and sate down and gathered the good into Vessels, and the bad they cast away: so shall it be at the end of the world.*

Matth. 22. 9, 10. *Go into the high ways, and as many as ye find, bid to the marriage* (or as Luk. 14. *Compel them to come in*) *so those servants went unto the high ways, and gathered all as many as they found both bad and good, and the wedding was furnished with guests. And the King saw there a man that had not on a wedding garment, and said, Friend. How camest thou in hither,* &c. (Mark, thus he will condemn wicked hypocrites themselves, but blameth not the *Ministers* that compelled them, or that let them in) Gal. 6. 1. *If a man be overtaken in a fault, ye that are spiritual, restore such a one in the spirit of meekness: considering thy self, lest thou also be tempted. Bear ye one anothers burdens, and so fulfill the Law of Christ, Let every man prove his own work.*

Note that *Paul* purified himself as having a Vow: He circumcised *Timothy*; He became a Jew to the Jews, and all things to all men, that he might win some.

Phil. 1. 15, 16. *Some preach Christ of envy,* &c. as aforecited.

Phil. 2. 1, 2, 3. *If there be any consolation in Christ,---fulfil ye my joy, that ye be like minded, having the same love, being of one accord and of one mind. Let nothing be done through strife or vain glory;*

glory; but in lowliness of mind, let each esteem other better than themselves-- 14. *Do all things without murmurings and disputings*---

Ch. 3. 15, 16. *Let as many as are perfect be thus minded: and if in any thing ye be otherwise minded, God shall reveal even this unto you. But whereunto we have already attained, let us walk by the same rule; let us mind the same things.*

1 Thes. 5. 12, 13. *We beseech you, brethren, to know them that labour among you, and are over you in the Lord, &c. and be at peace among your selves.*

Tit. 3. 10. *A man that is an Heretick, after the first and second admonition avoid, knowing that he that is such, is subverted, and sinneth, being condemned of himself.*

Jam. 3. 1, 2, 13, &c. *My brethren, be not many Masters, knowing that ye shall receive the greater condemnation, For in many things we offend all---who is a wise man, and endued with knowledge among you, Let him shew out of a good conversation, his works with meekness of wisdom: But if ye have bitter envying and strife in your hearts, glory not, and lie not aginst the truth: This wisdom descendeth not from above; but is earthly, sensual, devilish: For where envying and strife is, there is confusion, and every evil work. The wisdom from above, is first pure, then peaceable, gentle, easie to be intreated, full of mercy and good fruits; without partiality, without hypocrisie: and the fruit of Righteousness is sown in peace of them that make peace.*

Mat. 12. 25. *Jesus said, every Kingdom divided against it self, is brought to desolation: and every City or house divided against it self, shall not stand.*

I have cited so many Texts against division

and for the Unity of the Church and concord of Christians, as one would think by the very hearing of them, without expositions or argumentation, should utterly mortifie all inclination to divisions and hard censures, in all true believers; yea, so many Texts as I am perswaded many that most need them, will think it tedious to read them over. And yet I have cause to fear lest many such will *feel* as little of the *sense* and *authority* of them, as if there were no such words in the Scripture, and none of this had been set before them.

Out of all these you may gather these reasons of the necessity of Unity, and of the evil of schism or division.

First, It is *One God*, *One Head*, *One Saviour*, and *One Holy Spirit*, into whose name we are all baptized. Secondly, It is *One Covenant* which all in Baptism make with this *One God*. Thirdly, It is *One Spirit* by which we are all *regenerated*, and *One new Nature*, which is in all the truly sanctified. Fourthly, It is *One Gospel* or holy word of God, which is to us all, the seed of our new birth, the rule of our faith and lives; and the foundation of our *hope*; and must be our daily meditation and delight, and the food on which the children of Gods family must all live. Fifthly, It is *One Body* of Christ, whereof we are all members. As Christ is not divided, so his Body, that is his Church, both as Mystical, and as Visible, is but *One*; however the Members and their *Gifts* and degrees of grace are many. Sixthly, It is *One way* of Faith and Holiness which all must walk in. Seventhly, And it is *One end* and happiness

piness which we all expect: and in *One Heaven*, that we must meet and live for ever (so many as are sincere in the faith which we profess:) And in Heaven we shall have one mind and Heart, and One employment in the Love and praise of our Creator and Redeemer, and one felicitating fruition of his Glory for evermore. Therefore he that seeth not the necessity of *Unity*, knoweth not the *Nature* of the *Church*, or *Faith*, or true *Religion*.

The *Honours* and *Benefits* of *Unity*, and the *shame* and *mischiefs* of *Divisions*, may appear to him, that farther considereth the instances which follow.

First, Our *Union* with the *Church*, is a sign of our proportionable *union* with Christ: And our *separation* from the Church, doth signifie that we are separated from Christ. He that is united but to the *Visible Church*, is but *visibly* (by Baptism and Profession) united to Christ: such a union is spoken of in *Joh.* 15. 2. *Every branch in me that beareth not fruit he taketh away* He that is united to the *mystical Church*, of the Regenerate and spiritual, is united to Christ by *faith* and by the *spirit*: For his Union to Christ is at the same instant of time, with his union with the Church: but in order of nature goeth before it. He that is divided from this *mystical Church*, cannot possibly (at that time) be a Member of Christ in the spiritual sense: As the member which is cut off from the *body*, is also separated from the Head. And he that himself forsaketh the *Visible Church* as such, forsaketh the *mystical Church* and Christ himself. For to forsake the *Visible Church*

Of Church Unity.   67

is such, is to cease to be a *Professor* of Christianity. One may be a member of the *Visible Church*, and not of the *Spiritual*; but you cannot be a Member of the *spiritual* Church, if you forsake and refuse the visible Church as such. For though a man may be *regenerate by the Spirit*, before he make an *open profession* or be baptized (and without baptism in some few cases) yet so he cannot be, if he refuse to be a *Professor*. Its possible indeed to be a member of the Universal Church, both as *Mystical*, and as *Visible*; as *spiritual* and as *professing*, while we have not opportunity to joyn with any one particular Church, or to *separate* from some *particular Church*, without separating from the *Universal*: But to separate from the *Universal Church*, is to separate from *Christ*.

But then you must understand, that the Universal Visible Church is nothing else, but *all professing Christians in the world, as visibly subjected to Christ as their Head*: And that there is no such thing in being, as the Papists call the *Catholick* or *Universal Church*; that is, *the universality of Christians subjected to one Vicar of Christ as their Head* either Constitutive or Governing. Such a pretended Head is an Usurper and no true authorized Vicar of Christ; and therefore such a Church as such, is nothing but a company of seduced Christians, following such a traiterous Usurper. And to separate from the Pope, is not to separate from Christ or from his Church.

Secondly, Consider also, that *Union* is not only an *Accident of the Church*, but is part of its very *essence*, without which it can be *no Church*,

H 2   and

and without which we can be *no members* of it. It is no Kingdome, no City, no Family, and so no Church, which doth not consist of *United* members: as it is no house which consisteth not of united parts. And he is no Member which is not *united* to the *whole*. It is the great our of mens boldness in dividing wayes, that they take *union* to be but some *laudable accident*, while it may be had; which yet in some cases we may be without: and think that *separations* are *tollerable* faults, even when they are forced to confess them faults: But they do not consider that *Unity* is necessary to the *being* of the *Church*, and to the *being* of our own Christianity. Read 1 Cor. 12. *Ephes.* 4.

Thirdly, Remember also that our *Union* is necessary to our *Communion*, with *Christ* and with his *Church*: and to all the blessings and benefits of such communion, *Joh.* 15. 4. *Abide in me, and I in you: As the branch cannot bear fruit of it self, except it abide in the Vine; no more can ye, except ye abide in me: for without me, ye can do nothing. If a man abide not in me, he is cast forth as a branch, and is withered, and men gather them, and cast them into the fire, and they are burned.* And Col. 2. 19. *From the Head all the body by joynts and bonds having nourishment ministred and knit together, increaseth with th increase of God.* The member that is cut of from the body, hath no life or nourishmen from the head or from the body, but is dead He that is out of the Church is without the Tea ching, the holy worship, the prayers, and th discipline of the Church, and is out of th way where the spirit doth come; and out of the Society which Christ is specially related to: For he is the Saviour of his body; and if we leave his hospital, we cannot expect the presence and help of the Physician: Nor will he be a Pilot to them who forsake his ship: Nor a Captain to them who separate from his Army: Out of this Ark, there is nothing but a deluge; and no place of rest or safety for a soul.

Fourthly, The *Unity* of Christians is their *secondary strength*: Their *primary strength* is *Christ* and the *Spirit of grace* which quickeneth them: And their *secondary* strength is their *Union among themselves*: Separation from *Christ* depriveth men of the *first*; and *separation* from *one another* depriveth them of the *second*. An *Army* is stronger than a *man*: and a *Kingdom* than a *single person*: A *flame* will burn more strongly than a *spark*: and the *waves* of the *Ocean* are more forcible than a single *drop*. *A threefold Cord is not easily broken.* Therefore it is that weak Commonwealths do seek to strengthen themselves by confederacies with other States. The Church is likened to an Army with Banners; both, for their *Numbers*, their *Concord*, and their *Order*. And therefore Christ saith, that *a Kingdom divided cannot stand.* *Union* is the *Churches strength*: and what good soever they may pretend, *Dividers* are certainly the weakeners and destroyers of the Church: and as those means which best corroborate the body, and fortifie the spirits, do best cure many particular diseases, which no means would cure whilst nature is debilitated: So are the Churches diseases best cured, by uniting fortifying remedies, which will be increased by a *Dividing* way of Reformation : *Dividing* is *wounding*, and *uniting* is the *closing* of the wound.

There is no good work but *Satan* is a pretender to it, when he purposeth to *destroy* it : He resisteth *Light* as an *Angel of Light*; and his *Ministers* hinder *Righteousness*, as pretended *Ministers of Righteousness*: and he will be a *zealous Reformer*, when he would *hinder Reformation*. And this is the mark of *Satans way* of Reformation : He doth it by *dividing the Churches of Christ*, and teaching Christians to *avoid each other* : And to that end he zealously aggravateth the faults of every party to the rest ; that they may have odious thoughts of one another ; and Christian Love may be turned into aversation: As in the Plague time every one is afraid of the breath and company of his neighbour, and they that were wont to assemble and converse with peace and pleasure, do timorously shun the presence of each other ; because they know that it is an infectious time, and they are uncertain who is free : even so doth Satan break the Societies and converse of Christians, by making them believe that every party hath some dangerous infection, which as they love their souls, they must avoid.

And he destroyeth your *Love* to one *another*, by pretending *Love* to your *selves*: O how careful will he be for your souls! when the Devil would undo you, he will do it as your Saviour : And when his meaning is to save you from Heaven, and from Christ, and from his saving grace, and from Union and Communion with his Church, and from

from the impartial Love of one another, he takes on him that he is saving you only from *sin* and from *Church-corruptions:* Or rather that it is *Christ* and not *he* that giveth you counsel: And he can do much in *imitating Christ*, in the *manner* of his *suggestions*, to make you believe that it *is Christ indeed*. Perhaps his counsel shall come in in the midst of a *fervent prayer*, or presently after it, to make you believe that it is an undoubted answer of your prayers: and oft-times his impulses are vehement and much affecting, to make you think that it is something above nature: and the *pious pretence* will much perswade you to think that sure this can never come from an evil spirit: But if you had well studied 2 *Cor.* 11. 13, 14, 15. *Gal.* 1. 8. *Luke* 9. 55. 1 *Joh.* 4. 1,2. 2 *Thef.* 2. 2. you might be wiser, and be saved from this deceit. I will not recite the words, because I would have you turn to them, and seriously study them.

And in this *dividing work*, the Devil doth as make-bates do, who first goes to one man and tell him a tale what such a one said against him, and what a dangerous person he is, and then go to the other, and say as much of the first to him: So the Devil saith to the Presbyterian, O take heed of the Independents! and to the Independents, Take heed of these Presbyterians; To the Anabaptist he suggesteth, Avoid these Protestants: Take heed of them, for they Baptize infants: and to the Protestants he saith, Take heed of these Anabaptists, for they are against baptizing any till they come to full age: To one he saith, Away from that Church, or think not those persons to be religious; for they pray by the book: and to the other he faith, Take heed of those people, as whimfical and proud, and brainfick fanaticks; for they pray *without-book* by the *Spirit*. To one fort he faith, Take heed of those people, for they wear a Surplice, or Kneel at the Sacrament, or anfwer the Priefts in the Refponfes of the Common-prayer: To the other he faith, Take heed of thefe difobedient, ftubborn, felf-conceited people, that will fit at the Sacrament, and will not conform to the orders of the Church. I am not now minding whofe opinion is right or wrong, among all thefe parties, or any like them; But how charitable to your fouls the Devil is, when he would deftroy your *charity* and your *fouls*; and how *piouſly* and *kindly* he would have you *take heed* when he would lead you to *perdition*: and how great a *Reformer* he will be, if he may but do it by *Dividing*.

It may be the young unexperienced Schifmatick (of what fect foever) will diftafte thefe words, and think I fpeak like an adverfary to Reformation: and fo the Devil would make him think, of all other Chriftians as well as of me, except his party. But if one fhould give fuch counfel for the prefervation of his own health and bodily comfort, as the *Dividing* fpirit giveth him for the Church and for his foul, he would quickly underftand it, according to my prefent fenfe. If one fhould come in kindnefs to him, and bid him, [O take heed of that mouth and belly; for it getteth nothing, but devoureth all that the hands do get by labour: Cut off that hand, for it hath a crooked finger: Cut off that gouty foot, that it may not trouble
the

the whole body: Rip up those guts which have such filthy excrements, he would not swell against me if I advised him to suspect such kindness.

Fifthly, Remember also, that the *Unity* of Christians is their *peace and ease*, as well as their *strength* and *safety*. Psal. 133.1. *Behold how good and pleasant it is, for brethren to dwell together in unity!* As the amity and converse with friends, is pleasant, and the concord of families is their quietness and ease; so is it as to that amity and concord which is the bond of Church-society. And the *divisions* and *discord* of Christians, is their mutual *pain* and *trouble*. Do you not *feel* your *minds disturbed* by it? Do you not *see* the *Church discomposed* by it? The itch of contention, doth ordinarily make it pleasant for the time, to every Sect to scratch by zealous wranglings and disputes for their several opinions, till the bloud be ready to follow: But the smart and scab doth use to convince them of their folly. But if they will go more than *Skin-deep*, they may need a *Surgeon*. *Children* will *claw* themselves; but it is *Madmen* that will *wound* themselves. The hurt which we get in the Christian warfare, by mortifying the flesh, or by the persecution of the malignant enemy is tenderly healed by the hand of Christ, and usually furthereth our inward peace. But if we will hurt, and wound, and divide our selves, what pity or comfort can we expect.

Sixthly, Consider also that the *Unity* and *Concord* of Believers is their *Honour*, and their *Divisions* and *discord* are their *shame*: And consequently the

the honour or dishonour of Christ and the Gospel, and Religion is much concerned in it. Agreement among Christians telleth the world, that they have a certainty of the faith which they profess, and that it is powerful and not ineffectual, and that it is of a healing nature, and tendeth to the felicity of the world. But Divisions and discords among Christians perswade unbelievers, that there is no *certainty* in their *belief*: or that it is of a vexatious and destructive tendency; or at best that all its power is too weak, to overcome the malignity which it pretendeth to resist; where did you ever see Christians live in *undivided unity, undisturbed peace*, and *unfeigned Love*, but the very infidels and ungodly round about them, did reverence both them and their religion for it. And where did you ever see Christians *divided, unpeaceable* and bitter against each other, but it made them and their profession a scorn to the unbelieving and ungodly world? and whilst they despise and vilifie one another, they teach the wicked to despise and vilifie them all.

Seventhly, I may therefore add, that the *Unity* of *Believers*, is one of Gods appointed means for the conversion and salvation of *unbelievers*: And their *Divisions and discord* are an ordinary means of hardening men in infidelity and wickedness, and hindring their love and obedience to the truth. As a well-ordered Army, or a City of uniform comely building, is a pleasing and inviting sight to the Beholders; when a confused rout, or a ruinous heap, doth breed abhorrence: even so the very sight of the concordant societies of Christians, is amiable and alluring to those without;

without; when their disagreements and separations make them seem odious and vile. As a musical instrument in tune, or a set of musick, delight the hearer by the pleasing harmony; when one or more instruments out of tune, or used by a rude unskilful hand, will weary out the patience of the hearer; so is it in this case; and the difference is much greater, between concordant and dis-concordant Christians. Who loveth to thrust himself into a fray? And what wise man had not rather partake of the friendly converse, than joyn with drunken men that are fighting in the streets? Peace and Concord are amiable even to nature; And you can scarce take a more effectual means, to win the world to the Love of Holiness, than by shewing them that Holiness doth make you *unfeigned* and *fervent* in the Love of one another. 1 *Pet.*1.22. Nor can you devise how to drive men more effectually from Christ, and to damn their souls, than to represent Christians to them like a company of mad men, that are tearing out the throats of one another? How can you think that the unbelievers and ungodly should think well of them, that all speak so ill of one another? When the Lutheran flyeth from the Calvinist, and the Episcopal from the Puritan, and the Protestant from the Anabaptist, and the Presbyterian from the Independent, and all the other side implacably fly from them, Can you wonder if the Infidel and the Idolater fly further from you all? Mark well the words of Christ in his prayer, *Joh.* 17.20.21,22, 23. *For them which shall believe on me by their word, that they all may be one, as thou Father art in me, and I in thee, that they also may be one* *in us: that the world may believe that thou hast sent me: And the glory which thou gavest me, I have given them, that they may be one, even as we are one: I in them, and thou in me, that they may be made perfect in one, & that the world may know that thou hast sent me, and hast loved them as thou hast loved me.*

All these observations are obvious in these words. 1. That the unity of Christians must be *universal*, even of all that believe the Gospel of Christ. 2. That this Union should have some low resemblance to the Union of the Father and the Son. 3. That it is Christs great desire and intercession for his Followers, that they may be one. 4. That their glory is for their Unity. 5. That their Unity is their perfection. 6. That the Father and Son are the Head or Center of the Unity. 7. That this Unity is the great means of converting the world to the Christian faith, and convincing Infidels of the truth of Christ, as sent by God. Open but your eyes and you may see all these great doctrines in this prayer of Christs for his peoples Unity: O that all the Christian Churches would try this means for the worlds Conversion! (Not on the impossible terms of Popery, but on the necessary terms proposed by Christ.)

8. *External Unity* and peaceable Church-communion doth greatly cherish our *Internal Unity* of Love: And Church-divisions do cherish wrath and malice, and all the works of the flesh described by *Paul, Gal.* 5. 21, 22, 23. I pray you consider how he describeth the fleshly and spiritual man: *v.* 14, 15. *For all the Law is fulfilled in one word, even in this, Thou shalt love thy neighbour as thy self: But if ye bite and devour one another, take heed*
that

that ye be not consumed one of another. I say then, walk in the spirit, and ye shall not fulfill the lusts of the flesh. For the flesh lusteth against the spirit, &c. Now the works of the flesh are manifest, adultery, enmities or hatred, variance, emulations, wrath strife, seditions, (or as it may be read *Divisions* or *factions*) heresies, envyings, murders, &c. But the fruit of the spirit is Love, joy, peace, long-suffering, gentleness, goodness, faith, meekness, temperance: Against such there is no law. And they that are Christs have crucified the flesh, with the affections & lusts. If we live in the spirit, let us also walk in the spirit. Let us not be desirous of vain-glory, provoking one another, envying one another.

Obj. O but those that I separate from are guilty of this and that and the other fault.

Answ. Chap. 6. 1. *Brethren, if a man be overtaken in a fault, ye which are spiritual restore such a one, in the spirit of meekness, considering thy self lest thou also be tempted.* Instead of censorious disdain and separation, *bear ye one anothers burthen, and so fulfil the law of Christ:* which you think you fulfil by your unwarrantable separations, while you are but fulfilling your fleshly passions.

When once parties are engaged by their opinions in Anti-churches and fierce disputings, the flesh and satan will be working in them against all that is *holy sweet* and *safe*. When united Christians are provoking one another to Love and to good works, and minding each other of their heavenly cohabitation, and harmonious praise, and are delighting God and man by the melody of their concord; The contentious zealots in their separate Anti-churches, are preaching down
Love

Love and preaching up hatred, and making those that differ from them seem an odious people not to be communicated with, by aggravating their different opinions or modes of worship, till they seem to be no less than Heresie or Idolatry. If many thousands yet living in *England* or *Ireland*, had not heard this with their ears, yet *James* may be believed, *Chap*. 3. 1, &c. *My brethren, be not many Teaching-Masters* (for that is the word) *knowing that we shall receive the greater condemnation: For in many things we offend all* (which he addeth because the arrogancy of Sectaries was caused by the aggravating of other mens offences.) *If any man offend not in word, the same is a perfect man* (that is, If you will shew that you are prefecter and better your selves than those whom you account so bad; see that your foul back-biting, reviling, censorious contentious tongues, do not prove the contrary) 13. *who is a wise man and endued with knowledge among you, Let him shew out of a good conversation, his works with meekness of wisdome*: (that is, Let him that will be thought more knowing and religious than his neighbours, be so much more blameless and meek to all men, and excell them in good works) v. 14. *But if ye have a bitter zeal* (for so is the Greek word) *and strife in your hearts, glory not*, (in such a zeal, or in your greater knowledge) *and lie not against the truth.* 15. *This wisdome descendeth not from above* (as you imagine who father it on Gods word and spirit) *but is earthly, sensual* (or natural) *and devilish.* (O doleful mistake, that the *world*, the *flesh*, and the *Devil*, should prove the cause of that conceited spiritual knowledge and excellency, which they

thought

thought had been the infpiration of the fpirit) v. 16. *For where zeal and ſtrife is,* (that is, a *ſtriving* contentious zeal againſt brethren) *there is confuſion* (or *tumult and unquietneſs*) *and every evil work.* O lamentable reformers, that ſet up *every evil work*, while they ſeemed zealous againſt evil) v. 17. *But the wiſdome that is from above, is firſt pure, then peaceable, gentle, and eaſie to be intreated ; full of mercy and good fruits ; without partiality* (or wrangling) *and without Hypocriſie. And the fruit of righteouſneſs is ſown in peace, of them that make peace* : when peace-breakers that ſow in diviſions and contention, ſhall reap the fruit of unrighteouſneſs, though they call their way by the moſt religious names.

Thus I have briefly ſhewed you what Unity and Diviſion are, that wrong apprehenſions draw you not to ſin.

DIRECT. VIII.

When any thing needed amendment in the Church, remember that the beſt Chriſtian muſt be the forwardeſt to reformation, and the backwardeſt to Diviſion ; and muſt ſearch and try all means of Reforming, which make not againſt the concord of the Church.

I Do not here determine in what caſes you may or may not ſeparate, from any company of faulty Chriſtians. I only ſay that you muſt never ſeparate what God hath conjoyned ; the *Holineſs*
and

and the *Unity* of believers: If corruptions blemish and dishonour the Congregation; Do not say [Let sin alone; I must oppose it for fear of division] But be the forwardest to reduce all to the will of God. And yet if you cannot prevail as you desire, be the backwardest to divide and separate; and do it not without a certain warrant, and extream necessity. Resolve with *Austin*, I will not be the chaff, and yet I will not go out of the floor though the chaff be there. Never give over your just desire and endeavour of Reformation: And yet as long as possibly you can avoid it, forsake not the Church which you desire to reform. As *Paul* said to them that were ready to forsake a sea-wrackt vessel, *If these abide not in the ship, ye cannot be saved:* Many a one by unlawful flying and shifting for his own greater peace and safety, doth much more hazard his own and others.

DIRECT. IX.

Forget not the great difference between casting out the wicked and impenitent from the Church by discipline; and the godlies separating from the Church it self, because the wicked are not cast out. The first is a great duty: The second is ordinarily a great sin.

THe question is not, *Whether the impenitent* should be put away from Church-communion? That's not denied. But whether you should
sepa-

separate from the Church, because they are permitted: This is it which we call you to beware: Not but that in some cases, a Christian may lawfully remove from one Church to another, that hath more light and purity, for the edification of his soul. But before you separate from a faulty Church, *as such as may not lawfully be communicated with*, you must look well about you, and be able to prove that thing which you affirm.

Many weak Christians marking those Texts which bid us *avoid a man that is an Heretick*, and to have *no company* with disorderly walkers, and not to eat with flagitious persons, do not sufficiently mark their sense, but take them as if they call'd us to separate from the *Church* with which these persons do communicate. Whereas if you mark all the Texts in the Gospel, you shall find, that all the separation which is commanded in such cases (besides our separation from the Infidels or Idolatrous world, or Antichristian and Heretical confederacies, and no Churches) is but one of these two sorts. First, either that the *Church* cast out the impenitent sinner by the power of the Keys. Secondly, or that *private men* avoid all *private familiarity* with them. And both these we would promote, and no way hinder. Thirdly, but that the *private* members should separate from the *Church*, because such persons are not cast out of it, shew me one Text to prove it if you can.

Let us here peruse the Texts that speak of our withdrawing from the wicked. 1. *Cor.* 5. Is expresly written to the whole Church, as obliged *to put away the incestuous person from among them*, *and so not to eat with such offenders.* So is that in 2 *Thes.* 3. and that in *Tit.* 3. 10. *A man that is an Heretick after the first and second admonition avoid*: Unless it be a Heretick that hath already separated himself from our communion; and then it can be but private familiarity which we are further to avoid. In brief, there is no other place of Scripture, that I know of, which commandeth any more. I have before shewed that abundance of Church-corruptions, or of scandalous members, were then among them, and yet the Apostle never spake a syllable to any one Christian, to separate from any one of all those Churches: Which we cannot imagine that the Holy Ghost would have wholly omitted, if indeed it had been the will of God.

Obj. *But then why did* Luther *and the first Protestants, separate from the Church of* Rome, *and how will you justifie them from Schism?*

Answ. It's pitty that sloth and sottishness, should keep any Protestant (or Papist either) in such ignorance, as to need any help to answer so easie a question at this day! Let not equivocal names deceive us, and the case is easie. By the word *Church,* the Scripture still meaneth; first, either the *Universal Church,* which is the body or Kingdome of Christ alone: Secondly, or *particular Congregations* associated for personal communion in Gods worship: But the Pope hath feigned another kind of thing, and called it *The Church*: That is, *The Universality of Christians as headed by himself, as the constitutive and governing head*: Whereas, first, God never instituted or allowed such a Church. Secondly, nor did ever the
Univer-

Of our separation from Rome.

Universality of Christians acknowledge this usurping Head. Shew me in Scripture, or in Church-History, that either there ever was *de facto*, or ought to be *de jure*, such a thing in the world as they call the *Church*, and I profess I will immediately turn Papist. But if you ask why we separated from the Papal Church? I answer, Because, first, it was *no Church of Christ* (as such.) And secondly, It was a *Church of traiterous combination*, against the prerogative of Christ, and therefore by the Protestants called the Antichristian Church. We separated not from *Rome*, either as the *Universal Church*, (for that it was not) nor as *part of the Universal Church*; (for so we hold communion with those that are Christians in it still) Nor as a true worshipping *Congregation* (for they consist of many thousand congregations which we never had local communion with: and as true worshipping congregations *in specie*, we still hold communion with them in mind, so far as they are such indeed: But in two senses we separate from them: First, as a *Papal Catholick Church*; because in that sense they are *no Church of Christ*, but a pack of rebels: Secondly, as *particular Congregations in specie*, which have mixed Gods worship with false doctrine, and Idolatrous bread-worship, and other unlawful things, which by oaths and practice they would force those to be guilty of, who will communicate with them. And thus we disown them only as *neighbour Churches*, that never were their *lawful subjects*, but bear our testimony against *their sin*. And our fore-fathers who were members of their Churches,

I 2   depart-

departed to save themselves from their iniquity, and because they were refused by themselves, unless they would lie, and forswear, and be idolaters, and communicate with them in their sin. Nor would they then, nor will they to this day, admit any into communion of their particular Churches, as such, who will not first come in to their pretended Universal Church, which is no Church, and worse than none. If this answer seem not plain, and full to you, it is because you understand nor Christian sense and reason.

DIRECT. X.

Expect not that any one lawfully received by Baptism into the Christian Church, should be cast out of it, or denied the priviledge of Members, but according to the rules of Christian discipline, by the power of the Keys; that is, for obstinate impenitency in a gross or scandalous sin, which the person is proved to be guilty of: and this after private and publick admonition, and tender patient exhortation to repentance.

Here are two things which I desire you to observe. First, what is Christs appointed way, for removing members from the Communion of the Church. Secondly, how great a sin it is to remove them by a contrary and arbitrary way of our own presumptuous invention.

First,

Church-Justice necessary.

First, It is here supposed, that the person is not a professed *Apostate*: For there needeth no *casting out* of such. He that turneth *Turk* or *Heathen*, or openly renounceth Christianity, or ceaseth the Profession of it, doth go out of the Church himself, and needeth not to be *cast* out. Unless it be any Tyrant who will come to the Communion in scorn, while he professeth but to shew his lawless will. He that seeketh the Communion of the Church in sobriety, thereby professeth himself a Christian; and for such as being Baptized continue this profession, Christs way of rejecting them is plainly described in the Gospel. *Mat.* 18. 15, 16. *If thy brother shall trespass against thee, go and tell him his fault between thee and him alone. If he shall hear thee, thou hast gained thy brother: but if he will not hear thee, then take with thee one or two more; that in the mouth of two or three witnesses, every word may be established: And if he shall neglect to hear them, tell it to the Church: But if he neglect to hear the Church, let him be to thee as an Heathen man, or a Publican.*

Tit. 3. 10. *A man that is an Heretick after the first and second admonition, reject.*

1 Cor. 5. *Ye are puffed up, and have not rather mourned, that he that hath done this deed, might be taken away from among you: For I verily as absent in body, but present in spirit, have judged already as though I were present, concerning him that hath so done this deed, in the name of our Lord Jesus Christ, when ye are gathered together, & my spirit with the power of our Lord Jesus Christ, to deliver such a one to Satan--* V. 7. *Purge out therefore the old leaven--* v. 11, 12, 13. *With such a one no not to eat. ---Do not*

*not ye judge them that are within? ...
away from among your selves that w...*

By all this it is plain that the Ch...
ercise a regular course of justice, wi...
son that it shall reject: He must fir...
vately of his fault, and then before...
(unless, at least, the open notoriety...
vate admonition needless:) And t...
told the Church: and the Church m...
passion, tenderness and patience, an...
authority of the Lord Jesus, and the...
dence of truth, convince him and pe...
repent: And he must not be rejected...
this, he obstinately refuse to hear th...
is, to Repent, as they exhort him.

Note here, that no sin will warr...
out the sinner, unless it be seconded...
tency: It is not simply as a drunka...
cator or swearer, that any one is t...
but as an *impenitent* drunkard, or
swearer, &c.

Also that it is not all *impenitency*
rant their rejection: But only imp...
the Churches admonition.

Note also: that no private pers...
that any offender be cast out, eithe...
sin is known to him, or because he...
famed to be guilty, till the thing be
ficient witness.

Yea, that the admonition given...
proved, as well as the fault whic...
t:d.

Yea, if all the town do know him
and witness prove that he hath been

Objections against Church-Justice. 87

nonished, he may not be rejected till he be *heard speak for himself*, and till he refuse also the publick admonition.

This is Chrifts order, whose *wifdom*, and *mercy*, and *authority* are such, as may well cause us to take his way as beft. And yet the ignorance or rashness of many profeffors is such, that they would have all this order of Chrift overturned: and some of them muft have fuch a drunkard and fuch a swearer kept away and rejected, before ever they admonished them, or exhorted them to repentance, or prove that any one elfe hath done it; much more before they have told the Church, or proved that he hath neglected the Churches admonition. And some go so much farther, that they muft have all the Churches taken for no Churches, till they have gathered them anew; and muft have all the Parifh at once rejected (till they have gathered out some few again) without any fuch order of proceeding with them, as Chrift appointeth: It may be a thousand shall be caft out at once, when never a one of them was thus admonished.

Obj. *They were never members of a true Church, and therefore need no cafting out.*

Anf. Were they never baptized? or is not baptifm Chrifts appointed means of admiffion into his Church?

Ob. *They were baptized in their Infancy, & afterward bred up in ignorance & profanenefs, and know not what their baptifm is, nor ever foberly owned it.*

Anfw. Either they ftill profefs themfelves Chriftians, and attend Gods ordinances with the Church or not: If not, then they are Apo-
ftates:

of living contrary to it, you must proceed against them one by one as Christ appointeth; and first admonish them, and then tell the Church; and not say *they* are ignorant and profane, and expect upon your saying so, they should all be unchurched. Yea, if you prove them ignorant, if they be willing to learn, it is fitter presently to instruct them than to excommunicate them: nor do you read of any excommunicated for meer ignorance. But we confess that in gross ignorance, they may shew themselves uncapable of sacramental Communion, and may be denied it while they are learning to know what they do. But the mercy of God hath made points absolutely necessary so few, that this may be done in a short time, if the Persons be willing, and the Teachers diligent, and sufficiently numerous for that work. And though it is to be lamented, that in many great City-Parishes, the Ministers are not enough to catechize the twentieth part of the people, yet for the generality of Parishes through the Land, if Catechizing were used as it might be, there would not any great numbers be long kept away for meer ignorance. And he that is the cause of his Parishes ignorance, by neglecting Catechizing and personal conference, and then unchurcheth them for the ignorance which he is guilty of, but doth take a preposterous course, for his own account and comfort, or for the peoples good.

Obj. *But they refuse to learn or be instructed.*

Answ.

Anf. If that and their grofs ignorance be proved together, as you may delay them for the latter, so you may reject them for the former; because it sheweth their impenitence: But this must be *proved* of them and not affirmed without proof.

Obj. *But their Baptism made them members only of the Universal Church; and not of any particular Church: And therefore will not prove them such.*

Anf. True: But he that is a member of the Universal Church, is fit to be received into a particular Church; And there wanteth no more but mutual consent: And if he have statedly joyned with a particular Church in ordinary communion, Consent hath been manifested, and he is a member of that particular Church, and must not be rejected by it, but in Chrifts way. And this is the common cafe in *England*. The perfons who were baptized in infancy, were at once received into the Univerfal Church, and into fome particular Church, and have held communion at age with both; and have right to that communion till they are publickly proved to have loft their right.

And if we had no Churches, but particular Churches were to be gathered anew, yet he that is a baptized member of the Univerfal Church, and confenteth to communion with that particular Church in all the ordinances of Chrifts appointment, doth lay a fufficient claim to his admiffion, and cannot lawfully be refufed, unlefs he ftand juftly cenfured by a Church which formerly he was in. Yet this we confefs, that he can be no member of that particular Church, who fubjecteth not himfelf to the *particular Paftors* of it, and to the *neceffary acts or parts of their Office*

Office and Miniſtration: Becauſe he denieth his own conſent.

11. The ſinfulneſs of unchurching Perſons or Pariſhes, without Chriſts way of regular proceſs, conſiſteth in all theſe following parts. 1. It is a caſting off the Laws of the great Law-giver of the Church, and ſo a contempt of his authority, wiſdome, and goodneſs ; and a making of our ſelves *greater*, or *wiſer*, or *holier* than he. 2. It is groſs *injuſtice*, to deprive men of ſo great Priviledges without any ſufficient proof of their forfeiture! It is worſe than to turn whole Pariſhes out of their Houſes and Poſſeſſions: without any lawful proceſs or proof ; upon rumours or private affirmations that they are Delinquents. It is not doing as we would be done by: what if any ſhould ſay of you, that you are Heretical and deny Fundamental Truths? Or what if they ſhould ſay of a ſeparated Church: that they are generally Hereticks, or of wicked lives (as the Heathens did of the ancient Chriſtians) and therefore that they are *no Church*, nor to be communicated with; would you not think that they ſhould every one *perſonally* be accuſed, and proof brought againſt them, and that they ſhould ſpeak for themſelves, before they were thus condemned? 3. And it is an aggravated crime in them, that ſo much cry down *Church-tyranny* in others, to be thus notoriouſly guilty of it themſelves? what greater injuſtice and tyranny can there be, then that all mens Chriſtianity and Church-rights, ſhall be judged Null, upon the cenſures and rumours of ſuſpitious men, without any juſt proof or lawful tryal? That it ſhall be in the power of every one,

who

The aggravations of it. 91

who hath but uncharitableness enough to think evil of his neighbours, or to believe reports against their innocency to cast them out of the Family of God, and to unchristen and unchurch men arbitrarily at their pleasure? That any man that is but unconscionable enough to say [They are all *ignorant* or *prophane*] shall expect to have his Neighbours excommunicated. 4. It maketh all Churches to be lubricous and uncertain shadows: when a censorious person may unchurch them at his pleasure. What you say of others, another may say of you; and as justly expect to be believed. 5. It unavoidably bringeth in uncurable *divisions*: For there is no certain rule of justice with such persons: and therefore they know not who are to be received to their Communion, and who not: And the same man that one thinketh is to be rejected and kept out, another will think is to be received: And who knoweth which of them is to be obeyed. If one say that a Parish is a Church, and another say that they are to be unchurched, who knoweth which of them to believe. 6. It is a reproach to the Church and Christian Religion, when we tell the world that, that we have not so much *justice* and *equity* among us, as Heathens have in their worldly societies. 7. It depriveth the Church of the solace of her Communion, when the best man is not sure, but a censorious person may at his pleasure turn him out as unworthy. 8. It greatly wrongeth Jesus Christ, who so dearly loveth the weakest of his flock; and hath purchased their priviledges at so dear a rate: and whose body is maymed, when any of his members are cut off: and who taketh

the

the wrong that is done them as done unto himself. These are the great virtues of that censorious zeal, which un-churches Persons or Parishes without just tryal and proof, upon rumours of fame, or their own surmises.

DIRECT. XI.

Understand well what is the power of the Keys, and what the Pastoral office is, as they are the Governours of the Church intrusted by Christ with the power of admission and rejection; that so you may know how far you are to rest in the judgement of the Pastors, and may not attempt to take any part of their office to your selves.

THe power of the *Keys*, is the power of *taking* into the *Church*, and of *Governing* it, and of *casting* out: Both in respect to *present Order*, and in respect to future happiness, by a Ministerial declaration of the sense of the Gospel, concerning the state of such as they.

The power of *Baptizing*, is the power of the *Keys*, for *reception* into the Church. The private members have not the power of *baptizing*, nor were the Pastors ever appointed to do it, by their advise, consent, or vote. Therefore the private members have not the power of the Keys for admission. And it is most apparent in the Gospel, that the Keys for *admission* and for *exclusion* are

given

Pastoral power proved. 93

given into the same hands, and not one to the Ministers and another to the Flock: Therefore the people that have not the first, have not the latter.

For full proof of this observe the meaning of these Texts. Isa. 22. 22. *And the Key of the house of David will I lay upon his shoulder; so he shall open and none shall shut: and he shall shut and none shall open.* Isa. 9. 6. *The Government shall be upon his shoulder.* Mat. 16. 19. *I will give thee the Keyes of the Kingdom of Heaven; and whatsoever thou shalt bind on earth shall be bound in heaven,* &c. Mat. 18. 18. *Verily I say unto you, whatsoever ye bind on earth shall be bound,* &c. Joh. 20. 23. *Whosoever sins ye do remit, they are remitted to them; and whosoever sins ye retain they are retained.* Mat. 28. 19. *Go and teach all Nations baptizing them,* &c. Joh. 20. 21. *As my Father hath sent me, even so send I you.* Act. 1. 16, 17. *Judas was numbred with us, and had obtained part of this Ministry.* Act. 20. 28. *Take heed to your selves & to all the flock over which the Holy Ghost hath made you Overseers, to feed the Church of God.*---Rom. 1. 1. *Paul a Minister of Jesus Christ, called an Apostle, separated to the Gospel of God.* 1 Cor. 4. 1. *Let a man so esteem of us as of the Ministers of Christ, and Stewards of the mysteries of God.* Act. 14. 23. *They ordained them Elders in every Church.* Tit. 1. 3. *Ordain Elders in every City, as I appointed thee.* V. 7. *A Bishop must be blameless as the Steward of God.* 1 Tim. 3. 5. *For if a man know not how to rule his own house, how shall he take care of the Church of God.* 1 Tim. 5. 17. *Let the Elders that rule well be counted worthy of double honour*-- 1 Pet. 5. 2. *Feed the flock of God*

which

which is among you, taking the oversight thereof--
Heb. 13. 7, 17, 24. *Remember them which have the rule over you, who have spoken to you the word of God*--*Obey them that have the rule over you, and submit your selves; for they watch for your souls*--*salute them that have the rule over you*--- 1 Thes. 5. 12, 13. *We beseech you brethren to know them* (that is, acknowledge their power and labours) *that labour among you, and are over you in the Lord, and admonish you, and to esteem them very highly in love for their works sake, and to be at peace among your selves.*

Read these with judgement, and then believe if you can, that the power of the Keys or Government is in the People. Shew us what Text doth give them that power? and where the Scripture calleth them to exercise it by Votes? Or where God requireth ability in them for Church-government? or where he calleth them to leave their Callings and attend this work? When those that must perform it, he separateth to it as by office, and calleth them to *give themselves wholly* thereunto. 1 *Tim*. 4. 15, 16. Tell us when the people were authorized to baptise? or to rule the Church, that is, themselves.

Obj. Mat. 18. 15. *Tell the Church: if he hear not the Church,* &c. *Answ.* Many Expositors think that by the *Church there* is meant the *Ministers* only, by this reason: The Church that must *teach* must be *heard:* the Church that must be *heard* must be *told:* But that is only the Pastors and not the People: *Ergo*--- But I easily grant you, that the word [*Church*] there signifieth the whole Congregation (as Dr. *Taylor* in his second Dis-

swasive

[*swative* hath well shewed] But it is an Organized body only. And so the Office is to be performed only by the Organical part; and not by any of the rest. When I say to a man [*Hear me*] I do not mean that he should hear me with his *eyes*; but only with his *ears*: And when I bid him *See* or *Read*, I bid him not do it with his *ears*, but with his *eyes*. Nor do the eyes receive this power from the feet or hands, but immediately from the Head: Though if they were separated from the body they could not retain it. So if another Kingdome send to *England*, to desire an Army of men to help them, they mean the King only as the Commander of them, and the people as the executors of his Command. So when you are bid to tell the Church, it is *quatenus aurita*, that it must be told; And when you are bid to hear it, it is as *Teaching* that it must be heard. So that this talketh not of any Government in the people, either to use or to give.

Obj. 1 *Cor.* 5. *Paul* biddeth all the Church *to put from among them that wicked person.*

Answ. Note; that *Paul* passeth the sentence first himself [*I have judged as if I were present* (not that *you deliver*, but *) to deliver such an one to Satan*] And therefore he doth this himself [*in the name of the Lord Jesus*] and supposeth himself *among them in spirit and power* when they do it [*and my spirit with the power of our Lord Jesus Christ*] 2. And I have said, He speaketh to an organized Church, which had two parts, and accordingly two works to do: The *Ruling* part was to *put away the Offender* by *Judgement* or *Sentence*: And the people were all *to put him away,* by actual *shunning* his
Commu-

Communion, which is but the obeying of that sentence. If the King send to a Corporation to execute any Law, he meaneth not that *all persons* must do it in the like manner; but the Magistrates by Command, and the people by obeying them, and executing their Commands. If I desire a man to transcribe me a Book, and bring it me; I mean not that every part of him shall herein have the same office; But that he *read* it only with his *eyes*, and understand it with his *reason*, and transcribe it with his hand, and travel with his feet. The Pastors only excommunicate by Judgement or Sentence: and the people by obedient execution of it.

Obj. *Who then shall cast out an Heretick or pernicious Pastor, if he himself must be rejected?*

Answ. 1. The neighbour Pastors shall *renounce Communion* with him, and reject him from their *neighbour Communion*. And they shall warn that people to avoid him (by virtue of the common relation which they have to the universal Church of Christ.) 2. The people (as *Cyprian* determineth) are bound to *forsake him*: not by an act of *Government* over him or themselves; but by an act of *obedience to God*, and of *self-preservation*; As Souldiers must forsake a trayterous General, or Seamen a perfidious or desperately unskilful Pilot that would cast them all away. As the people did alwayes choose their Pastors to Govern them, so may they in such a case refuse them, without usurping any Government themselves.

Well! Now let us see what influence this truth

truth should have upon your Church-Communion.

Do you say that your neighbours are not to be accounted members of the Church, nor to be communicated with? Who took them into the Church by Baptism? Was it not a Minister of Christ? If you say no, you must prove your accusation. If you grant it, was it not his *Office* so to do? Hath not God made his Ministers Judges whom they are to baptize? And afterward also whom to catechise and instruct and admit to the communion of the Church? There is no doubt of it. If then they are admitted by an entrusted Officer, will you venture to usurp the place, yea and to do them the wrong to say that they are no members? Is it any of your trust or work? I pray you mark what a mercy it is to you, that the Officers and not the private members are intrusted with this work. First, if it were *your work*, you must *study* and be able to perform it. Secondly, you must *watch for it*, and *constantly attend* it. If a Heretick pervert the text of Scripture, you must convince him by your skill in the Originals or in the sense. How many hundred or thousand persons are there in a Parish to be tryed? The worst of them must have a hearing and just trial at least, before you can refuse him lawfully: And how accurately must this difficult work be done, that the weakest be not denied his right, nor the unfit admitted? How long must a sinner be admonished and exhorted to repentance? And are *you able* and *willing* to leave all your callings, to do all this?

If the *Minister* that doth it, must lay by the

business of the world, how think you
do the same without laying by you[r]
siness? If *he* must have so many year[s]
preparation, can *you* do it *without* ?
it is not for *Sermons* only, that min[isters need]
their learning and labour; but also
pline and *guidance* of the flocks. T[he]
it be *your work*, you must be *account*[able be]
fore God. And do you not fear suc[h]
And if these busie people had their
they not be in a worse case than t[he]
and lazy Minister?

Consider it well, and you will fin[d]
not at all bound *to know* what the sp[irit of]
any man is, as he is to joyn in Ch[urch]
nion with you, but upon your P[astors]
word. Whether their understandi[ng be suffici]
ent at their admittance, you are n[ot]
called to try: but the Pastor is: A[nd when he hath]
admitted them, you are to rest in [it]
(unless you would undertake th[em your]
selves) whether the profession o[f re]
pentance be serious and credible, [you are not]
called to try and judge: But if yo[ur Pastor hath]
admitted them, he hath numbred [them with]
visible Christians: And it is the cr[edit of the]
Pastor that you have to consider; a[nd he]
must judge of the credibility of the p[rofession,]
not immediately by your own tri[al of all]
the persons that you shall meet a[t Sacrament]
or in publick Communion, you ar[e not re]
quired to try; And if you never sa[w them]
or heard them speak, you may per[form your du]
ty nevertheless: Indeed if as a *nei*[ghbour]

called to instruct or counsel or comfort them, you must do it: But there may be five thousand in one Church with you, whose names or faces you are not bound to know; but to rest in the knowledge of them to whom the keys are committed, who according to their office take them in.

Obj. *But what if they are notoriously wicked? Must I be blind?*

Answ. No: you must do your best by neighbourly watchfulness and help (though not by Pastoral Government) to reform all about you whom you are able to do good to. And if you know them to be so bad, you must privately admonish them, as is proved; and then if they hear not, tell the Church: But if you see a man in the Church at the Sacrament, or a thousand men, who are unreformed, and you know it not, you have no reason to avoid the communion of such: And if there be a thousand in the Church whose case you are strangers to, this may be no sin of yours, and should be no impediment of your communion.

Obj. *But what if carnal negligent Ministers will let in all into the Church by Baptism, and give them the Lords Supper? Shall it be thus in their power to corrupt the Church: And must we joyn with them and take no care of it?*

Answ. There is no person in any office or trust, but may too easily abuse it: And the more noble the work and trust is, the greater is the sin and calamity of such abuse. And no doubt but a bad unfaithful Minister is one of the greatest sinners on earth, and one of the most pernicious plagues to the Church. Which could not be, unless

less it were in his power to do very much hurt. But it will not follow that therefore you must take his place, and become the Church Governours, or try all the peoples fitness your selves. If a Judge be bad, you may say what an intollerable thing is it, that one man shall have power to give away mens estates, and take away the life of the innocent, and to acquit the guilty.] But for all that you must not mend it, by stepping up into the judgement seat your self, and saying, that you or the rest of the People will do it better. Some body must be trusted with it. If you are fittest, offer your self to the office. The thing that you must do is, to do your best to deliver the Church from so bad a Pastor: Use all your wisdom and diligence to amend him: And if you cannot do that, use all your interest to get him out, and get a better: And if you cannot do that, deliver your own soul from him, by removing to a better if you are free; But if as servants, or children, or wives, you are under another Government which restraineth you, be patient, and use such means as God provideth for you. This is the true way of your Church-duty, and not to think that you must have a knowledge of the Godliness of all that you communicate with: or that you must refuse communion if the Pastor be remiss and negligent.

Obj. But will it not be my sin if I communicate with such as I know to be notoriously wicked? when a little leaven leaveneth the lump.

Answ. It will be your sin if you obey not Christ, *Mat.* 18. 15. in admonishing them; and so if it belong of you, that they are not removed:

or

or if you do not your duty to reform the Pastor or remove him: But otherwise if they be there without your fault, it is no more your sin to communicate with such men, than it is to live and converse with fellow servants that are wicked; when it is not *you*, but your *Master* that hath the choice of them.

And the *leavening* of the *lump* which the Text speaketh of, is the tempting of others to the like sin; and not that the innocent shall be held guilty of it: nor were the words spoken to the people to perswade them to do the Pastors work, or to separate from the Church; But to the Pastors to perswade them to cast out the sinner; and to the people, to perswade them to execute their Sentence, (and the Apostles in particular.)

It would rule and quiet people, if they knew the trust and work of the Pastors, from their own.

DIRECT. XII.

Well study the gracious Nature and Office of Jesus Christ, and his great readiness to receive those that come to him, though weak in faith; and his backwardness to refuse such commers; that so you may desire a Church-discipline that is suitable to the Nature and Office of Christ, and to the design and tenor of the Gospel.

CHrists outward Discipline is agreeable to his inward. As those that come to him by faith, he *will in no wife caft out* or reject; so those that come to him by *profession* of faith, he would not have his Ministers in any wise reject. And *coming to Chrift* when he was personally on earth, did signifie the following of him in presence, as well as believing in him: Just so far as men will come, so far they shall be received by Christ: If they will come but *towards* him, he will not put them back. If they will come but to his *visible Church* by a dead profession, he would not have his Ministers repulse them. The outward priviledges of the visible Church which they come to, they shall possess. If they will come over to the Church of the regenerate, they shall be saved. But where ever they stop it shall be their own doing. Many came to Christ when he was on earth, whom he never repulsed, though he was marvelled at and grudged at for entertaining them. Some came so far as to own his Name, and did Miracles by it, that yet did not follow him: whom the Apostles would have hindered, but Christ reproved them, *Mar.* 9.38. *Luk.* 9.49. Some came only to receive a Cure of their Diseases from him, whom his Disciples sometimes repulsed, but so did not he: when little children were brought to him, his Disciples rebuked those that brought them, as thinking them unfit for his reception: but Christ rebuked them for their forbidding of such guests. When he eat and drank with publicans and sinners, and when he received a kindness of a woman that had been a great sinner, the Pharisees censured him therefore as ungodly: But yet he would not abate his clemency. Many at this day can scarce digest it, that he sent forth a *Judas* to preach

preach the Gospel, when he knew that he was a thief and an hypocrite, and foreknew that he was a Son of Perdition, and would betray him, and that the Devil would enter into him; yea, knew that he was a Devil, *Joh.* 6. 70. and 13. 2. yea, that this *Judas* should be one of the twelve select Apostles, and one of the Family of Christ. Yet Christ repulsed him not; And if he did not partake of the Sacrament at his last Supper, it was not because Christ did turn him out, but because he went away himself. And accordingly the Apostles received 3000 at once into the Church, upon their sudden profession of repentance, even of such as had killed the Lord of Life. And though *Simon Magus* would not come out of the gall of bitterness, and bond of iniquity, yet was he not kept out of the visible Church, when he professed to believe and desired baptism.

Indeed if men will not come so far as to the *profession* of *true faith* and *repentance*, they are not to be received into the Church; Because the Church is a Society of *such Professors*: And if they will not come, they cannot be received. The Church and Sacrament must not be altered, and made another thing than Christ made it, for the receiving of another sort of men. We must not do as some that would have no *profession* of *saving faith and repentance*, but only a *consent to learn*, required of them that are baptized; and so baptism changed into another sort, which Christ never instituted and the Church never used to this day. But if Christians had well studied the compassions of a Saviour, and the tenour of his Gospel, and his practise upon earth, and instead of a surly flying from their neighbours, and groundless censuring them, were possessed themselves, with that love and tenderness which is the Evangelical temper, and the image of their Lord; it would put an end to many of our divisions, and bring us nearer the truth, and one another.

DIRECT XIII.

Yet, lest you run into the worse extream, remember still that the destroying of sin, and the sanctifying of mans nature and life by recovering us to the obedience and Love of God, was the design and work of the Redeemer: And that holiness and Peace must go together: And that the outward order and discipline of the visible Church, must be subservient to the inward spirituality and prosperity of the regenerate Church: And no such favour must be shewed to sinners, as favoureth and strengtheneth their sin, and hindereth the increase of holiness.

IT is woful work which ungodly Pastors make in the visible Church, under the name and pretence of *Unity, Concord, Peace,* and *Order*; when an enemy to true holiness, hath the manageing of these, you may easily imagine how they will be used: But sad experience hath told the *Christian* world, these 1300 years more doleful things than could have been otherwise imagined. The compassion which Christ shewed to sinners was to convert

and

and save them from their sin: But the compassion which carnal Pastors shew them, is to harden them in their sin, and make them believe that repentance and holiness are but hypocrisie or needless things. The *Unity* and *Concord* which Christ intended was a *Unity* in himself and a *Concord* in holy obedience to his Laws: But it is a *Unity* in the will of man and a *Concord* in obeying the Dictates of the proud, which Treacherous Pastors do require. It is a *Peaceable* progress of the Gospel, and *unanimous* endeavour to convert and sanctifie and save the world, which Christ requireth us to promote: But it is a *Peacable* enjoyment of their own prosperity, wealth and honour, and a *peaceable* forbearance of a holy life, which Wolvish Pastors do desire. It is an *Orderly* management of holy doctrine, worship and conversation, for the edification of the flock, and the increase of godliness, which Christ commandeth. But it is an absolute obedience to their wills, and exact observance of their new made Religious, and needless scandalous inventions, and adoreing of their titles and robes of honour, covering their ignorance, pride and sensuality, which Church-tyrants call the *Order* of the Church. All Christs indulgent tenderness and Discipline, are but to further his Holy design, of killing sin and sanctifying souls. But the *Images* of Piety, Government, Unity, Peace and order, which Hypocrites and Pharisees set up, are devised engines to destroy the life and serious practice of the things themselves, and are set up in enmity against spirituality and holiness, that there might be no
other

ges.

It is far from the mind of Christ, that no difference should be made between the *Holy* and the *profane*, the precious and the vile: Or that serious piety should be suppressed or discouraged; or faithful preachers hindred from promoting it, or ignorant graceless Ministers countenanced, under pretence of *Peace* or *Order*. The design of Christ was not like *Mahomet's*, to get himself an earthly Kingdom, and numerous followers meerly to cry up his name: And therefore he will not indulge men in their sins: nor abate, or alter the conditions of his Covenant, to win disciples: He will have his Ministers deal plainly with all to whom they preach, and let them know that without *self-denial* and *forsaking all* (in estimation and resolution) and a willing exchange of earth for heaven, they cannot be his true Disciples: Nor without a *Profest consent* to thus much, they cannot be his *visible profest* Disciples: But all that will not repent must perish. And therefore in their Baptism they must profess a renunciation of all competitors. His Ministers also must impartiality exercise the Keyes which he hath committed to their trust, and must not fear the faces of men, who at most are able but to kill the body. *Luk.* 12. 4. They must discern between the righteous and the wicked: and draw all scandalous sinners to repentance, or else exclude them from the communion of Saints, that the world may see that Christ is no freind to prophane persons, or sensual fleshly bruits. As *Chrysostome* comman-

commandeth the *Presbyters* not to give the body and blood of Christ to the unworthy, though he were the greatest Commander or wore a Diadem, and professeth that he would suffer his own blood to be shed, before he would give the blood of Christ to the unworthy: And as blessed *Paul* would become all things to all men to win them, and commandeth us not to please our selves, but to please our neighbours for their good to edification: And yet when it came to the flatterring of men in their sins, he saith that if he shoud so *please men*, he should be no longer the servant of Christ. And as to his *own interest* in mans esteem, he saith, *with me it is a small thing to be judged of you, or of mans judgement.* Rom. 15. 1, 2, 3. 1 Cor. 10. 33. Gal. 1. 10. 2 Tim. 2. 4. 1 Cor. 4. 3. Take heed therefore of pretending Unity, order, peace, or charity, against the strictest obedience of Gods laws, or against the faithfull preaching of the Gospel, and exercise of true Church-discipline, or against the necessity of the ancient profession of saving *faith and true-repentance* in all that will be admitted to the communion of the Church: It is not an ungodly unity, peace or order that we plead for.

DIRECT

DIRECT. XIV.

Though your Governours and not you, must judge what persons shall be of your Publike Church-commnion, yet it is you that must judge who are fit or unfit for your private company and familiarity. Here therefore excercise your strictness in your own Part.

As it is not *you*, but the King that must judge who shall be of the *same Kingdome* with you: nor the *servant* but the *Master*, that must choose who shall be in the *family* with him: Nor the *Scholler* but the *Schoolmaster* that must choose who shall be of the *same School* with him: So it is not *you*, but your *Pastor* that must judge who shall be of the *same Church* with you. As to the Universal visible Church, this is confest by all: And there is no reason why it should be denied of *particular Churches*, as is proved. But who shall be your *Pastors* or your *Masters*, your husbands or your wives, if you are yet *free*, you your selves must be the choosers: And who shall be your intimate companions, or your bosome freinds: Here therefore make as strict a choice as you can. If you meet a prophane person at the *Lords Table*, it is his own fault or the Pastors: But if you keep company needlesly with such, or *marry* such, it is your *own* fault. If the Pastor do not excommunicate them, you may choose not to be *familiar* with them: Though you must meet them at the *Church* and *pray* with them; you need not meet

them

them at the *Ale-house* and *drink* with them. Though you may not with a few of the most godly separate from the publike communion of all the rest; yet may you keep a more intimate familiarity with those few than with all the rest. And if you will consider, this is all that is necessary to your own duty, and that which is best for your own edification. Keep thus to a strictness within the bounds of your own place and calling, and God will bless you in such a strictness.

DIRECT. XV.

Understand well how much it hath pleased God, to lay all mans good or evil, happiness or misery, upon their own choice: And observe the reasons of it, that you may not oppose this order of God.

THough God by his grace must change the perverse disposition of mens wills, before they will make a gracious choice; yet it is most certain, that the teachings, commands, exhortations and reproofs of God, are directed to the *Will* of man: And that the promises and threatnings, mercies and judgements, are used to move and change the will: And that in the tenor of his Laws and Covenants, Christ hath set Life and Death before men, and put their *Happiness* in their own choice; and that no man shall have better or worse than he made choice of: that is, none shall be either happy or miserable, but as they

they did *choose* or *refuse*, the *causes* of happiness or misery. And the reason of this is, because *Natural free-will*, was part of the *Natural image* of God on *Adam*; and it is as natural to a man to be a *free-agent*, as to be *Reasonable*. And God will govern *Man as Man*, agreeably to his *nature*.

Therefore do not wonder if *Church-priviledges* are principally left to mens *own wills* or *choice*; when their *salvation* is left to it.

Indeed God would not have any man admitted into the Church and to its communion, in *his own way*, and *on his own terms*: The *way* and *terms* are of Christs appointment: That they must *Profess faith and Repentance* is his appointed *condition*: that the *Minister* must be the *publike judge* of this profession; and accordingly receive them solemnly by *baptism*, and that they must enter under the hand of the *Key-bearers* of the Church; All this is of Christs institution. But whether they will make this profession or not? and whether they will make it in *truth* or in *falshood*; and whether they will live according to it, or play the hypocrites and live contrary to it; These are at their own choice. And good reason; for the *gain* or *loss* must be their own. If any be in the Communion of the Church, who either *never made profession* of Christianity, or who is *proved* before them to have *apostatized* from that profession, or to live *impenitently* in any *gross sin*, after the *Churches admonition*, it is the Pastors fault; & yours if it be by the neglect of *your* duty. But if any *other* be there it is their *own fault*, and the loss and hurt must be their own. If any one that professeth

fesseth Christianity ignorantly, unbelievingly, and hypocritically be there: or if they come to the Sacrament whilest they live in secret or open sin, before they have been openly admonished by the Church, it is their own sin; and not you but they shall bear the blame. God leaveth such matters to their own choice: and as they choose they speed. And for us to grudge at this order of God, is but to quarrel at wisdome and goodness, and to correct Gods order by our disorder. The man that came in without a wedding garment, is blamed, and bound hand and foot, and punished: But the Minister that called him in and admitted him, is not blamed; because he did as he was bidden: He went to the high-ways and hedges and compelled them (by importunity) to come in, that the House might be filled: Nor are any that came in *with him* blamed, for having communion with such. For *they* were in *their places*, and did as they were exhorted to do. And so will it be in the case that is before us.

DIRECT. XVI.

Though the profession of Christianity which entituleth men to Church-communion, must be credible: yet remember that there are divers Degrees of credibility; and that every Profession which is not proved false is credible in such a degree as must be accepted by the Church.

PRofession of Christianity is every mans Church-title. No man is to prove the sincerity of his own profession; nor may the Church require such proof at his hands; For how can a man prove to another the sincerity of his *own heart?* But the *fuller* testimony he giveth of it, the *better* it is: And therfore none should *refuse* to make his own profession, as *fully credible* to the Church as he is able, nor is the Church to be blamed for enquiring after the *fullest credibility*, so be it they do it but *ad melius esse*, and not *ad esse*; not laying his *title* upon it, nor refusing him for want of it. But every *profession as such* is *credible* in some degree, which is *not disproved*. Because men are under God, the only competent judges of their own hearts: And the belief of one another is the ground of humane converse: And it is an injury to any man to account him a lyar, without sufficient proof. He that will disprove a mans profession, must prove first, that he doth not tolerably understand what he saith; secondly, or that he speaketh not seriously, but in jest; or not voluntarily:

Grace how far necessary. 113

luntarily, but in hypocrisie by constraint, or for some by end: Thirdly, or that he contradicteth his own words by some more credible words or deeds. And if you never yet thus disproved mens profession of Christianity before the Pastors of the Church and yet cry out against the Pastors for admitting them, you are not *true Reformers*, but *disorderly Mutineers*, and peevish censurers in the Church of Christ. Christs orders, and mens right, and all Church-justice, must not be trodden down and sacrificed to your humour, and arbitrary way.

DIRECT. XVII.

Know how far either Grace or Gifts are necessary to a Minister; that you may give both Grace and Gifts their due.

THere have been two great questions which long have troubled the Church, whether we may take him for a true Minister of Christ, that is *ungodly*? And what measure of *Gifts* is necessary to the being of the Ministry? I have carefully answered them both in my *Disputation of Ordination* long ago, and shall now only say in brief: First, that no *ungodly man* is *so called* to the Ministry, as to *excuse himself* before God for his usurpation and hypocritical administrations. Secondly, But many an ungodly man is *so far* called to the Ministry as that his administrations are all *valid to the Church*, and the *innocent people* shall not

L have

have the *loss*. Thirdly, no people should *choose* and *prefer* such an ungodly Minister before a better. Fourthly, but they should rather *submit* to such than have *none*, when a better cannot (by them) be had. *Judas* had a *place in the Ministry* with the Apostles, *Acts* 1. 17. And his ministration might be valid to others, though his hypocrisie might turn it into sin to himself. And his ministry might have been accepted of the people though they had known his hypocrisie as Christ did: But a *sincere Apostle* was to be *prefered* before him.

And for *Gifts*, First the greatest degree is best, and secondly, God maketh so great use of them that many a hypocrite with excellent gifts, doth edifie the Church more than many good men that are ungifted. Thirdly, but that measure of Gifts only is necessary to the *Being* of a Minister without which the *essential parts* of his *office* cannot be performed.

Learn therefore to prefer them that have more grace and gifts; but not to take them for no Ministers that want *Grace totally*, or want only *greater degree of gifts*. And marvel not that Gifts are more necessary to the validity of ministration than Grace is. He may perform the office of Minister to the benefit of the Church, that hath no saving grace at all: so did *Judas*: so did those in *Math.* 7. 21. that prophesied and cast out devils in Christ name, to whom he will yet say depart from me ye workers of iniquity, I know you not: For *Grace* is to save him that possesseth it: But Gifts are to teach and profit others. Yet *Grace* is an exceeding furtherance of the righ-

and succesfull use gifts: For ordinarily he that speaketh from the heart speaketh to the heart; when an unexperienced hypocrite speaketh without life. But sometimes a dulness and want of utterance in the sincere, and a natural and effected fervency in the hypocrite, with a voluble tongue, do obscure this difference; and make the hypocrite the more profitable to the Church.

DIRECT. XVIII.

Understand well the necessity of your Communion with all the Universal Church, and wherein it consisteth, and how far to be preferred before your Communion with any particular Church.

With the *Universal Church mystical*, you must have communion by the *same spirit*, the *same regeneration*, the *same Faith* and *Love*, and the *same Laws of God*; and *obedience* thereto.

With the *Universal Church visible*, you must have communion, in the *same Profession* of faith and repentance, and the same *baptism*, and the same *sort* of *ministry* and *publick worship*, so far as they are *universally determined* of by Christ. And though you are absent in body, you must be as present in spirit by consent, with all the Churches of Christ on earth. You must have *spiritual communion* with the whole *spiritual Church*, and *visible communion* in *kind* (in the same Rule of faith, and kind of worship) with all the *visible* Church; and

Local-presential communion with that *particular Church* where you are present, and with any other where your presence afterwards may be needful; unless they hinder you by unlawful terms.

So that it is not the same *kind* nor *measure* of Communion which you are obliged to hold with all; But you must have Communion with all *men as a man*; and with *neighbours* as a *neighbour*, and with *relations* according to the relations civil or domestical; and with all *true Christians*, as a *true Christian*; and with all *professed Christians*, as a *professed Christian*, and with the *particular Church* of which you are a part, *as a part* of that Church. And with your bosome Friends and intimate Companions, as a *Friend* and *Companion*.

And yet in all this, you must communicate with no Church or person in their sin it self: and yet not refuse their Communion in good, though mixt with sin. You must own all the *prayers* of all the Churches in the world, so far as they are good, and joyn in spirit by consent, as if you concurred with them in presence, and made all their prayers to be your own (As you do by the prayers of the Church where you are present.) If there be disorders or imperfections or sinful blemishes in their prayers, you must disown all those faults, but not therefore disown any part of all their prayers which are good, but desire to have a part in them and desire the pardon of their failings.

And here you may perceive what a mischief peevish separation is on both sides. It hindereth you from praying aright for others, as the members should do for all the body; And it hindereth

eth you from partaking in the benefit of the prayers of moſt of the Church of God on earth. Indeed God may hear thoſe prayers for you which you your ſelves diſown: But whether this may be expected, according to the ordinary courſe of his dealing, is much to be doubted: ſeeing he hath made every mans *will* or *choice* the ordinary condition of his participation of ſuch benefits, it is hard to conceive, that he that abhorreth the prayers of other men, or taketh them for ſuch as God abhorreth, or will not accept, and in his mind diſowneth all participation, and communion in them, ſhould yet have a part againſt his will. But of this more anon.

As your *Baptiſm* maketh you Members of the Univerſal Church, in order of nature before you are members of a particular Church; ſo your *relation* to the Univerſal Church is more *noble*, more *neceſſary*, and more *durable*, than your relation to any particular Church: It is more *noble*, becauſe the Society is more *noble*.

The *whole* is more excellent than a little part: It is more *neceſſary*, becauſe you cannot be ſaved and be Chriſtians, without being members of the Univerſal Church: But you may be Chriſtians and be ſaved, without being a member of any ſtated particular Church. It is more *durable* becauſe you can never ſeparate from the Univerſal Church, or ceaſe to be a member of it, without being ſeparated from Chriſt: But divers occaſions may warrant your removall from a particular Church. Live not therefore in thoſe narrow and dangerous principles, as if your Congregation or your party were all the Church of Chriſt; or

L 3

as if you had no Christian relation to any other Ministers or People, nor owed any duty to them as members of the same Body. But remember that all Christians, Persons and Congregations, are but the Members of the Kingdom of Christ.

DIRECT. XIX.

Take heed of ingaging your selves too far in any divided Sect, or of espousing the interest of any party of Christians, to the neglect or injury of the common interest of the Universal Church, or cause of Christianity.

I Doubt not but among several ranks of Christians, the soundest and most upright are to be best esteemed, and *(cæteris paribus)* their Communion to be preferred, before theirs that are more unsound and scandalous. But tis one thing to prefer the eye or hand, before the foot; a noble member before a more ignoble, and another thing to own a *Sect as such*, or a *party* as they either divide from others, or take up a dividing opposite interest. You are sure that the *Universal Church* of Christ can never erre against the *essentials* of Christianity, nor against any truth or duty necessary to their salvation. For then the Church were no Church, and then Christ were not its Head. And then the body of Christ might perish: And then Christ were not the Saviour of his body. But you cannot say of any *one part*, that you

you are sure *that part* shall never fall away and perish. There may fall out a necessity which may warrant the Body to cut off a hand or leg, to save the rest: But no corporal necessity can warrant you to destroy the whole; nor any one member to forsake the Body, before it is forcibly cut off.

He that seeth not how the espousing of parties and divided interests, doth corrupt most Christians in the world, and lacerate and deface the Church of Christ, doth not understand or not observe the condition of mankind. It is somewhat rare to meet with any serious Christians, who are not so deeply engaged into some *Sect* or *Side* of *party*, as to darken their judgements, and pervert their affections as to all the rest, and to corrupt their converse in the world: how blindly do such look on all that is good in those that differ from them? How partially do they judge of the judgements and practises of others? How small a thing will serve the turn, to excuse the faults of any of their party? And how small and common a good seemeth excellent in them? And how perversely do they aggravate the faults of all that are against their way? As if every infirmity were a crime, and had no excuse? yea, they are oft glad to hear of some miscarriage in them, for which they may speak against them. And very readily take up such reports, and are the willing-tongues of slanderous fame: and in all this their faction maketh them impenitent: For they think it tendeth to the disgrace of the other Party, and so of their Cause, which they account an errour; and consequently that God hath use for their

their malicious Calumnies to his glory.

What company can you come into of forward Christians, but they are talking against those of other parties?. (except a few true entire Christians, who are throughly possessed with the loving compassionate spirit of their Lord, and have received the true impression of the Gospel.) And if you mark the cause, you will find it is a *sectarian spirit*, that prevaileth against the *Catholick spirit* of *Christianity*. And in no sect more, than in those that pretend to be the *only Catholicks*, and to do all this against the Sectaries as such! What bitter lies do the Popish sects under the name of Catholicks daily vent not only against *Luther*, *Calvin*, and other Reformers, but any that stand against the peculiar interest of their party. And they that can get the upper hand and by worldly advantages become the domineering sect, do think that thereby, they are exempted from the name and number of sectaries; and that all are sectaries that question their authority, and do not absolutely obey them.

In all their discourse the stigmatizing of dissenters is an ordinary part! One side reproacheth the other as Hereticks and Schismaticks; And the other reproacheth them as hypocrites, formalists, and pharisaicall persecutors: And every party think that all this is a part of Christian zeal; and if they did it not they should be guilty of lukewarmness and neutrality, and consenting to the sins of others, And thus the Church of Christ is engaged in a war against it self: And when all men should know them to be Chrifts disciples by loving one another; most men may

perceive

perceive that they have too much contrariety to the Christian nature, by their endeavouring to make each other odious. And all because instead of distinguishing the members of the *same Body* by their several offices and degrees, we are grown to make *several Bodies* of them, and to set one part against another. How many a Kingdoms conversion from Infidelity hath been hindered? and how many a faithful Minister silenced or reproached? and how many excellent Christians slandered and vilified? and how many blameless customs, forms, and practices accused? and how many infirmities aggravated as mortal crimes, by a siding factious disposition, and to promote the cause and interest of a Sect. Therefore as you love your integrity and peace, keep up an impartial universal love and honour to all Christians as such, and take heed of a dividing spirit.

DIRECT. XX.

Be very suspitious of your Religious passions; and carefully distinguish between a sound and a sinful zeal; least you should father your sin on the spirit of holiness, and think that you are most pleasing God, when you offend him.

WE are seldome more mistaken in justifying our selves than in our *Passions*: And when our *Passions* are *Religious* the mistake is both *most easie* and *most perillous*: *Easie*, because we are apt

apt to be most confident, and not suspect them, the matter seeming so *great* and *good*, about which they are exercised. And *Perilous*, because the *greatness* and *goodness* of the *matter*, doth make the errour the *greater* and the *worse*. I have shewed before how easie it is, to think that our *Religious passions*, are all the works of the spirit of God: For we are apt to estimate them, by the depth and earnestness which we feel. But excellent persons have been here mistaken, as *James* and *John* were. And not only so, but when the passion is up, the judgement it self is seldom to be far trusted; For it inclineth us to err in all things that concern the present business. Therefore still remember the difference between *true zeal* and *false*: And know that he that is upright in the main, and whose zeal for Christianity is sound, may yet have much zeal that is unsound with it.

First, it is an ill sign when your zeal is raised about some *singular opinion* which you have owned, and not for the *common salvation* and substance of the Christian faith or practise. Or at least, when your odd opinion hath a *greater proportion* of your zeal, than many more plain and necessary truths.

Secondly, when your zeal is moved by any *personal interest* of your own: By honour or dishonour; By any wrong that is done you, or any reputation of wisdom or goodness, which lieth on the cause. Or at least when your *own interest* hath too large a *proportion* in your zeal.

Thirdly, when your zeal is more for the *interest* of your *party*, than for the Universal Church, and the common cause of Godliness, and Christianity; and can be content that some *detriment*
to

to the *whole*; may further the interest of the party.

Fourthly, when your zeal tendeth to *hurt and cruelty*, and would have God rather to glorifie his *Justice* by some present notable judgement; than his *Mercy* by patience and forgiving: And when your secret desire of *fire from heaven*, or some destruction to the adversaries is greater than your desire and prayer for their conversion. The sure mark of true zeal is, that it is *zealous Love*: It maketh you *love your neighbours and enemies* more *fervently* than others do: But *false zeal* maketh you more inclined to their *suffering*; and to reproach and *hurt* them.

Fifthly, it is an ill sign when your *zeal* is beyond the proportion of your *understanding*: And your *prudence* and *experience* is as much *less* than other mens, as your *zeal* is *greater*. True *zeal* hath some *equality* of *Light* and *Heat*.

Sixthly, It is an ill sign when it is a zeal which is easily kept alive, and hardly restrained: For that sheweth the flesh and the Devil are too much its friends. The true zeal of the spirit doth need the fewel of all holy means, and the bellows of meditation, and prayer to kendle it: and all is too little to keep it up in the constancy that we desire. But carnal zeal will burn of it self without such endeavours.

Seventhly, It is an ill sign when some *Sect* or *false-teacher* was the kindler of it; and not the sober preaching of the truth.

Eighthly, And it is an ill sign when it burneth in the same soul where *lust* and *wrath* and *pride* and *malice* burn; and when it prospereth at the same time

time, when the love of God, and a heavenly mind and life decay. The zeal of a sensualist, of a proud man, of a covetous man, of a self-conceited empty person, can hardly be thought a spiritual zeal.

9. And it is an ill sign when it carrieth you from the *holy rule*; and pretendeth to come from a spirit which will not be tryed by the Scripture: Or when it driveth you to use means which God forbiddeth in his Word: and putteth you upon wayes which the sealed Law and Testimony condemn: It cannot be of God, which is against Gods Word.

10 Lastly, it is a suspitious sign, when it is contrary to the judgement, experience and zeal of the generality of the most wise, experienced, tryed, sober, godly Christians; and so to the ordinary working of Gods Spirit in other men, who are as good as you. For Gods Spirit is not contrary to it self.

By all these signs you may easily perceive, how the dividing zeal of a Sect as a sect, doth differ from the genuine Christian zeal. The one is a zeal for some *singular opinion* : The other is a zeal for *Godliness* and *Christianity*. The one is kindled by some *interest* of our *own* religious reputation: the other is kindled by the interest of the *will* and *glory of God*. The one is for the strengthning of a *Party*: The other is to increase the Church Universal, and promote the common cause of Christianity: even when some particular truth or duty is the *Matter* of it, yet the *general cause of godliness* is the *end*. The one is a *burning, hurting zeal*, even the same which hath made matter for so

many

many Martyrologies, and frightfull Histories, by inquisitions, torments, prisons, flames, massacres and bloody wars: And the same which hath silenced so many faithful *Ministers*, and disturbed so many states and Churches: The other is a *zeal of Love*, which maketh men fervent in *doing good* to others: The one causeth men to revile and despise and censure and backbite, and zealously to make all dissenters seem odious, that the hearers may abate their love to them. The other maketh us value all that is good in others, and to hide their nakedness, and to make them better, and to provoke the hearers to love and to good works. The one tendeth to divisions and sidings and separations and distances from our bretheren: and to feed contentions: The other is a zeal for *unity, amity* and *peace*. The one is the complexion of the weak, and childish, the proud, and self-conceited, the peevish and surly sort of Professors: The other is the zeal of solid knowledge, and of the prudent, humble, meek and well grounded sort of Christians. The one is a zeal which flyeth most outward, against the sins of other men, and can live with pride, and covetousness, and selfhness, and sensuality at home: such *serve not the Lord Jesus, but their own bellies*, Rom. 16. 16, 17. The other beginneth at home, and consumeth all these vices in the heart; and as zeal increaseth humility, and meekness, and love, and self-denyal, and temperance, and heavenly mindedness increase. The one is easily got and easily kept, and hardly kept under! O how easie is it to get and keep a contemptuous, censorious, backbiting, dividing or persecuting zeal! But

the

the other is not so much befriended by Satan or the flesh, and therefore must be preserved by prayer and meditation, and very great diligence. How *hard* is it to keep up a *zealous love of God and Man*? and a fervour in all our heavenly and spiritual desires? Abate but your *diligence* and this will presently decay: when the fierce, contending, hurting, separating and persecuting zeal doth need no such fuel or labour to maintain it: The one is kindled by the enflaming censures of some rash and passionate Preacher that knoweth better how to *kill Love* than to *cause* it; or by the singular conceits of some Sectary or Divider; or by the backbitings of some *Doeg*, or malicious Calumniator: The other is kindled by the humble, and heavenly preaching of the Gospel, and by the meditations on Christs example, and a study to imitate him and his Saints in patience, forbearance, forgiving others and doing good. The one is a zeal which carrieth men *from the Scripture*, to pretenses of such revelations, and inspirations, and impulses as have no proof, but the feeling and fancy of the person: or at least, to abuse the Word of God, and plead it for that which it condemned: It provoketh men to some unlawful practise, under pretense of misinterpreted texts, and of good ends and meanings. The other still putteth you upon good, and striveth against evil, and goeth for tryal of every cause to the Law and to the testimony. Lastly, the one is a zeal which pretendeth the spirit, and yet goeth contrary to the common workings of the spirit, in the most part of the best and wisest Christians. But the other is the common vital heat, which animateth

all

all the body of Christ, and actuateth all his living members; and keepeth up love and holiness in the Church? and is the same in all humble heavenly Christians in the world. It will be of great use to you, in order to your own and the Churches peace, to understand and observe the difference between these contrary sorts of religious zeal.

DIRECT. XXI.

Lend not a patient ear to back-biters; much less must you hastily believe them when they speak ill of others: But shew your detestation of that sin, though they should be most religious people that use it, and do it upon a religious pretence.

I Do not say that it is *alwaies* unlawful to speak that which is ill of another behind his back. Sometime wicked men will take occasion to justifie sin it self, by the advantage of a sinners name: And sometime they will magnifie the vertues of some wicked man, or of some of their sect, on purpose to cast reproach on godliness, or to make others odious by the comparison. Yet in such cases we must repress their malignity more by a *defensive* than an *offensive* opinion. But the usual course of back-biting in all sorts of men, is sinful. The back-biter (how great or learned or religious soever) is but the devils minister, to
preach

preach down the love of others, and to exhort you to hate your brother, or to abate your charity to him. And he that patiently hearkeneth to such, is a partaker of their sin. And he that believeth them, hath taken the infection. Most of our odious thoughts of others, and our false and uncharitable censures, do come in this way. For the most part, men censure and separate and persecute most, where they are acquainted least, but go by hear-say, and judge of men by back-biters mis-reports : And acquaintance and familiary usually reconcileth them, and sheweth them their error. You think it is a fair excuse for you, when you either believe or report evil of another, to say, that you heard it from very honest and religious, or reverend persons; or you heard it from many, and confidently uttered. But God hath not allowed you to receive back-biters, because they are *godly*, or because they are *many*. This very age and time doth experimentally confute this excuse : In which it is so common a thing, for false reports and news to be uttered with confidence, and that by multitudes, and many of them religious, and yet neither truth nor ground at all, for what is said. *Back-biters, and haters of God* are conjoyned, Rom. 1. 30. *He that back-biteth not with his tongue, nor doth evil to his neighbour, nor taketh up a reproach against his neighbour,* is one that hath the mark of a Citizen of Zion. Psalm 15. 3. *An angry countenance must drive away a back-biting tongue.* Prov. 25. 23. Paul was afraid of that which we all now feel the evil of, even this evil spirit, which I am now detecting. 2 Cor. 12. 20. *Lest there be debates, envyings*

ings, *wraths*, *strifes*, *back-bitings*, *whisperings*, *swellings*, *tumults*, and so God would humble him among them. Rebuke *back-bitings* and *whisperings*, or you will hardly avoid the rest of these iniquities. It may be the reports which you hear may be all false: Or it may be it is some little matter made much greater than it is. Or it may be some part of the truth is concealed and some circumstance which would make it better understood. However, if it be true, when the reporter hath no call to speak it, or when the accused is not heard speak for himself, and you never heard what he hath to say, there is sin and injustice in the back-biter, the believer and reporter.

DIRECT. XXII.

Make not your selves judges of other mens actions, much less of their state, before you have a call, and before you have sufficient acquaintance or proof, of the person and of the case.

Very common reports and very confident presumptions, may all prove injurious and false. You may hear that such a family is prophane, and that such a person hath no religion, that such a one is covetous, and such a one erroneous, &c. and when it comes to the tryal, it may all prove false. However it must be as false to you, till you know, or prove it to be true: you may be ignorant of another

ther mans faults, without any faultiness of your own: But you cannot rashly censure another without being your self faulty though the matter should prove true. Justice must be observed as well in *private* as in *publick* judging. As no Judge in any Civil or Ecclesiastical Court, must condemn any man without sufficient proof (which made Christ say, *Matth.* 18. 15,16. Take one or two more, that in the mouth of two or three witnesses, every word may be established) so no man in his own *thoughts* must condemn his brother, by any rash or groundless sentence. It is safer for you to judge better of another than he is, than it is to judge worse of him than he is. In many cases it may be your duty to judge better of him than he is; because you must judge according to proof; And if the evidence or proof deceive you, it is none of your fault to be so deceived. And yet you are not hereby bound to believe a falshood: All that you are bound to believe is, that it is *probable* that such a person is vertuous, innocent, or sincere: and this no falshood: for that may be *probable* or *likely* which is not true.

Few well consider of the meaning of Christs words in *Matth.* 7. 1, 2. *Judge not that ye be not judged: For with what judgement ye judge, ye shall be judged: and with what measure ye mete, it shall be measured to you again:* I doubt not but part of the sense may be, He that judgeth without mercy of another, shall have judgement without mercy from God: as St. *James* expresseth it. But that's not all: but the rest of the sense is [And he that judgeth cruelly rashly and falsly of his brother, shall be so judged of by other men himself.] Not that

that God will *cause* it, but he will *permit it* ; and therefore can *foretell* it ; and make a righteous punishment, of the sin which he doth permit. Do you not know that other men will censure and backbite you, as boldly and as busily as you do censure and backbite others ? Is it such a pleasure to you to imitate the Devil, the great accuser, as that you will be as much accused your selves, and as hardly thought of, rather than you will give it over?

And see here how sin doth cross it self. Most of the censorious, are *proud* persons, who think others much worse than themselves, and therefore speak worse of their common and more ignorant neighbours, that they may be thought to be no common nor ignorant persons themselves, and they are offended with the Pastor of the Church, for admitting such persons into communion with such as they: That so their piety may be more conspicuous than their neighbours: when all this while they are but preparing for their own dishonour; And others will judge as bad of them. When usually the meek and humble and merciful Christian who judgeth hardly of himself and tenderly of all others, is tenderly and lovingly judged of by all. The Prelatist saith, [what obstinate persons are these Nonconformists, They do all to keep the approbation of their party] And are they not requited by many of them whom they censure, who say [What temporizing hypocrites are these Formalists and Latitudinarians ! They would turn Papist or any thing to save their skins, or get preferment. What perjury or other heinous crime will they no-number with *things* indifferent.] The Papist thinks the Protestant a Heretick unworthy to live on earth and therefore thirsteth for his blood; And is he not requited by the censures of them that think that he is but a blood-thirsty limb of Antichrist himself? If he think that the Protestant cannot be saved, because he is not a member of the Pope, or Roman Church; the Protestant requiteth him oft times with concluding, that a Papist cannot go beyond a reprobate, nor a worshipper of the Beast be saved. If the Independant censure the Presbyterian as a favourer of loosness and formality, the Presbyterian can requite him, by censuring him to be an enemy to order, government and peace, and a turbulent cause of all confusion. The same I may say of all other sects: It is not now my purpose to take part with any of them, nor to speak against any one of them more than the rest: but to tell them all of their mistake in their censorious way, and how certainly they prepare for the same measure and judgement which they give to others. *Rom.* 14. 4. *Who art thou that judgest another mans servant ? To his Master he standeth or falleth : Yea he shall be holden up, for God is able to make him stand.*——*But why judgest thou thy brother, or why dost thou set at nought thy brother ? We shall all stand before the judgement seat of Christ*——*So then every one of us shall give an account of himself to God.* It is strange that those men that can understand a text against swearing and drunkenness, can see no light, nor feel no power in such words as these.

DIRECT.

Mistake not the nature of the sin of scandal: Think not that it is the bare displeasing or grieving of another; For it is the laying of a stumbling block, that is, a temptation, or occasion of sinning before another.

INdeed the word [*offend*] hath occasioned the mistake of many in this point, to the great ensnaring of themselves and others. *Offending sometime* signifieth only *Displeasing* or *grieving* another: And this is not the *scandal* which the Scripture speaks against. But it signifieth also the laying of a *stumbling block* before another, upon which he may be occasioned to fall into sin; And this is the *offence* which is called *scandal*. Abundance of well meaning people, have thought that they must not use any form, or words, or order, or action (especially if it be indifferent in it self) which others are displeased or grieved at: Because they think that is *scandal*: Indeed there is a *grieving* others which is scandal; that is, when by grieving them we occasion them *to sin*. But consider I beseech you these two things.

First, what a wretched person that is, who will sin against God every time that his brother doth not humour him? Durst these persons profess this openly with their tongues? Dare you say, Do not you use such a form of prayer, or such a ceremony for if you do, I will sin against God? What else do you mean, when you blame men for scandalizing you? I hope you do not mean that no body must *displease you?* If not, you must know that this only is true scandal, to *occasion you to sin?* And is it not a shame that you will sin so easily?

2. And if bare *displeasing* had been scandal, then *peevishness* and *ignorance* would have advanced all that had them to be the Governours of the world. For what is it to govern, but to have all others obliged to fulfill your wills? And if no man must *displease* you, than all must fulfill your wills: And he is scandalous that is not ruled by you. And if this were so, the most childish and womanish sort of Christians, who have the weakest judgement and the strongest wills, and passions, must rule all the world: For these are hardliest pleased, and no man must displease them.

But I beseech you remember that *scandal* lieth in Pleasing men as well as in *displeasing them*, when it may harden them in an error, or tempt them to any sin: I will instance to you but in two *scandalous* acts of *Peter* himself. The first was to Christ in *Matth.* 16. 22, 23. Where he thought to please Christ and save him from suffering, and would have had him to spare or favour himself. And Christ saith, Get thee behind me Satan, thou art an offence to me: the Greek word is, *A scandal:* that is, Thou wouldst do as Satan did, even tempt me to sin, and neglect the work which I came into the world about. The other was in *Gal.* 2. 12, 13. Where *Peter* did scandalize the *Jews* by *pleasing* them! For fear of offending the weak Judaizing Christians, he separated from familiar communion with the Gentiles. By which he laid a stumbling

bling block or temptation before them, to harden them in the sinful opinion of separation. If it had been done in our dayes many would have been drawn away with *Barnabas*, and thought that *Peter* had not given *scandal* to the *Jewish Christians*, but only separated for fear of scandalizing them. Many a time I have the rather gone to the Common prayers of the publick assemblies, for fear of being a scandal to those same men that called the going to them a scandal: that is, for fear of hardning them in a sinful separation and error: because I knew that that was not scandal which they called scandal, that is, *displeasing them* and *crossing* their *opinion*: but hardning them in an error or other sin, is true scandalizing. Understand this or you will displease God under pretence of avoiding scandal.

DIRECT. XXIV.

Make conscience of scandalizing one party as well as another: and those most, who are most in danger by your offence.

MAny persons pretend the *avoiding* of *scandal*, only to flatter one party, and to preserve their own reputation and interest with that side which they are lothest to displease. And perhaps discern not the deceit of their own hearts in all this; but think that it is indeed the sin of scandal which they avoid. But why make you no conscience of scandalizing others, on the contrary side?

side? Who perhaps are more in number, and whose salvation should be as much desired by you? The Papist perhaps will not deliver the Lords Supper in both kinds, nor will forbear his Image-worship, lest he offend the Roman-Catholicks: But he careth not much that by so doing he offendeth the Protestants and other Churches; Nor that his Images are a scandal to all the *Mohometans*, and keep them from the Christian faith. And thus every *sect* saith; If you do this or that, you will scandalize and offend many good people: Meaning their *own side:* But they never regard how many others they shall readily scandalize by the contrary: One saith, It is scandalous to use extemporary prayers; And another saith, it is scandalous to pray by forms and books: And both sides usually mean no more, but that their own party will be displeased and take it for a sin. But as he is not scandalized by me, who only taketh *my action* to be *a sin*; but he that is ensnared by it in any sin himself; so whether it be *displeasing* or *tempting* that you mean, you must regard one side as well as the other. The heavenly wisdom is *without partiality* and *without hypocrisie*. Jam. 3. 7.

And usually they talk most against scandalizing those whom they account to be the *best:* And the *best* are least in danger of sinning. And so they accuse them to the world, or else they know not what they say. For suppose a Separatist should say, If you hold communion with any Parish minister or Church in *England*, it will be a scandal to many good people! I would ask such a one why call you those *good people* that are easily drawn to sin against God?

know not what *scandal is*, *scandal* is not *troubling men*, nor making men take *me* for a sinner, but occasioning *them to sin themselves* by some unlawful or needless act of mine. Therefore if you know what you say, you make the separatists almost the worst of men, that will sin against God because another *will not sin*: yea if they would but sin, because another *sinneth* it were bad enough. I would ask you therefore, whether you take not the people of the Parish Churches to be more than you? and to be *worse* than you? If you took them not for much *worse* than your selves, you would not separate from them. And if you do think them worse, you must think that they are more in danger of sinning, or being turned from the liking of godliness and of the Gospel. And if so, then we are bound to be more afraid of giving scandal *to them* than unto *you*. Are not men most afraid of overthrowing the *children* and the *weak*, rather than those that are *stronger* than themselves? If you are apter to sin and turn from Christ than the people of the Parish Churches, we should rather *separate from you* than from them. If not, we must more take heed of scandalizing them than you.

   Obj. *But Christ pronounceth a woe to them that offend his little ones.*

   Answ. If by [*offending them*] be meant only *persecuting* and *hurting* them as many think, then it is nothing to the question in hand. For I hope
commu-

communicating with others is not a *persecuting you*. And bare [*displeasing them*] it is certain that the text doth not mean at all. But if by [*offending them*] be meant *scandalizing* them, that is, laying snares before them, whether by fraud or persecution, to turn them from Christ, and draw them to sins, then it confirmeth all that I say: And the term [*little ones*] conteineth the reason of the words: Because as *little children* are easily overthrown and easilier *deceived*, so the *young* and *weak* believers of little faith, are most in danger of being turned away from Christ, or ensnared in any sin or errour. And therefore if you think the Parish Churches to consist of weaker persons than your selves, the wo is to you or us if we *offend them*.

The truth is, *offending* and *giving scandal*, is commonly taken in the Gospel, for any action (which is not our necessary duty) by which either Heathens and Infidels and enemies to Christ, are like to be drawn to harder thoughts of the Christian faith; or any wicked man is like to be kept from a godly life; or else by which the young ungrounded and unsetled sort of Christians, may be tempted to turn back and forsake the faith which they have professed, or fall into any dangerous sin. And therefore seeing the separatists profess to be setled in the faith already, and many in the Parish Churches are weak, and many averse to some duties of Religion, and more in danger of being turned away, we are bound to be much more afraid of giving scandal to the Parishes, than to the separatists,

Obj. *But Christ cared not for offending such perverse*

verse ones as Herod *or the Pharisees.*

Answ. Christ feared not to displease the greatest, when it would be done by doing good: No more must you or they be pleased by our neglect of any duty. But Christ was against laying any trap before either *Herod* or the Pharisees, to make them sin.

And it is not your censure of others that will warrant us to use them as Reprobates, forsaken of God. If every man that can be uncharitable enough, to call his neighbours Pharisees or enemies of Christ, without proof, shall keep us from communion with them, then the worse any man is, the more he shall be Lord of all other mens consciences.

DIRECT. XXV.

Be not over-tender of your reputation with any sort of men on earth; nor too impatient of their censures, displeasure, or contempt.

THe fangs of the censorious are a common scandal; and as strong a snare or temptation to some men, as worldly preferments are to others: When we come among men whom we take for the most Religious, and hear them keenly censure all for hypocrites, or formalists, profane or schismaticks, who are contrary to them in opinion or practise; at the first we are in danger of being carried away as *Barnabas* in dissimulation, and to say as they say, or at least comply with

with them by our silence and practise, lest we should be censured by them as others are. Especially Ministers are greatly in danger of this snare. For the prophane hate them for their doctrine and their holy lives; And it is the godly that are the fruit of their labours, and the satisfaction which they have for all their sufferings, and the comfort of their lives: and if these forsake them and despise them, with whom shall they find any comfort in the world? Therefore they are very much in danger of complying too far with their errours and weaknesses, to keep their interest in them: And they think it is that they may do them good. And perhaps this was the case of *Peter* and *Barnabas*, with the weak Judaizing Christians. For *Paul* telleth us *Rom.* the 14. that it was the use of the weak (who thought those things to be duties and sins which were not so) to *judge* the strong, who knew their liberty; And it was the custom of the strong to *despise* the weak: Just as at this day, the mistaken superstitious Christian, saith, They are prophane that are not against all that he is against: And those that see his errour say what giddy whimsical fanaticks are these? So was it then, and so it is like to be, till God give the world a better mind. Many a faithful Minister I have known, who have freely confessed to me, that the censures of the peevish self-conceited Christians, enclined to separation, was a far stronger temptation to them to forsake or over-run their own understandings, than all the offers of honours, or riches could be on the other side. It is a hard thing, when we have spent our labour and lives to bring men to Christ, and have got
them

trials which God will have his servants undergo: And both Ministers and private persons must be above the praise and the dispraise even of self-conceited Religious persons, before they can be fit to follow Christ, as tried and firmly setled men. Stand your ground if you are in the right. Truth will bear all your charges at the last, and will defend it self and you : If you *please men* (whoever they be) contrary to God and conscience, you *are servants of men*, and *verily you have your reward. Math.* 6. But you are *no longer the servants of Christ. Gal.* 1. 10. And you will never be setled, but change as the Moon, as the parties or opinions of the *censurers* change. But if you stick to the words of truth and soberness, at last the sober part of the Religious will be your encouragers, and many of the giddy will come to you by Repentance, when experience hath shewed them that which they would not learn of you. That which is vertiginous will at last settle its rest on that which is permanent and firm : As boyes when they have made themselves wheel-sick with turning round, will lay hold on the next post, to keep them from falling. Therefore bear the censures of the ignorant. Please them in all things lawful for their good and edification; and become all things to all men in a lawful way: But depart not from the principles or practise of *Christian-unity, Communion, Charity*, or *Sobriety*, to please a dividing hot-brain'd party, nor to

escape

escape their sharpest censures. He is unfit to be a Physitian that cannot bear a madmans railings, or the harsh expressions of his friends, when a phrensie or feavour makes them brain-sick. When you have followed them in their violent heats a while to avoid their censure, either you must come back with sorrow, or run to the end with them, as many in this age have done to their own, and to the Churches, and the States confusion; or which is worst of all, God may justly give you up, to be of their minds, and to think that way right and necessary at last, which at first you only yielded to, in compliance with the heats of other men. And when you have sinned against God to avoid their censures, and keep an interest in them, it's two to one, but they will turn on still further and further, till you are forced to let them go, and you shall in the end be more censured and despised by them, than if you had never humoured them at all. These things are written in an age of full experience, by one that hath seen the proof in multitudes.

For my own part, I will be so ingenious and thankful, to the disingenuous and unthankful world as to confess, that they have used me with unusual moderation and civility; in that they have still mixed too high commendations with their blind unreasonable Censures. But yet I must say that he is worse than a fool who would not be taught, by so much experience as I have had, of the vanity of the judgings of the vertiginous world, to choose a more stedfast seat for his rest, than a windmills-sails. The *malicious cen-furers* and railers on one side, and the *peevish cen-*
furers

surers on the other side, have taught me to stand to the judgement of God, and to pity the poor hypocrite, who hath no better a reward, than, the thoughts and praise of mortal men.

Do I speak according to the most common judgment of Divines? The Sectary saith, my light is divine: I speak but by rote, and not by true illumination. Do I pretend to add any clearness to the methods or points received, or to correct any errour which hath got the major Vote of the injudicious? Then I am self-conceited, and a novellist; and if not a Heretick, it's well! And the honour of all the Divines which are of a contrary mind, must be engaged to promote the Censure. And the fear that sober Christians have of novelty and errour, must be called up to make them abhor any truth which the grave and ignorant censurer doth not understand: And they that confess that they never seriously read what I have written, on such or such a subject, yet have wisdom and honestly little enough to say behind my back, O take heed of such a mans Books, for they are *tantum non* heretical: Though in *presence* they are as gentle as Lambs, or as quickly silenced (or worse) as the Owls at the aproach of day-light: If such a judicious Writer, as *Camer*, or *Davenant*, or *Usher*, or *Grocius*, or *Bergius*, or *Amyrald*, or *Placæus*, or *Capellus*, or *Testardus*, or *Blondel*, or *Dallæus*, or *Le Blanc* (in his late excellent impartial judicious Theses) or *Julius*, or *Vossius*, or *Strangius*, &c. do tell any of the unstudied or injudicious sort of Divines, any more than they have received from that party of Teachers, who are in greatest reputation with them; you shall
have

dities they speak: And it all goes down with deluded auditors, as if the Speaker were an Oracle; or at least, knew what he said.

And to teach you to despair of the hypocrites reward, let me tell you; that till God make the world another thing than now it is, there is no hope that even the *honester sort of Christians* or *Teachers* (much less the dishonester) should ever come to so high attainments, that the major part should be truly judicious in judging of deep and difficult controversies! And that there is as little hope, that either of them should know how little they know, till their knowledge in the matter it self increase; or that ever the world (whether Christians or Heathens, Pastors or People) should cease to overvalue their own apprehensions; till greater Light and study bring them first to *Doubting*, and lastly to separate the *certainties* from the *uncertainties*, and to *fasten* upon one, and lay by the other. But I have been long upon this instance.

And it is so in almost all things else. Scarce a day or hour that I spend, but I must sin or be censured for it. If I neglect my most publick labours, my conscience and those at a distance censure me. If I do not, those at hand who expect all my time should be spent in private converse with them, censure me: If my publick duty command me away, yet he that expected that hour in conference, thinks that I disdainfully neglect him;

And

And if I should cast off preaching and writing, it is almost all one: For that hour which I have been spending with one, another hath been that while expecting; and censuring me as sharply for his frustration.

If I had a benefit to do or give, which I can give but to one, ten shall censure me, because they have it not, when the one that had it is scarcely thankfull. If you would give all that you have to the poor, when all is given, many that had nothing will censure you more than those that had it will be gratefull. Expectations with most men are high, and they understand not your inability: And mens necessities are many and great; And every one will say, why I look but for so much; when all set together is ten times more than you have to give.

And as to the *Manner* of our duties, the censures will be as sure and many. If I would cure any hearers of an error, instead of a cure, they make me know they feel the smart; And that they came not to be *taught*, but to be *pleased*. (So dangerous a thing is it for men to come into the School of Christ, as *Judges* and not as *Scholars*, (or *Disciples*.) Its two to one but there are present many persons of contrary opinions! what shall I do to please them all? shall I first preach for *Separation*, *Anabaptism*, *Antinomianism*, *Popery*, to please those on those sides; and then preach against them all again to please those on the other side? This would displease them all: (and God and Conscience who are more than all.) If I speak on one side, I lose the other. If I meddle with no Controversie,

I muſt meddle with no truth: For one or other controverteth all things; (the Immortality of the Soul, Chriſtianity and the Deity, not excepted.)

If in prayer it ſelf I let fall a confeſſion of the controverted ſin, which any are guilty of who are preſent, they cenſure that Confeſſion, and inſtead of repentance, are ready to ſay they will joyn with ſuch a one no more; And it is the Confeſſion which muſt be the ſin.

But if once we have to do againſt the ſin, of any that are *Great* or *Godly*, that *power* or *piety* is made a patron of the error; then it may be a ſmarting cenſure indeed, which we may expect: One crieth out, He is a peſtilent fellow, and a mover of ſedition, as they did of *Paul*, though I hate and preach againſt ſedition. Another ſaith, he is bitter and ſpeaketh againſt the Godly, when I ſpend my ſelf to preach up Godlineſs.

But if it be a *party* that is engaged in the error, you muſt expect the cenſure of all the *party*. And what error is it that hath not a *party*? or that hath neither *Greatneſs* nor *Godlineſs* for a refuge?

If in doctrinal or practical conſultations of great moment you have to do with injudicious unskilful men, if you contradict their way (be it never ſo modeſtly) you are proud and ſelf-opinionated, and muſt have your own way: If you follow their miſtakes, and contradict them not you may wound the Church and Cauſe of Chriſt and be more generally cenſured at the laſt.

In a word, when ſuch a multitude of things & matters of *Controverſie*, as many may be the matter of Censure. One will censure me for praying with a form, or book, and another for praying without it. One for being too long; and another for being too short: one for this gesture, and another for that: One for preaching when I am silenced; another for not preaching more. One for being too gentle to dissenters, and another for being too severe: One for being too narrow in my principles, and communion; and another, for being too large and universal.

And if in the sense of the sin and misery of some Christians Love-killing principles and practises, I have spent the best of twenty years, in writting preaching (while I had leave) conferring and praying for the Union of Christians and the Churches peace; I have but made a wedge of my bare hand, by putting it into the clift; and both sides have closed upon me to my pain. But I have turned both parties in the fray, which I endeavoured to part, against my self; when each side had one adversary, I had two.

Nay this is not the worst to be expected: But moreover I must add, that I was never more accused of any thing as a crime, than of that which I did most against, and even for doing so. Never more suspected of Cornal compliance, than when I exercised the greatest self-denial: Never more accused of unpeaceableness, than for labouring for the Churches peace. Never was I more accused of Schism, than for striving with all my power, to have united the Ministers, and healed the Church, or at least prevented further divisions. Never more accused of enmity against the true Discipline of the Church, than when I have done most (and at the dearest rates) to stablish it, and to prevent its fall.

In all this I meddle not with my Civil Superiours, as thinking it meeter patiently to bear, than to aggravate their censures, though not all so tolerable as private mens.

I might give you as many instances of the matters of common Converse: He that hath much to do in the world, shall hardly escape the censure of many. The buyer will say he sells too dear: The seller will say, he would buy too cheap. Every one that expecteth a commodity, will censure him that hindereth it, and steps in before him.

If I have a friend or kinsman unworthy of any office or preferment, he is nevertheless peremptory in his desires and expectations, for being unworthy. If I will not speak for him and further his suit, I am censured as unnatural and unkind, and turn a friend into an enemy: If I do speak for him, I am false to my conscience and the common good; and I must look to be censured accordingly by many.

But I will add no more instances, lest what I intend for instruction, seem to be but a complaint. But to what purpose is all this?

It is to let the Reader know, that man is not God, nor his judgement to be rested in, nor his favour to be over-valued. To call to you, O cease from man whose breath is in his nostrils; whose heart is deceitfull and desperately wicked! For wherein is he to be accounted of! Look up to God, and take him for your *God indeed*: Rest in his Love, and be satisfied in his approbation:

Despise

Despise not man, nor lay any *stumbling-blocks* befor them, but as to your *own interest* in their esteems (farther than Gods service and *their* benefit requireth it) account it but a shadow, and a thing of nought: And say of it as *Paul, With me it is a very small thing, to be judged of you or of mans day (or judgement) For I have one that judgeth me even the Lord.* 1 Cor. 4. 3.

It is GOD (Christians) it is GOD, it is only GOD, whose infallibility, justification, and unspoted *truth* and *goodness*, you must make your rest. It is *Heaven*, it is *Heaven*, it is only *Heaven*, where perfect truth, and impartial righteousness, and the full vindication of all the just, and the fruition of perfect Love and Concord, is to be expected, and where malice, and lies, and discord, and the father of them, are totally and finally shut out.

As you would not be used as Hypocrites by God, and deprived of the true reward of faith, O seek not after the hypocrites reward! What is the applause of mortal man! Can you not bear the censure of such a shadow? How then would you suffer martyrdom for Christ? Over-value not the esteem of High or Low, of the Great or of the Godly, of the many or of the few. Gods approbation is sufficient to be your reward. See that *you be Godly*, and then be more indifferent though you are *thought ungodly*. See that you *be loyal*, and *peaceable*, and then you may bear it, if you be called the contrary. Abhor all unwarrantable divisions, and then you may bear to be reputed schismaticks. Study you to be *good*, and not to be *accounted* good.

And what if I should look further, to historical fame when I am dead! Away with the over-valuing of that too, as part of the hypocrites reward! I confess God usually blesseth the memory of the just, and sets their names above the power of the greatest tyrants, and causeth the names of the wicked to rot: But this is but a temporal and uncertain thing. If one write in my praise to the highest, and another write a volumne of false reproaches, how shall posterity know which is true, who knew neither party nor the cause?

But yet the nearer reason of all this admonition is, to let you know that as contention comes by pride, so over-valuing the esteem and censures of men (though Good or Great) is a dreadful snare, and cause of schisms: For then you will be stretching your consciences, and using your wits to please the party whose censures you must escape: And you will wound the truth, and be warping to their errors and extreams: And though by this you may think, that some present necessity may be satsfied, and some inconveniencies avoided, yet at the long running, the wound will be found to be increased; and the cure the harder because of the delay. Converse with all men as those that must be finally judged by God: and remember that the Judge is at the door.

DIRECT.

DIRECT. XXVI.

Use not your selves needlesly to the familiar company of that sort of Christians, who use to reproach and censure them, that are more sober, Catholick and charitable than themselves: Unless you also be as much or more with the soberer sort, who will shew you the sin and mischiefs of uncharitableness, censoriousness, and divisions.

Nothing is more experienced, than the power which the converse of chosen familiars hath upon the minds of the injudicious and unsetled. Which maketh education and the converse of our youth, to have so great a hand in choosing mens opinions and Religion: And is the cause that Religion is as Languages are, diversified by the territories or bounds of Countreys. They that are bred among such as use to speak of dissenters, as odious, as hypocrites, as hereticks, as schismaticks, as ungodly, as proud fanaticks, are very like to be possessed themselves with the same spirit of malice and detraction. The words of those whom you respect, especially when you hear them not confuted, will make you believe that it is so indeed, and that the persons are as mad or as odious as they make them. And thus, the Papists think odiously of the Protestants, and the Lutherans of the Calvinists; and the Arminians and Anti-Arminians, the Diocesans and the Presbyterians, the Pædobaptists and Anabaptists of one another: because they converse only with such as paint them in an odious shape. And thus if you use only or chiefly to converse with the *censorious Separatists*, you shall hear so many invectives against them that are truly Catholick, and sober, as will make you think that Love and Peace and Catholick Communion, are some sinful and mischievous things. Sometimes they will deride them as ridiculous, and sometimes they will call them temporizers, formalists, or luke-warm hypocrites, who will do any thing in compliance with their own commodities, and for the saving of their flesh. And sometimes they will thunder out some terrible threatnings against them and their way, as heinously sinful. And this language will form the belief and affections of ignorant Christians, into its own uncharitable mold, as a necessary part of Christian zeal. As it was the common way of the success of the Quakers, to come into Christian assemblies, and in a prophetical strain, like men commissioned from heaven, in the name of the most high God to denounce his judgements against the faithfullest Pastors and their flocks, and pronounce them condemned enemies of the light; and so by the very terror of their words, they frightned many women and boyes into their sect, before they understood at all what it was that they were against or for: so do the Separatists declaim against the sinfulness of Parish Assemblies and communion, and of forms of prayer and such like, till they have frightned the ignorant into their mistaken zeal.

There-

Therefore, though I am not perswading you to separate from these feaverish persons, as they do from others, yet I would advise all the younger and unsetled sort, that love themselves, not needlesly to choose the familiar frequent company of such: Our private company is at our own chocie.

And as the company of fierce self-conceited dividers, is so very dangerous, so on the contrary, the company of grave, experienced, sober, charitable and judicious Divines and other Christians, is exceeding helpful to settle the minds of the younger and weaker sort: with them they shall hear the unity of the Church, and the doctrine of Christian Love and Concord, humility, meekness and moderation opened; and the sinfulness and lamentable consequents, of schism, self-conceitedness, censoriousness and discord; which among others they should never hear.

And let me leave this warning to the Church of God, that *if ever it may be hoped that Unity, Love and peace shall be recovered, it must be by the training up of the younger Christians, under the precepts and examples of such grave, judicious, experienced and peaceable guides, instead of educating them in the smoaky scorching chimney, of young, unexperienced, self-conceited teachers, who burn with the ambition of applause.* And let the sober be-think them whether our times and preachers are better and purer than theirs, to whom *Paul* said, *Acts* 20. 30. *Of your own selves shall men arise, speaking perverse things, to draw away disciples after them.* And *Eph.* 4. 14. He gave the Church Pastors and Teachers, for its Unity and perfection [*That we henceforth be* no more children, tossed to and fro, and carried about with every wind of doctrine, by the slight of men and cunning craftiness, whereby they lye in wait to deceive.]

DIRECT. XXVII.

Take heed of mis-judging of the Answers of your prayers, and of taking those things to be from God, which are but the effects of your prejudice, passion or weakness of understanding.

THis is a sin, which I know not whether I may say is *more common* with many godly persons, or more *injurious to God*, or more *pitiful* as to themselves.

It is so common, that it is hard to meet with many women and passionate Christians, who are earnest in prayer, but sometimes they run into this mistake, and judge ungroundedly of the answer of their prayers, by such feelings and strong apprehensions of their own, as never came from the spirit of God at all.

And it is a great *wrong* to God, to be made the author of mans infirmities and errors, and of that which is contrary to his word.

And yet it is a very *pitiful* case as to the offenders; because it is usually the sin of persons that are very upright and honest in the main, and that are very serious in their prayers to God; and of such as have naturally such weakness of reason and

strength

strength of affection, as that they are less *blameable*, though less *curable* than others are.

To understand this matter the better, I pray you consider, that Prayer is not to change Gods mind; but to make us the meet receivers of his mercies: and this it doth by exciting and exercising those apprehensions and desires, which make us fit by valuing them to improve them. Therefore such principles, dispositions and desires as are in us, Prayer doth excite and exercise: And every man prayeth according to his own judgement, disposition and affection. And that apprehension and affection, which is most stirred up and exercised, is most *felt*. And that which is most *felt*, doth most take us up, and is most observed: And so we think that it is the impulse of Gods spirit, and the answer of our prayers, when it is but the operation of our own spirits, and the sensible activity of our formal principles.

There are very few that take their impulses and resolutions, for the spirits answer of their prayers, but they had before an understanding most inclined to that opinion, or else a byas upon their affections, bending them that way; or something in themselves which occasioned the scales to turn that way.

Obj. But *I did bring my mind to a pure impartiality, and prayed to God that he would shew me the truth, be it what it would be: and that if this were not right, he would blast it and never suffer it to go on: And the more I prayed, the more I was confirmed, that this is the right.*

Answ. All this may be, without any of Gods appro-

approbation of the conclusion which
his answer to your prayers. For whil
ed that God would turn your mind fr
were not right; yet at that time you
was inclined to it; or your affectio
And it is an easier thing to speak imp
in prayer than to get an impart
diced mind. And when you think th
is brought to an impartiality, alas,
many deep roots of prejudice which
not: And there is scarce one of a tho
thinketh that He prayeth with a pure
but his opinion, disposition, inclinati
or secret affection, doth byas and p
mind, more to one side than to the otl

But if you were never so willing
truth, yet there are passions in you,
ptions and ignorance and former erro
may all do much to hinder you from
and may breed many false apprehens
mind; and yet may cherish them wit
espousal and affection, as if they w
from God.

And moreover, you have been guil
sins: And whether God for any of
leave you to run into mistakes, you kn
whether any present self-conceitednes
sion him to leave you to mistakes.

But the principal part of my ans
God hath no where promised to re
truth to you, because you desire him t
is not every prayer of yours, which h
mised to hear and grant; but only tho
agreeable to his will: His will is eit

ree, his *Command*, or his *Promise*. Though the first be not it that is meant in the text, yet it is certain that your prayers cannot change Gods decrees. The will of his command doth more concern the sense of the text; but it is only a negative which may hence be gathered; that is, that if your prayers be contrary to Gods commands, they are your sins and have no promise of his grant. But it will not follow that God will grant all the prayers which are put up in obedience to his laws: But only that you shall be no losers by such obedience; but he will give you that, or something which shall be as good for you. It may be Gods command that godly children should pray for the lives of their sick parents; and that parents pray for the conversion of their ungodly children, and that we pray for all men: And yet it doth not follow that we shall have the very thing which we obediently pray for. But it is his *Promising will* which is the measure of our *hope*, as his *Commanding will* is the rule of our *obedience*. Whatsoever he hath *promised*, he will certainly give us. Now God hath no where promised in his word, that he will reveal the true meaning of every text of scripture, to every godly person that asketh it. *Praying* is but one of the means which God hath appointed you to come to knowledge. Diligent reading, hearing, and meditation, and councel of the wisest is another means. Even to dig for it as for silver, and to search for it, as for hidden treasure, and to continue so doing, and wait at the posts of wisdoms doors, that knowledge may come into you by degrees in time. God hath not promised you

true

true understanding, upon your prayers alone, without all the rest of his appointed means: Nor that you shall attain it by those means, as soon as you desire and seek it; For then prayer would be a notable pretense for laziness, and they that would not be at the labour, of study, meditation, or conference, might save all their pains; and go to God and ask wisdom of him and he would give it them. Even as idle beggers think without working, to get an alms to maintain them in their slothfulness. If instead of all our reading, hearing and meditation, we could but *pray*, and so get al the knowledge which other men study, labour and wait for, it would be too cheap a way to wisdom. *Solomon* that got it by prayer extraordinarily, commandeth us very great diligence to get it.

It is very considerable, not only that Christ increased in wisdom in his youth, but also that he would not enter upon his publick Ministery (as is aforesaid) till he was about thirty years of age. When it had been more easie for Christ to have got all knowledge by two or three earnest prayers, than for any of us.

Moreover you must pray according to Gods *will of precept*, not not only in the *matter* but in the manner of your *prayers*. And there may be more selfishness, and many other corruptions in the *manner* of them that you discern.

And there are many things which submissively you may lawfully pray for, which God hath never promised you at all: You may pray for the life of the sick, and for the conversion and salvation of all your relations, and of thousands of
others

whether this or the other be the meaning of such a text of scripture? or whether you should joyn with such a Church, in the use of such preaching and prayers or not? And when you have prayed earnestly, you are confirmed for one way and against the other. And perhaps all this is but to be confirmed in your error: For first, you came with a secret prejudice; secondly, or you came with distempered affections; or with such a *fear* of going one way rather than the other, that the very *fear* doth much to cause your apprehensions. Thirdly, or you come with the guilt of former sin. Fourthly, or you have some partiality on your spirit, and a secret inclination to one side more than to the other; or some overvaluing of your own understandings, persons or prayers. Fifthly, Or you are lazy and presumptuous; and think God must teach you that in one hour, and at a wish or prayer, which others better than you must learn with prayer and twenty years study, diligence and patience. Sixthly, or you think God must needs resolve you of that which he never promised to resolve you in. Where hath he promised upon all your prayers, that ever he will teach you in this life the sense of *every text of Scripture?* If ever he *promised* this, he will perform it. And is it to *One Christian*, or *to every praying Christian* that he hath promised it? If to *every one*, why are we not *all of a mind?* Why be not all as wise as you? What need we Com-
mentaries

why do not *those some*, condefcend to write an infallible Commentary upon all the Bible, when they themfelves are taught it of God, that fo we may doubt and differ no more?

But if you fay that it is not the meaning of *every text* that God hath promifed to make known to you when you pray, but of *some few*, how will you know which *thofe few* be? and where is the promife which maketh this difference? Except only that to all true Chriftians, he hath promifed to reveal fo much as is neceffary to their falvation. But if you will pray for more, your belief of your fuccefs muft not go beyond the promife. If you will promife to your felves, you muft perform for your felves?

Obj. *But hath not God bid us believe that we shall receive what ever we ask, and promifed to believers that they shall receive it?*

Anfw. He hath firft made a Law to command you prayer, and then made a *promife* to grant, what you pray for, according to his *will*, that is, according to his *command and promife*, and hath made your *believing* of this *promife*, one of the conditions of his fulfilling it to you. So that if you believe not his power and promife you fhall not have right immediately to the thing promifed. But if you *pray* and *believe* and withall ufe thofe other means with diligence and patience which God hath appointed you, you fhall know in that meafure, as is fuitable to your ftate (For God hath

not

How to judge of Prayers. 161

not promised the same measure of *knowledge* to all true believers.) So that this is all that the promise giveth you, and not that you shall know all that you pray to know, and that immediately.

Obj. *But then you leave us at utter uncertainty, whether we have the answer of our prayers or not?*

Answ. Not so. But the answer of your prayers must not be tried by *your* conceits but by Gods rule. If you pray for that which you have neither a *command* nor *promise* for, your prayer is sin, and your answer can be nothing but Gods rebuke, or your own delusion. But if you pray for that which you have a *command* for, but no *particular promise*, then you have only the *General promise* that your prayer shall not be lost, but shall bring down either the thing you pray for, or something else which the wisdom of God seeth to be best for you and others; and to his ends. And this is all that you can warrantably *believe*. But if you pray for that which hath both a *command*, and a particlar *promise* (as the pardon of sin, and necessary grace and life eternal to a believer) you may be sure that this prayer shall be granted in kind. So that you are not to judge of the answer of prayers, by your *feelings* and *passions* and *impulses*, but by the *promise* of God, which you must *believe* will be fulfilled whatever you *feel*: Faith and not *feeling* must tell you whether your prayer be accepted.

Nay if you should *receive* health or wealth or gifts for your selves or others, when you have prayed for them; you cannot tell whether it be a *merciful* answer to your prayer, or a *judgement*, unless you try it by *faith* according to the *promise*. I have nothing now to say of the case of miracles, but this: If God *promise* a *miracle*, you may believe it because it is *promised*. If he perform it without a promise, then either you must not believe it till it is done, or else your faith must be a *miracle* also; And then the faith it self is its own justification. But miracles are now so rare, that all sober Christians will take heed how they expect them, or overhastily believe them; and especially how they take their *own belief* for a *miracle*. All the talk that some men make of a *particular faith*, may by tryed by what I have here said.

To conclude, the warning which I give you in this case, is from long and sad experience. I have known too many very honest hearted Christians, especially *melancholly* persons and *women*, who have been in great doubt about the opinions of the Millenaries, the Seperatists, the Anabaptists, the Seekers, and such like, and after earnest prayer to God, they have been strongly resolved for the way of error, and confident by the strong impression, that was the spirits answer to their prayers, and thereupon they have set themseves into a course of sin. If you say, how know you that they were mistaken? I will tell you how. First, Because they have been resolved contrary to the word of God. And I know, that Gods spirit did first make a standing Rule, to try all after-impulses by; And whatever impulse is contrary to that Rule, is contrary to Gods spirit. The Law and the testimony are now sealed, and all spirits to be tryed by them. *Isa* 8. 20. Secondly, Because I have found their impulses contrary to one another. One hath been resolved for Infant baptism, and another against it: One hath had a revelation for a prelacy, like the order of *Aaron*, and the Priests, and another against all Prelacy.

One hath been confident of an answer of prayers for Antinomianism, and another against it for Arminianism: One for publick Communion, and another to detest it: And both came in, in the same way. And Gods spirit is not contrary to it self. Thirdly, Because I have seen abundance of prophesies of things to come, which people have this way received with the greatest confidence to prove all false. Fourthly, Because I have staid till many of the persons have found by experience that they were deceived, and have confessed it with lamentation. And fifthly, because perhaps I know more of the nature of prejudice, affection, melancholy, feminine weakness, and self-conceit, and of tempting God in the way of prayer, and of Satans transforming himself into an Angel of light, than every Reader will know till they have paid for their learning.

DIRECT.

DIRECT. XXVIII.

Do not too much reverence the impulses or revelations or most confident opinions of any others, upon the account of their sincerity or holiness: but try all judiciously and soberly by the Word of God.

Many that have no such impulses themselves are yet so much taken with the reverence of others, that they are very apt to be seduced by their confidence. When so great a man as *Tertullian* was deceived by *Montanus* and his prophetess: when such a one as *Hacket* could deceive not only *Coppinger* and *Arthington*, but abundance more, some taking him for the Messiah, and some by his breathing on them thinking that they received the Holy Ghost! When *David George* in *Holland*, and *John* of *Leyden* in *Munster*, and *Behmen Stiefelius* and so many more pretended Prophets in *Germany* could deceive so many persons as they did? When the pretended revelations of the Ranters first, and the Quakers after could so marvellously transport many thousand professors of religion in this land; I think we have fair warning to take the counsel of St. *John*, *Believe not every spirit; but try the spirit whether they be of God.* It is a pitiful instance of the good old learned *Commenius*, who so easily believed the prophesies of *Daubritius* and the rest which he hath published: Yea, when he saw the prophesies fail, yet when he adjured the Prophet to speak truth, and

got

with the nature of Melancholy and Histericall passions as many others are, he would have known that as strange things as that he recordeth of the man or woman, may be done without any Divine inspirations: and that it is no wonder if that person swear that his words are true, who is first deceived himself, before he deceived others. For a crackt brain'd person to believe his delusions to be real verities, is little wonder.

I have many a time my self conversed with persons of great honesty and piety (though of no great judgement) who have some of them affirmed that they had angelical revelations, and some of them thought that the Spirit of God did bring this Scripture or that Scripture to their mind in answer to their prayers; and were so very confident that what they affirmed was the certain truth or voice of God, that I have been stricken with a reverence to their professions, and with a fear lest I should resist God in resisting them. But resolving to take none on earth for the master of my faith, but to try the Spirits whether they be of God, by going to the Law and Testimony, I was constrained to turn my reverence into pity. For I found that their seeming revelations were some of them *Scripture-doctrine*, and some of them *contrary* to the Scripture: As for that which is already in the Scripture, what need I further revelation for it? Is it not there sufficiently revealed? Can their words add any authority to the Word of God? And have I not Gods own Ministers and means

means to help me to the knowledge of his word? And as for that which is *contrary* to Scripture, I am sure that it is contrary to the will of God: And if an Angel from Heaven should preach another Gospel to me, I must hold him accursed: *Gal.* 1. 7, 8. so that if these persons should have the appearance and voice of an Angel speaking to them, I would despise it as well as the words of a mortal man, if they be against the recorded word of God.

But by what I have seen and heard, I know that it is a great temptation to some weak Christians to hear one that is much in prayer, say, *Take heed what you do: Have no communion with this sort of men, nor in this or that way of worship; nor in this or that opinion, for I am sure it is against the mind of God: I once thought as you do, but God hath better made known his mind unto me.*

But saving the due respect to the honesty of such persons, ask them, How shall I know that you are in the right? If they say, *I will not reason the case with you, but I know it to be the mind of God;* Tell them, that God hath made you reasonable creatures, and will accept no unreasonable service of you; and you have but one Master of your Faith, even Christ: Therefore if they believe that themselves, which they can give you no reason to believe, they must be content to keep their belief to themselves, and not, for shame, perswade any other to it, without proof! If they say that God hath revealed it to them, Tell them that he hath not revealed it to you, and therefore thats nothing to you, till they prove their divine revelation: If God reveal it to them but *for themselves* they must keep it to themselves: If he reveal

reveal it to them *for others*, he will enable them to make some proof of their revelations, that others may be sure that they sin not in believing them. If they say, that the Scripture is their ground, Tell them that the Scripture is already revealed to all; And if indeed what they speak be there, you are ready to believe it: But if they pervert the Scripture by false interpretation, or abuse it and misapply it, none of this is the work of the Spirit of God.

If they say that the spirit hath told them the meaning of the Scripture, say as before, that is not told for you, which is not proved to you. The Scripture is written in such words as men use, of purpose that they might understand it; and is to be understood by all men that hear it, though they have no revelation: God hath set Pastors in his Church to teach it; If therefore revelations be still necessary to the understanding of the Scripture revelations, then the Scripture seems to be in vain; and these last revelations must again have new revelations to the right understanding of them also.

The truth is, it is very ordinary with poor fanciful women and melancholly persons, to take all their deep apprehensions for revelations. And if a text of Scripture come into their minds, they say, *This text was brought to my mind, and that text was set upon my spirit*; as if nothing could bring a text to their thoughts, but some extraordinary motion of God? And as if this bringing it to their mind, would warrant their false exposition of it.

To conclude, Decry not the necessity of the ordinary sanctifying work of the spirit, to bless the Scripture to your true illumination and sanctification: And if any pretend to any other revelations or inspirations, or expositions of the Scripture which they cannot *prove* to you, *despise them not*, but modestly leave them to themselves: But take heed that the reverence of any ones holiness, tempt you not to depart from the certain sufficient word of God and draw you not into any Sect or Heresie, or Separation, or Opinion contrary to Gods standing Law.

DIRECT. XXIX.

Take heed lest the trouble of your own disquieted doubting minds do become a snare, to draw you to some uncouth way of cure, and so make the fancy of some new Opinion, Sect or Practice, to seem your Remedy, and give you ease, and thereby perswade you that it is the certain truth.

THis is the pitiful Case of the ignorant, and ungrounded, and troubled sort of religious persons; that they are looking every way for ease and comfort: And having not wisdom enough to fetch true grounded satisfaction from the Scriptures, and from the solid truth, in the use of Gods appointed means; they hearken to any one that will promise them comfort and salvation, by what means soever. Like ignorant people in their sickness: some of them know not an able

Physi-

Physitian, and some of them will not be at the cost; and some of them will not take such unpleasing Medicines; and most of them have not patience to stay for a Cure, unless the Medicine at twice or thrice taking do give them ease, they will not believe that it will do them any good: And so in their foolish ignorance, and the weariness of their pain, they will go to any ignorant woman or unskilful fellow, who will take cheapest of them, and be boldest in his undertakings: And those that dye by it, are out of sight, and forgotten by the living: And those that by the strength of nature do recover, do magnifie their ignorant Physitian as if there were none such, and so entice others to their Graves.

Thus many troubled unquiet souls, either *know not* found Doctrine and Teachers from deceit, or else will not be at the *pains* or *patience*, to wait on God in the use of the right means; or most commonly spoil the Remedy offered them, by their own misapplications; and then for ease they hearken to any ignorant Sectary, that will fiercely cry out against sound Teachers, and revile all that are wiser than himself, as if he knew more than all the Ministers in the Country. O saith the deceiving Papist, you will never have settled comfort while you follow these Ministers, and till you come to us, who are the true Church——Saith the Anabaptist, you will never be well setled while you follow these Preachers: They have not the Spirit, but speak only by the book: Come to us and be baptized, and you will have peace. And thus saith the Quaker, the Familist, and other Sects.

I

turned to another. I have known those also that have lived many years in timerous complaints, and fears of Hell; and they have turned to the Antinomians, and suddenly been comforted: And others have turned Arminians, which is clean contrary, and been comforted: And others have but heard of the Doctrine of *perfection in this life*, and suddenly been past their fears, as if hearing of perfection had made them perfect: And from thence they have turned *Familists*, and at last shew'd their perfection by *fornication* and *licentiousness* and meer Apostacy; who yet liv'd very conscionable and blamelesly, as long as they lived in their fears and troubles.

The reason of all this is plain to any juditious Observer. 1. The persons are ignorant and never had the right knowledge and skilful improvement, of the sound doctrine which at first they seemed to embrace. And 2. the power of conceit and fancy brought them comfort or quietness in their change. For they thought before, that if they had not somewhat extraordinary they could have no assurance of salvation: And while they held that sound Doctrine which all about them held as well as they, and found no *extraordinary* power of it on their hearts, they perceived no difference between themselves and others: But when they had entertained new opinions, and entered into a new Sect, which confidently told them, that they only were in the right, they had

then

then *something extraordinary* to trust their souls on. And the novelty of the matter, and greatness of the change with the conceited excellency of the opinions and party, did make them think that they were now grown very acceptable to God.

To this may be added, that as a life of holiness hath far more opposition from the Devil, the world and the flesh, than the changing of an opinion or joyning with a party hath; so it must be harder to get and keep that comfort which is got and kept by faith and holiness, than that which is got by such an easie change.

We see among us what abundance of persons can live like beasts in most odious whoredoms, drunkenness and rage; or like devils in bloody cruelty against the good, and yet be comforted, because they are of the Church of *Rome*, which they think is the true Church. As if God saved men for being of such a side or party! And why may not Separatists, Annabaptists and others easily take such kind of comfort?

O therefore labour for well-grounded faith and solid knowledge, that you may attain the true Evangelical comforts; and your ignorance may not prepare you for deceit? and you may not be like children tossed to and fro and carred up and down with every wind of doctrine by deceived and deceitful men. Nor may not have need to go to the devil to be your comforter, nor to steal a little unlawful peace from parties and opinions, as if there were not enough to be had in Christ and holiness and eternal life.

DICECT.

DIRECT. XXX.

Keep in the rank of an humble Disciple or learner in the Church of Christ, till you are fit and called to be your self a Teacher.

CHrist owneth no Disciples, which are not in one of these two ranks; either *Teachers* by office upon a lawfull call, or *Learners* who submit to be taught by others. When his Ministers have made men his *Disciples*, they must afterward Teach them *to observe all things whatsoever he hath commanded them*. Matth. 28. 19, 20. And a *Learner* must hear and read and discourse in a *learning* way, by humble asking the resolution of his doubts, acknowledging the weakness of his own understanding, and the superiority of his Teachers. This is the common ruine of raw professours, that they presently grow proud of a poor ignorant head, as if it were full of knowledge and spirituality: and while they continue Hearers, they continue not *Disciples* or *Learners*, but come with a proud and carping humour, to quarrel with their Teachers as poor ignorant men, in comparison of them; And therefore choose them a *heap of Teachers* according to their own opinions: And all this while they have such list to be some body and to vent their seeming wisdom, that they can hardly stay from being Teachers themselves, till they have any thing like a lawful call. Whereas if they would have kept in the rank of humble Learners till they had

grown

grown wiser, they might have preserved the Churches peace and their own.

DIRECT. XXXI.

Grow up in the great substantial practical truths and duties, and grow downwards in the roots of a clearer belief of the word of God and the life to come; And neither begin too soon with doubtful opinions, nor ever lay too much upon them.

HE that taketh this course will have all these advantages. First, He will be himself a solid Christian, and will make sure of the main, which is his own salvation. Secondly, He will have so fast hold of the necessary points, that no controversies or opinions, will shake his faith or destroy his love to God or man. Thirdly, He will honour God by *upright practise*, and shew forth the power and excellency of religion in the true success upon the heart and life: His Religion which begins in solid faith, will grow up into sincere Love and good works. Fourthly, He will be without *partiality*, a Lover of all the servants of Christ, and therefore escape temptations to faction and division, because his Religion consisteth in those common truths and duties, which all profess. Fifthly, he will not only safely receive all further truths from these principles, but all his knowledge and disputes will be sanctified, as being all subservient to faith and love and holiness.

Where-

Whereas he that taketh the contrary course, and presently falleth to the study of by-opinions, and layeth too much upon them, will prove too like a superficial hypocrite, and a deceiver of himself, by thinking that he is something when he is nothing. *Gal.* 6. 5, 6. And he will make a pudder in the world for nothing, as children do in the house about their babies and their bawbles: He will make but an engine of his by-opinions, to destroy true Piety and Christian Love in himself first, and then in all that will believe him. He will first make himself, and then many others, believe that Religion is nothing but proud self-conceipt and faction; And he will be the shame of his profession, and the hardner of the wicked in their sin and misery; by perswading them that the Religious are but a few ignorant whimsical fanaticks. These are two sad experienced truths.

DIRECT. XXXII.

Lay not greater stress upon your different words or manner of Prayer, than God hath laid: And take heed either of scorning, reproaching or slighting, the words and manner of other mens worship, when it is such as God accepteth from the sincere.

IT is an easie thing to turn the native heat of Religion, into a feavourish out-side zeal about *words*, or *circumstances* or ceremonies, whether it be be *for them* or *against* them. O what a wonder is it, that by so palpable a trick as this, the Devil should deceive so many, and make such a stir and disturbance in the Church. I know that one party will cry up *Order*, and the other will cry up *Spirituality*, and both will say that God maketh not light of the smallest matters in religion, nor no more must we: And in this general position there is some truth. But if *nothing* could be said for both their errours, they would then be no deceits, nor be capable of doing any mischief. Some things that you contend about, God hath left wholly undetermined and indifferent; And some things in which your brother erreth, his errour is so small a fault, as not at all to hinder his acceptance with God, nor with any man that judgeth as God doth. Had you ever understood, *Rom.* 14. & 15. you would have understood all this.

It would make a knowing Christian weep between indignation and compassion, to see in these times, what censures and worse are used on both sides, about the *wording* of our prayers to God! How vile and unsufferable some account them, that will pray in any words which are not *written down for them*? And how unlawful others account it to pray in their *imposed forms*: Some because they are *forms*, and some because they are *such forms*; and some because that *Papists* have used them, and some because they are *imposed*! when God hath given them no command, but to pray in faith and fervency, according to the state of themselves, and others, and in such order as is agreeable to the matter, and in such method as he hath given them a Rule and Pattern of. But of all
qarrrels

quarrels about *forms* and *words*, he hath never made any of their particular determinations, no more than whether I shall preach by the help of Notes, or study the words, or speak those which another studied for me.

It is a wonder how they that believe the Scriptures, came first to make themselves believe, that God maketh such a matter as they do, of their several words and forms of prayer: That he loveth only *extemporary* prayer as some think, and hateth all prescribed forms: Or that he loveth only *prescribed Forms* as others think, and hateth all extemporary prayers by habit; Certainly in Chrifts time both Liturgies by *forms*, and also prayers by habit were used: And yet Christ never interposed in the Controversie, so as to condemn the one or the other. He condemneth the Pharisees for making *long prayers* to cover their *devouring widdows houses*, and for their *praying to be seen of men*: but whether their prayers were a Liturgy and *set form*, or whether they were *extemporary*, he taketh no notice, as telling us that he condemned neither! (And its like the Pharisees long Liturgy, was in many things worse than ours, though the Psalms were a great part of it: And yet Christ and his Apostles oft joyned with them, and never condemned them.)

Nay as far as I can find, the Pharisees and other Jews were not in this so blind and quarrelsome as we; nor never made a controversie of it, nor ever presumed to condemn either Liturgies or Prayers by habit.

I shall now pass by their errour who are utterly against publick prayers from a habit as having

ing spoken of it at large elsewhere when I had opportunity, I shall now only answer the contrary extream.

Obj. *Where hath God given any men power to prescribe and impose forms for others ? or commanded others to obey them ?*

Answ. First, where ever he hath given any power to *teach* their *inferiours* to *pray*, who cannot do it in a *better way*. He hath given *Parents* this power where he hath bid them, *Bring up their Children in the nurture, and admonition of the Lord*: Is it not by the Law of nature, the Parents duty to teach their children to pray ? And is not the learning of the *words* first, profitable to their learning of the sense ? May they not teach their Children the *Lords Prayer* or a *Psalm*, though it be a Form ? And why not then *other words* which are agreeable to their State ? And he that taught his own Disciples a Form and Rule of Prayer, and telleth us that so *John taught his Disciples*, and saith to his Apostles, *As my Father sent me, so send I you*; by making them *Teachers* to his Church, did allow them to teach either by *forms* or *without*, as the cause required. All the Scripture is now to Preachers, a *form of Teaching*: And when we read a Chapter, we read a *prescribed form of Doctrine*: And it hath many *forms of prayer* and *praise*, and forms of *Baptizing* & *administring* the *Lords Supper*.

If you say, that the Apostles had an infallible spirit, I answer, True: And that proveth that their Doctrine was *more infallible* than other mens: but not that *they only* and not other men may teach by the way of *forms*. All the Books of Sermons now written are so many *prescribed words* or *forms* of teaching: And if we may use *forms* of *Teaching* as well as the Apostles, why not also forms of *praying*.

If you say that the Apostles prescribed the Church no Liturgy, I answer, That only proveth that no one is *universally necessary*, nor to be *universally imposed*: but not that therefore no use of *forms* of *prayer* are *lawful*; May we not now use the *Lords Prayer*, or pray in some other *Scripture form*?

Obj. But *the Apostles compelled none to use them*.

Answ.. Christ and his Apostles assumed not the civil Sword, and therefore so compelled men to nothing: But yet their authority bound the conscience; when Christ said, *when ye pray, say, Our Father*, &c. he bound them in duty to do as he bid them, though he forced them not.

But Secondly, tell me if you can where God *forbiddeth* you to use good and lawful words in prayer, meerly because the Magistrate or Pastor bids you use them. Is this the meaning of all the Precepts of honouring and obeying your Superiors [Do nothing which they bid you do, though otherwise lawful.] O strange exposition of the Fifth Commandment? If you command your Child to learn a Catechism or Form of Prayer before his meat, or for other times, will you teach him to say Father or Mother, it had been lawful for me to use this Form, if neither you nor any body had bid me; But because you bid me, now it is unlawful.] O whither will not partiality lead men!

Obj. But *though it be lawful to impose forms on*

children, yet not upon aged Christians.

Answ. Aged persons have too many of them as much need of such forms as children. Age maketh not the difference: We are fain to teach many aged persons *forms of Catechism* as well as children; Why not therefore forms of prayer?

Obj. *But it is not lawful to impose forms publickly on whole Congregations of Believers.*

Answ. All sects in the world do it. I never heard any Separatist or Anabaptist or any other publick Minister, but he *imposed a form* of prayer upon all the Congregation. He is void of common sense that thinketh that his extemporary prayer is not as truely a *form* to all the people, as if it had been written in a book. The *order* and *words* are not of your *own invention*, but invented by *another* to your hand; and *imposed* upon you to use: For I hope you come together to *pray*, and not to *bear a prayer* only. But the difference is, First, that one *imposeth* every day a *new form* on you, and the other imposeth every day the same: Secondly, And that one telleth you not what words you shall pray in, before you hear them: and the other writeth them down for you to know before hand. For my part I wonder why wrritten or unwritten, long-premeditated or suddenly expressed prayers should be taken for unlawful. But however do not think the difference to lie where it doth not: For doubtless to the *people*, they are both *forms*, and both *imposed*, though not *imposed* by the same persons and authority.

Obj. *But at least you have no proof for imposing*
P 2 *forms*

forms on the Ministers themselves.

Ans. First, I know no man that questioneth but some form of prayer and praise were imposed by God himself, on the *Jewish Ministers*; And *one* was taught by Christ to his Apostles: And a *form* of *Profession* of *faith*, and of *Baptism* and the *Lords Supper* is imposed on all the Ministers of the Church. And *Joel* 2. 17. a form of prayer is taught the Priests: Secondly, But we are not now pleading for the needless imposing of any forms, nor the causless restraint of extemporary prayers. I have fully born my testimony against that in due season: But many things are lawfully and necessarily obeyed, which are not lawfully commanded, as I shall shew you more anon. I could heartily wish that we could say that all Ministers (of any party) were such as were wholly above the *need* of forms. Or at least such whose own composures were better for the Church, than any that could be offered them by others (If it were not a contradiction.)

But all that I now expect from the Objectors is, that they tell me or themselves, what proof they have that it is a sin for a *Minister only* to use an *imposed form*, when *all the Congregation* else may use it? Answer this well before you go.

And I pray let all the people note here, that it *is not*, nor *cannot* be *denied*, but that a form (even a new one every day) may be lawfully *imposed upon all them*; and that the question is only of the *Ministers* use of imposed forms.

Obj. *But our Ministers do not impose their prayers by force.*

Ans.

Of Ministerial gifts in Prayer. 181

Answ. Do you think that there is no imposition but by force ? Your Pastor is your guide in the worship of God; and God hath imposed it on you to follow him, and joyn with him in lawful prayer. And what the *words shall be,* and what the *matter* and *order* chosen for that time, the Speaker *chooseth* for you! And so he bindeth you by his Ministerial authority (which is a true and lawful imposing) though he compel you not by the sword or force.

Obj. But Christ *hath given gifts to all his Ministers and commanded them to use them. And they use them not when they use imposed forms : Therefore we must not obey men against Christ.*

Answ. No doubt but all that are lawful Ministers, have such gifts as are necessary to the *essential works* of their office. But the *degrees* of their gifts have very great variety, as *Paul* fully sheweth in 1 *Cor.* 12. and oft elsewhere.

And the necessary *gift* for hearty acceptable prayer, is *true Desire* excited by the spirit of supplication, which sometime venteth it self but by *sighs* and *groans,* Rom. 8. 16, 26.

But the *Ministerial gift* of *prayer* is *Knowledge* and *Utterance*; by which a Minister may be able to express the desires and wants of the people unto God : which includeth *memory* in some degree. Even as *Knowledge* and *Utterance* are his *Gift* of *preaching.*

And some have *more Knowledge,* and *worser Utterance*; And some have *better Utterance* and *less Knowledge*; And some through want of *memory* are defective in both.

The lowest rank of lawful Ministers, may be so defective in their *own gifts*, both of *Knowledge*, *Memory* and *Utterance*, as to have need of the help of the gifts of others, who much excell them.

As a Minister who hath *tollerable Gifts* for *preaching*, may yet need the writings of other men before hand; and may bring both their *Matter* and *Method* into the Pulpit, yea and oft times their *words*; so that though he have *Gifts*, yet being *weak*, he may use the gifts of others. I have been counselled since I was silenced, to compose Sermons my self, and give them in writing to some weak Minister, that hath an excellent Voice and utterance, and to let him preach them. And really if I had not known that such have good books enough at hand for such a use, I think I should have done it: And who can prove that this had been his sin? And yet this was a using of another mans gifts instead of his own. And I have heard men that are much against Parish Churches and Liturgies wish that some unlearned men of good utterance, might read some excellent Sermon-books to the people, in ignorant places that can get no better: And who can prove the reading of a Homily unlawful.

Moreover, Christ hath given to *all his members* such gifts as are suitable to *their places*, as well as to *Ministers* such gifts as are suitable to *theirs*. And the place of a Master of a family requireth the gift of Catechising and instructing the family? And they are as truly obliged to use *their gifts*, as Ministers are *theirs*. And yet who doubteth but it is lawful for Parents to teach and

and catechize their children, by such books and forms of Catechisms as are composed by the gifts of abler men?

Moreover *Prayer* is the duty of every one, and specially of the heads of families: and therefore every true Christian hath gifts procured by Christ, for so much as is his duty. And he is bound to use his gifts. And yet those gifts are so low in *many*, that I fear not to call that man effectively an enemy to families, souls and prayer, who forbiddeth *all such*, to use such forms of prayer as are composed by the gifts of others.

The famousest Divines in the Church of God, even *Luther, Zwinglius, Melancthon, Calvin, Perkins, Sibbs*, and abundance of Non-conformists of greatest name in *England*, did ordinarily use a form of Prayer of their own, before their Sermons in the Pulpit, and some of them in their families too. Now these men did it not through idleness or through temporizing, but because some of them found it best for the people, to have oft the same words: and some of them found such a weakness of memory, that they judged it the best improvement of their own gifts. Now besides the *first composure* of these prayers, (which perhaps was done 20 years before) none of these men did use their own gifts, any more than if they had used a form composed by another. For the memory and utterance is the same of both.

These all were famous worthy men, whom no wise man judgeth to be insufficient for the Ministry for want of gifts. But if such as these may so many years forbear the exercise of their gift of extemporary prayer, much more may far weaker

Ministers do it. Abundance of young Ministers are trained up under aged experienced Divines, what if one of these should sometimes make use of the same words of prayer, which the aged Minister used the day before, as finding them fitter than any that he could devise himself. Must he forbear to *do better*, because he cannot do so well, by the use of his own gifts alone?

And in some Ordinances as Baptism and the Lords Supper, &c. the same *things* must be daily prayed for: And he that thinketh he must not frequently speak the same things, will quite corrupt the Ordinance of Christ. And he that will *imagine* that he must have alwayes *new words*, will at last have *new things*, or worse than nothing. If then it be meet to use often the *same words*, why may not a weak Minister use the *better words* of others, when he hath none meerly of his own that are so fit?

Nay is it not the *Duty* of such to do it? Every man is bound to do Gods service in the best manner that he can: (Cursed be the *deceiver that hath a better in his flock, and bringeth that which is corrupt*) But to utter prayers and praise to God, in a full, methodicall and congruous manner, and in the words suitable to the Majesty of the worship of God, is *better* (to the people and to the honour of Religion) then to do it in a more *confused, disorderly, broken* manner, with barrenness and incongruity of speech. But this *last* is the *best* that *many* honest Ministers can do by their *own gifts*, when they may do it in the *former better manner*, by making use of the *words* and *gifts* of others. Therefore it is *a duty* for *such men so far* to use

others

others *gifts of inventing words*, before their own.

And among us there is no man forbidden in the Pulpit to use his *own gifts* to the *utmost*, and pray without any set form of his own or other mens.

And I would at last desire any of the Objectors but to name the text of Scripture which directly or indirectly commandeth every Minister, to use his gift of inventing words and method, or his gift of extemporary prayer, every time that he prayeth to God: Or which forbiddeth to use the gifts of others, though better than his own.

Obj. But *what if the forms imposed be worse than the exercise of our own gifts.*

Answ. First, that may be *below* one mans *own invention*, which is *above* anothers. Secondly, And that may be more defective than your own invention could reach to, which yet may be more desirable for other advantages. As if all the Church for some good ends, should agree to use one mode or method or form, (as now we do in singing Psalms) the benefit of that concord might do more for the Churches service than my singular better form or words could do. And if the lawful Rules commanded me that which perhaps I could somewhat exceed my self, I should do much in obedience to their command: Or if the people had a greater *averseneß* or *unfitneß* for my more congruous words than for others more defective, I should take that for the best food or physick, which is most agreeable to the stomack and disease. But especially if I am restrained from the publick preaching of the Gospel, or exercise of any of my Ministry, unless I will use a more disor-

disordered or defective form, I shall take it for my duty then to use it. Because it is more to the Churches edification.

In a word, God hath bound all his Ministers to use all their gifts to the Churches greatest edification: but to use a more *defective form* with liberty to use my *best gifts also*, and to exercise my Ministry *publickly to all*, is more to the Churches *edification*, than to use my *own gifts* only a *few dayes* in a *corner*, and then to lie in prison and use them no more. Though no man must of *choice prefer* the less congruous before the more congruous, when he is free (which I confess is a sin) yet it is a *duty* to prefer a *less congruous* order before *none*, or before a better for a day, with a restraint of that and all our Ministry hereafter.

For my part I have often truly professed, that I look at many Liturgies which I have read as I do at the prayers of some honest men, who use little method, nor very meet words and often toss Gods name through weakness; who put that last which should be first, and that first which should be last but, yet the *matter* is honest and good. I would not *prefer* such a man in a *Congregation*, before an abler man, who will speak more composedly and agreeable to the matter: But yet I would not be so peevish, as utterly to refuse to joyn with such a one. But as God doth not reject his prayers notwithstanding all his weakness, no more would I. And I had rather have such prayers, than none at all.

O that men would discern what is the true worth of prayer! and how little God is taken with the Oratory of them, in comparison of the faith

faith and love and desire which is the soul of prayer. And O that men would lay no greater stress on their *peculiar modes and words* than God doth; and condemn no mans prayers further than they are condemned by God; nor separate from any further than God rejecteth them or commandeth our separation.

I cannot forbear telling you the aggravation of this kind of sin. It seemeth to me a kind of blasphemy against God. As if you would make the world believe that God is so much for your *mode* and *words*, that he overlooketh all the desires of the Spirit, and all his promises, and all mens interest in Christ, and forgetteth all his love to his people: so that Christ shall not intercede for them, or shall not prevail, unless they pray to God in the *words* and *mode* which you have fancied to be best, whether with a Book or without, in *these* words or in *those*. Me thinks you are renewing the old controversie, whether in this Mount or at *Jerusalem* men ought to worship? and knew not that the time is come that God will neither accept men for worshipping at this Mount or at *Jerusalem*, here or there, with a Book or without Book; but the true worshippers whom he chooseth, do worship him as a Spirit, in Spirit and in truth, as well with Forms as without them.

And yet some are more wicked than barely to *condemn* their brethrens prayers, because they be not cloathed just as their own. They will also *break jests and scorns* at them, and take this for the ingenuity of their piety. Like men of several Countreys who think the fashions of all Countreys save their own, to be ridiculous, and laugh

at

at strangers as if they were cloathed in fools Coats. So many do by the cloathing of other mens devotions. Some scorn at *extemporary* prayers, and some scorn at *Forms* and *Liturgies*: And the Litany they call *conjuring*, and the Responses they take for a formal jocular playing with holy things, when in all these, the humble heavenly Christian, is lifting up his soul to God.

By this petulant carnal kind of zeal, I remember our divisions were here raised at the first: To *deride* the *Common prayer*, and deride them that used it, was too common with some kind of religious people: And they excused it by *Elias* his example, As if *Idolaters*, and the true *worshippers of God*, that differ from us in a *Form*, or Ceremony, were all one.

I remember how some of the contrary mind were inflamed to indignation by such scorns, when they were going into the Churches in *London*, and heard some separatists that lookt in at the Church door, say, [*The Devil choke thee, art thou not out of thy pottage yet ?*] Because the Common Prayer was not ended. So little do men know what spirit they were of. But wise and holy Mr. *Hildersham*, Mr. *John Ball*, Mr. *Bradshaw*, Mr. *John Paget*, and other learned Non-conformists of old, did foresee and greatly fear this Spirit.

It is a dangerous thing to scorn and jest at any thing that is done about Gods worship, though it should be it self unwarrantable; while you scorn at one anothers worship of God, you raise a bold unreverence and contempt of holy things in the *hearers*, and perhaps before you are aware in *your selves* too. And you will teach the Atheist to scorn

scorn you all; unless it be the worship of an Idol, where the very object is to be derided, as being no God, you should be very suspicious of this way. I am afraid of making a mock at the grossest erroneous worship of the true God. It is fitter to confute it in a way that more expresseth our reverence to the Object, God himself, and our respect to that pious affection which may be engaged, in it: I have seldom seen the best temppered people inclined to this way of jesting at other mens manner of worship? nor have I observed much good come by it: But I have oft seen that it is the way by which young proud self-conceited persons do kindle a carnal dividing zeal, and a contempt of their brethren, and quench all holy sober zeal and love together.

DIRECT. XXXIII.

When you are sure that other mens way of worship is sinful, yet make it not any other or greater sin, than indeed it is: and speak not evil of that much in it, which is Good; And accuse not God to be a hater or rejecter of all mens service which is mixed with infirmities.

AS St. *James* faith, 3. 2. *In many things we offend all, but be that offended not with his tongue is the perfect man.* So we may here say in the same sense, *In many particulars of our prayers and other worship we all offend God: But he that* bridleth
not

not his *tongue* from the reproaching of his brothers different way of worship, may prove the greatest Offendor of all. It would move a charitable understanding hearer to grief and pity, to read and hear one party call all prayer by habit, no better than *crudities, whinings, bold talking to God and nonsence*; and whatsoever bitter scorn can speak: and to read and hear many on the other extreme, to call the *Liturgy*, no less than *Idolatry!* I desire the Reader to peruse a judicious Treatise of Mr. *Tombes* in answer to one of this language: As much as he and I have written against each others opinion about Infant Baptism, our consenting admonition to you should so much the rather be accepted in this.

And what pitiful arguments have they to prove this charge of *Idolatry? False worship of the true God is idolatry as well as worshipping a false God: But such is the Liturgy: Ergo* ——

This is all that these rash preachers must trouble the Church, and seduce men into a hating factious zeal with. But what mean these men by *false worship?* Do they mean *worship contrary to Gods word?* That is, which is *sinful?* And do they mean *all such sinful worship or some only?* If they mean *all such sinful* worship, than *these words* of theirs are *Idolatry*; For they are part of their *preaching*, which is part of *Gods worship*, in their own sense: And it is *false doctrine*, and tendeth to mens perdition. And so they and all false Teachers should be idolaters. By this they would turn *all* sins in worship into *one*: It is *all Idolatry*. Is not every *confused* prayer *sinful*, which hath unmeet expressions and disordered, and hath wandering

as *Idolaters?* Yea and every man for himself; that is, He must give over praying becaufe its all *Idolatry?*

But perhaps they will fay: *This fin is but in the manner and not in the matter.*

Anfw. Very good; It feems then that fin in the manner of worfhip is not *Idolatry.* And how prove you that the faults of the Liturgy are not as far from the *Matter* of the worfhip, as your *own* are? Will you find *fome words* which you can call *falfe* in the *matter?* Suppofe it were fo? When an Antinomian, an Anabaptift, a Separatift, or any one that erreth doth drop fome of his errours in his prayers, (as I think none will deny that they ufe to do) muft we needs believe that his prayer is *Idolatry* therefore, as being *falfe worfhip?* And is it unlawful to joyn with fuch? Then we fhall have more feparation than you yet plead for, or practife your felves. No two men in the world muft joyn together if *finfull worfhip*, or worfhip *falfe* fometime in the very *matter* doth neceffitate a feparation: At leaft where no one knoweth before hand what another will fay with his tongue, when I know that every man hath fome falfe opinion in his mind.

But where did thefe men learn to call their brethrens worfhip *falfe* any more than their *own*, upon the account that God hath not commanded the *manner* of it; when he hath neither commanded us to *ufe a form*, nor to *forbear* it; but by general precepts of doing all to edification?

on; If one man preach in one method and another in another; One by written Notes to help his memory, and another without; one by his own gifts only, and another by the help of others; which of these is the false prophet, the false worshipper or Idolater? Hath God said *you shall use Notes in preaching?* No more hath he said, *you shall preach without Notes*: yet hath he commanded both, to severall persons where *edification* variously requireth it. Is he an Idolater that useth Meeters, Tunes, Versions, Translations, Directories, Pulpits, Cups, Table-Cloaths, Fonts, Basins, *&c.* which God commandeth not. O Lord pity thy poor Church, whose Pastors themselves are so peevish in their ignorance, and tempt other men by their follies, to justifie all their severities against them and others.

But what Text of Scripture is it that ever told these men that *all false worship is Idolatry?* what text do they name, but such as if they did it on purpose, to shew their boldness in adding to Gods Word? The second Commandment is the chief which they insist on. But what ever Expositions they may forge, there is no such word nor sense in the Commandment. We all hold that as the *gross direct Idolatry*, is the worshipping of a *false God*, against the first Commandment, so to make any *such false representation* of the *true God*, by *words or deeds*, as maketh him *like an Idol*, and contradicteth his *nature*, and *so to worship him*, this is also a *secondary* kind of *Idolatry*: Because God is *none such* as they represent him, and therefore it is not God indeed, but an Idol which they worship. And because God is not like to any thing corporeal

real in heaven or earth, therefore he that maketh an image of any thing in Heaven or earth as like to God, or to represent him, he maketh an idol of God by blasphemy. *To what will you liken me, that I should be like unto it, saith the Holy one?* This is the idolatry forbidden in the Second Commandment: It is not *all false worship, but one sort of false worship*, which is idolatry: what else that Commandment forbiddeth, is neither called *Idolatry*, nor can so be proved.

It is an odious found, to hear an ignorant, rash, self-conceited person, especially a Preacher, to cry out, *Idolatry, Idolatry*, against his brethrens prayers to God, because they have something in them to be amended; while perhaps his own prayers have to much false doctrine in them, or such fire of carnal passion and uncharitableness, as maketh it a much harder question, whether it be lawful to joyn with such as he is, while he abhorreth so much to joyn with others. All that know me know that it is not my own case and interest, that I fit this reprehension to. It is twenty times harder to me to remember a Form of words, than to express what is in my mind without them. But we must not fit our opinions of all our brethrens prayers, to our own temperament.

DIRECT.

DIRECT. XXXIV.

Think not that all is unlawful to be obeyed, which is unlawfully commanded.

Many a Ruler sinneth in his Commands, when it is no sin but a duty of the inferiour to obey them. He that hath but a *bad end*, or bad circumstances may sin in commanding: As if a Magistrate command Religious Duties in meer Policy for his own Advantage, or if he enforce a lawful Command with unlawful Penalties: And yet it will be the Subjects Duty to obey. Yea, as to the *matter* it self, it may be unlawful for a Ruler to command a thing that will do no good, (because it is a vain Command, and maketh men spend that time in vain:) and yet it may be the Subjects Duty to do it.

If the Magistrate choose an inconvenient place for publick worship, or an unfit hour, or if the Pastor choose a less fit translation, meeter or tune, or other circumstances of worship, it may be their sin to do so, and yet the peoples duty to obey them. If a Father bid his Child but carry a straw from one place to another, it is his fault so to imploy his time in vain; but the Child is not faulty in obeying. Indeed if the thing commanded be such as is simply evil, and forbidden us by God, in all cases whatsoever, than no ones commands can make it lawful. But if it be a thing that is only inconvenient, or unlawful by some lesser accident, then the command of autho-
rit

rity may preponderate as a more weighty accident. If it be lawful to give a Thief my purse, to save my life, which is not lawful for him to demand or take; Then sure it is lawful to obey a King, a Parent, a Master or a Pastor, in things not evil in themselves, though they unlawfully command them. I say not that we must do so in *all things* which are evil but by accident: For *some* accidents may make it so great an evil, as no mans command can preponderate and make it lawful: But in *some cases* it is so, though not in all.

Therefore remember that you do not prove it sinful in you to do such things, by proving it a sin in the imposer, unless you have some better reason, and can shew a Law of God forbidding you.

DIRECT. XXXV.

Think not that you are guilty of all the Faults of other mens worship with whom you joyn; no not of the Ministers or Congregations; Nor that you are bound to separate from them in worship; because of all the faults in their performance.

THis Error is a common cause of separations; but such as will suffer no two men to joyn together, but will turn all Churches into confusion, and crumble them to dust, if it be fully practised. For there is no man alive that worshippeth God without some sin, as I said before.

fore. Do you ever pray your selves in secret or in your families without sin? Must all separate from you for this? Or may not you bear anothers failings as patiently as your own? Your own you are still guilty of, because they are your own: but not of another mans which you cannot help. If I believed that I were partaker of the guilt of all the false doctrine, or faulty preaching, or prayer which was used in the Church where I am, I would flye from all the Churches in the world: But whether to go I could not tell.

Obj. *But if I joyn with them that worship God amiss, do I not approve of their sin or signifie my consent to it?*

Answ. Approving and consenting are acts of your own mind: and whether you do so or not, is best known to your self: But it is a *Profession* of consent that we have now to speak of. And I say that our presence at the prayers of the Church, is *no profession* of *consent* to all that is faulty in those prayers. Why do you not offer to *prove* it to be so, but barely affirm it without any proof? I never heard a word of proof for this bare assertion to this day. But its easily disproved.

First, No man can in reason and justice take that for my *Profession*, which I never made by word nor deed, according to the common sense of words and actions: But according to this common sense I never did by word or deed profess that I consent to all which is uttered by the Pastor in the publick prayers.

Secondly, When the profession which we make by our Church-communion is publickly declared

(to

to be another thing, totally distinct from this, no man may justly interpret it to be this which is quite different: But it is another thing which we profess by our Church-communion; That is, I profess my self only to be a *Christian*, in my Baptism when I enter into the Church, and in my daily communion with it: And I profess to be a member of a Christian Society, and to hold Communion with them in Faith and Love and in worshipping God according to his word: And I profess subjection to the particular Pastors of that Church, as Christian Pastors, who are to teach the people that word of God, and guide them in worship and discipline according to that word. This is every mans profession in his Church-communion and no more; unless he make some further particular expression of more, as every Sect used to do, in professing the opinions of their party. Why then should any lyar charge me to make a profession which I never made, when my profession in my Christian communion is described by Christ himself who instituted it? And why should I turn lyar against my self, and say that my presence is a profession of that consent which I never made the least profession of?

Thirdly, The wording of the publick prayers, is the Pastors work and none of mine: It is part of his office, as the wording and methodizing of his Sermons is: And if he do it well the praise is not mine but his: And if he do it ill the dispraise is not mine but his. Why should any hold me guilty of another mans fault, which I neither can help, nor belongeth to any office of mine to help, any further than to admonish him.

Fourthly, I do not profess an approbation and consent to all the faults of *my own* secret or family prayers: Much less to another mans, who is not in my power. I have disorders, and defects and incongruities and other faults in all my prayers; And if my very *speaking* and *committing* them signifie not my *approbation* of them, how much less is it signified where it is not I but *another man* that speaketh and committeth them.

Fifthly, And as I have said, This opinion would make it unlawful to joyn with *any* Pastor or Church *on earth*, because no *sin* must be *approved of* and *consented* to; and every one mixeth sin with their prayers.

Obj. But (*say those* on the one extream) *if I joyn with one that is known to be a Separatist, an Anabaptist, an Antinomian, an Arminian,* &c. *his own profession doth before hand bid me not to expect not only that the manner but the matter of his prayer be erroneous.*

Answ. First, it is granted that no man may in his choice, preferr an erring person or mode of worship before a better. Secondly, But when the question is not, whom you should *prefer* but whom you may *joyn with*, it is not *his* errors *that are yours*, nor his profession that is *yours*. I come to joyn with him as a *Christian Pastor* whose office is to preach the Gospel: And while men are the agents I know that all that they do will be imperfect and faulty: And it is not *my knowing* their faults that makes them *mine*, but rather may preserve me from them.

Obj. *But for ought I know he may put heresie or blasphemy into his prayers, when I know*
not

Objections against praying by habit. 199

not what he will say, before I hear it.

Answ. For ought *you know your Phsitian*, or *your Cook*, may give you poison, and your Nurse may poison your child: But though that should make you careful whom you trust, yet some body must be trusted for all that. You go not upon certainty in any case where man is to be trusted, but upon *probability*. Men are not to be distrusted in their own profession, if they be lawfully called to it, by cautelous and able triers, till they have forfeited their trust: And as he would not mend the matter who should make a Law, that no Physician shall give any medicine but one and the same to all in such diseases, and that fetcht from the Kings Apothecary; And no Cook shall sell any meat but what is drest by the Kings Cooks; for fear lest they should poison men; so he that would say, No Pastor shall preach or pray but in prescribed words, lest he should speak heresie or blasphemy, would but destroy the Pastoral office, for fear lest it should be abused.

But here you have no great temptation to this error; Because though a man may poyson your bodies against your wills, yet no one can poyson your souls but by your own consent. If he speak words of heresie or blasphemy, if you disown them in your minds, and consent not to them, they are none of yours, nor can do you hurt: They may be your temptation and your grief, but they are not your sin.

And yet I shall tell you in the next direction, how far they are to be avoided.

Ob. But (say those on the other extream)

When I know before hand by their Common-Prayer-Book, what their error in worship is, and yet joyn in it, do I not seem to approve it?

Ansr. Do not barely *affirm*, but *prove*, that all *fore-known faults* of the Pastors words in prayer are *mine*, if I separate not: How doth fore-knowing them make them mine. Take heed that thus you make not God the greatest sinner and the worst being in all the world.

For God *fore-knoweth* all mens sins; and God is *present* when they commit them; and he giveth them all that life and time and strength and breath, by which they do them: and he hath communion with all the prayers of the faithful in the world, what faults soever be in the *words* or *forms*: he doth not reject them for any such failings. Will you say therefore that God *approveth* or *consenteth* to all these sins?

I know before hand (as is said before) that every man will sin that prayeth (either by defect of desire, love, faith or fervency, or by wandering thoughts, or disordered words, &c.) And I know that every erroneous person (commonly) doth use to put his errors into his prayers and preaching. But how doth all this make it mine? I am bound to hold communion with all Gods people on earth as I have occasion; not as they are *sinners*, but as they are *Saints*: And I come as to the Communion of Saints: And though both they and I do bring our sins to that communion, and I fore-know them; yet I lament both theirs and mine; and so far am I from consenting to them, that they are my grief, and I beg forgiveness both for them and me.

Obj.

Obj. But you said that it belonged to the Pastors office to word his own Sermons and Prayers: Therefore prescribed forms destroy the Pastors office: And I may not consent to such usurpations by tyrannical men.

Answ. First, the Pastor is the mouth of God to the people, and of the people to God: And he doth word his own Sermons and Prayers; or else his voice could not conduct you. But if he that is conscious of his own infirmity, to take the help of others in wording them, that doth not destroy his office, but help him in the exercise of it. If a weak Minister learn a prayer out of the writings of some abler Divine and use it in the Pulpit, this is no destroying of his office.

Secondly, and if they that fear the effect of Ministers weakness shall force them to use the words of others, the speaker still maketh them his *own words* before you joyn with him. And if it did hinder the *free exercise* of all his office, it doth not *destroy* it.

Obj. But he doth it voluntary, whereas the weakness of conceived prayer is voluntary.

Answ. It is with more probability said, that a man is *involuntary*, in doing that which another compelled him to do, than that which no man but himself only is the author of: It is said to him that readeth the Liturgy [Do this, or *nothing*] But no body saith to an erring, weak, confused Minister, [*Put in your errours into your prayers, or pray disorderly or you shall be punished.*] Every Separatist, Anabaptist and Antinomian doth too willingly put his errours into his prayers.

Obj. But the Liturgy is imposed on the ablest

as well as on the weakest Ministers.

Answ. Whether it be well or ill imposed, is none of the question now in hand: No nor whether it be lawfully used by the Speaker: But whether *you* may lawfully *joyn* in it. And however it be imposed, till the Minister consent to use it, you shall not be put to joyn with him in it. And when he doth consent, he maketh it his own words, and (for reasons which seem good to him) he doth choose those expressions rather than others: (Even because he must use those or none) so that he is still in the exercise of this office; And it is his personal fault, if be a fault, to use those words, and none of yours: Whether he do it willingly as the best, or do it with a half will as of necessity, or whether there be tyranny in the imposing them or not; you are not guilty of any of this, by joyning with a Christian Chruch that useth them.

DIRECT. XXXVI.

Yet know what Pastors you may own, and what not, and what Church communion you may remove from or forbear: And think not that I am perswading you to make no difference.

THis is a point that I have more largely handled elsewhere, and can give you now but these brief hints, lest I be too tedious.

First, He that is not *at all able* to do the essential

tial works of the Miniſtry, that is, to teach the people the Chriſtian faith, and a holy life, and to pray and praiſe God with them, and adminiſter the Sacraments, and in ſome meaſure overſee the manners of the flock, is not miniſter, nor to be owned: For he wanteth the eſſential qualifications: As an illaterate man can be no Schoolmaſter, nor be a Phyſitian, a Pilot, an Architect, who is utterly ignorant of their work.

Secondly, he that preacheth Hereſie, that is, denieth any eſſential point of Chriſtianity or Godlineſs, after the firſt and ſecond admonition is to be avoided.

Thirdly, he that in his application, endeavoureth to diſgrace a Godly life, and to diſſwade the people from it, on falſe pretenſes, and encourage them to a life of wickedneſs, is a traytor to Chriſt, and not to be owned in the Miniſtry: In a word, *Any one whoſe Miniſtry is ſuch, as tendeth to deſtruction more than to edification and to do more harm than good.* But then remember, that it is not partiality and paſſion that muſt here be judge: Nor is every one an oppoſer of Godlineſs, who oppoſeth the errours of a party, or the faults or follies of godly men.

Fourthly, that Paſtor or Church who will not let you have communion with them, unleſs you will ſay or ſubſcribe ſome falſhood, or commit any ſin of wilful choice, doth drive you from their communion by their unlawful terms; and it is not you that are the Separatiſts, but they.

Fifthly, When you are to chooſe what Miniſter or Church you will ſtatedly have your ordinary communion with, you ſhould not prefer a
leſs

less reformed Church or a less worthy Pastor, or one that is erroneous, before a better, but choose that which is most to your true edification.

Sixthly, if you live under a worse and unreformed Church, or unprofitable Minister, if necessity hinder not, you may remove your dwelling to a better.

Seventhly, and where Churches are near and there is no great hurt or disorder will follow it, you may joyn with another Church without removing your dwelling: But this you may not do, when the hurt to the publick is like to be greater than the good to you.

Eighthly, and you must not conclude that the more faulty Church and Minister *may not lawfully be communicated with* though for your benefit you choose a better, for this is the true crime of sinful separation.

But surely a mans soul is so precious, that all men should prefer the greatest helps for their salvation before the less? and think no just means too dear to purchase them.

DIRECT.

DIRECT. XXXVII.

In your judging of Discipline, Reformation, and any means of the Churches good, be sure your Eye be both upon the true End, and upon the particular Rule, and not on either of them alone: Take not that for a means, which is either contrary to the word of God, or is in its nature destructive of the End.

There are great miscarriages come for want of the true observation of this rule. First, If a thing seem to you very *needful* to a good *end*, and yet the *word be against it*, avoid it: For God knoweth better than we, what means is fittest, and what he will bless. As for instance, some think, that many self-devised wayes of worship, contrary to *Col.* 2, 21, 23 would be very profitable to the Church: And some think that striking with the sword as *Peter* did, is the way to rescue Christ or the Gospel: But both are bad, because the Scripture is against them.

Secondly, and if you think that the Scripture commandeth you this or that positive means, if Nature and true Reason assure you that it is against the End, and is like to do much more harm than good, be assured that you mistake that Scripture. For first, God telleth us in general that the *means as such are for the End*, and therefore are *no means* when they are against *it*. The Ministry is for edification and not for destruction. The Sabbath

Sabbath is for man and not man for the Sabbath. Secondly, God hath told us, that no positive duty is a duty at all times. To pray when I should be saving my neighbours life, is a sin and not a duty, though we are commanded to pray continually. So is it to be preaching; or hearing on the Lords day, when I should be quenching a fire in the town, or doing necessary works of mercy: Wherefore the Disciples Sabbath-breaking was justified by Christ; and he giveth us all a charge to learn what this meaneth, I will have mercy and not sacrifice which must needs import, I prefer mercy before sacrifice and would have no sacrifice which hindereth mercy. Therefore if a Sermon were to be preached so unseasonably or in such unsuitable circumstances, as that according to Gods ordinary way of working, it were like to do more hurt than good; it were no duty at that time. Discipline is an Ordinance of Christ: But if sound reason tell me, that if I publickly call this man to Repentance, or excommunicate him, it is like to do much hurt to the Church and no good to him, it would be at that time no duty but a sin. As Physick must be forborn where the Disease will but be exasperated by it. Therefore Christ boundeth our very preaching and reproof, with a [*Shake off the dust off your feet as a testimony against them. And give not that which is holy to dogs*, &c. *When treading under foot, and turning again and rending us, is likest to be the success*, the wisdom of Christ, and not that of the flesh only, requireth us to take it for no duty. This is to be observed by them that think that Admonitions, and excommunications,

and

and exclusion from the Sacrament, must be used in all places and at all times alike, without respect to the End, come of it what will: Or that will tempt God by presuming that he will certainly either bless or at least justifie, their unseasonable and imprudent actions, as if they were a duty at all times. To be either against the *Scripture*, or against the *End*, is a certain proof that an action is no duty, because no means.

DIRECT. XXXVIII.

Neglect not any truth of God, much less renounce it or deny it: For lying and contempt of Sacred truth is alwayes sinful: But yet do not take it for your duty to publish all which you judge to be truth, nor a sin to silence many lesser truths, when the Churches peace and welfare doth require it.

TO speak or subscribe against any truth, is not to be done on any pretence whatsoever: For lying is a sin at all times. But it is the opinion of injudicious furious spirits, that no truth is to be silenced for peace. Truth is not to be sold for carnal prosperity, but it is to be forborn for spiritual advantage, and true necessity.

First, if the publishing of all truthes were at all times a duty, then all men live every moment in ten thousand sins of omission, because there are

are more than so many truths which I am not publishing: Nay which I never shall publish whilest I live.

Secondly, Positives bind not alwayes and to all times.

Thirdly, while you are preaching that opinion which your zeal is so much for, you are omitting far greater and more necessary Truths. And is it not as great a sin to omit them as the lesser.

Fourthly, Mercy is to be preferred before sacrifice: What if the present uttering some truth would cost many thousand mens lives? Were not that an untimely and unmerciful word? And is it not as bad if (but accidentally) it tend to the ruine of the Church, and the hurt of souls? It were easie to instance in unseasonabe and imprudent words of truth spoken to Princes, which have raised persecutions of long continuance, and ruined Churches, silenced Ministers, and caused the death of multitudes of men.

Fifthly, And where is there any word of God which commandeth us to speak all that we know, and which forbiddeth us to forbear the utterance of any one truth.

Sixthly, And for the most part those men, who are most pregnant and impatient of holding in their opinions on the pretense of the preciousness of truth, do but proudly esteem their own understandings precious, and who vend some raw undigested notions, vain janglings or errors, under the name of that truth which must by no means be concealed, though the vending of it tend to envy and strife, and to confusion and every evil work. When those that have the Truth indeed,

have

have more wisdom and goodness to know how to use it.

It is not *Truth* but *Goodness* which is the ultimate object of the soul. And God who is infinite *Goodness* it self, hath revealed his *Truths* to the world to do men *Good*, and not to hurt them. And the Devil, who is the Destroyer, so he may but do men *hurt*, will be content to make use even of *Truth* to do it; Though usually he only pretendeth *Truth* to cover his *lies:* And this Angel of Light, hath his ministers of Light and Righteousness; who are known by their fruits: whilst the pretences of Light and Righteousness are used to Satans ends and not to Christs, to hurt and destroy and to hinder Christs Kingdom, and not to save and to do good: As the Wolf is known by his bloody jaws, even in his sheeps cloathing.

DIRECT. XXXIX.

Know which are the great duties of a Christian life, and wherein the nature of true Religion doth consist; and then pretend not any lesser duty, against these greater; though the least when it is indeed a duty, is not to be denyed or neglected.

Heaven-work and *Heart-work*, are the chiefest parts of Christian duty. Christ often giveth us his summaries of the Law, and inculcateth his great Command; *John* 13.35. *Matth.* 22

37, 38, 39. *Luke* 10. 27. And so doth the Apostle *Rom.* 13. 10. 1 *Pet.* 1. 22. 1 *John* 3. 11, 14, 23. & 4. 7, 11, 12, 20. 2 *John* 5. And the fruits of the spirit are manifest *Gal.* 5. 22, 23. *James* saith, that *pure Religion and undefiled before God even the father is this, to visit the fatherless and widows in adversity, and to keep our selves unspotted of the world,* Jam. 1. 27. *Paul* saith, 1 *Tim.* 1. 5. *The end of the Commandment is Charity out of a pure heart, and of a good conscience, and of faith unfeigned:* And then addeth, *From which some having swarved, have turned aside to vain janglings*———

In a word [*The effectual belief of pardon and eternal Glory given through Christ, and the Love of God and man, with the denial of our selves, and fleshly desires, and contempt of all things in the world which are competitors with God and our salvation with a humble patient enduring of all which must be suffered for these ends*] is the nature and sum of the Christian Religion.

Do nothing therefore as a duty which is a hinderance to any of this. Contentious preachings and factious tidings which weaken *Love,* are not of God. *The servant of the Lord must not strive, but be gentle to all men,* 2 *Tim.* 2. 24. When you come into a family and find that their Religion consisteth in promoting some odd opinion, and pleading for a party, and vilifying others, be sure that this is a Religious way of serving the devil, being contrary to the great and certain duties of a godly life. When you fall into company, which stifleth all talk of Heaven, and all *Heart-searching* and *Heart-humbling conference,* by pleading for this or that opinion, be sure that it is but one
way

way of enmity to Holiness, though not so gross as scorning and persecuting. That which I said before of *Truth*, is appliable to this of Duty.

It is one of the most important things in the world, for the resolving of a thousand cases of conscience, and the directing of a Christian life, to know which *Duties* are the *Greater* and which are the *lesser*, and so which is to be preferred in competition; For that which is a duty at another time, is a sin, when it is done instead of a greater! as Christ hath resolved in the case of the Sabbath. If *Good* must be loved as Good, then the Greatest Good must be most loved and sought. Sacrifice instead of mercy is a sin: Our gift must be left at the altar, while we go to be reconciled to 'our brother. *Math.* 5. Never hearken to those men who would set up their controverted duties, or any positives or lesser things, against the duties of nature it self, or the great substantial parts of godliness.

DIRECT.

DIRECT. XL.

Labour for a sound judgement to know good from evil, lest you trouble your selves and others by mistakes: And till you grow so judicious, forsake not the guidance of a judicious Teacher, nor the company of the agreeing generality of the Godly.

ALmost all our contentions and divisions are caused by the ignorance and injudiciousness of Christians; especially the most self-conceited. They are for the most as children, that yet need to be taught the very principles of the divine Oracles, and to be fed with milk, when they think themselves fit to be teachers of others. *Heb.* 5. 11, 12. And therefore as children they are tossed to and fro, and carried about with every wind of doctrine. *Eph.* 4. 14. And when they have many years together been crying up an opinion, and vilifying dissenters, at last they turn to some other opinion, and confess that they did all this upon mistake. And was it not a pitiful life that they lived that while? and a pitiful zeal which did set them on? and a pitiful kind of worship which they thus offered to God? Alas to hear a man pray and preach up Antinomianism one year, and Arminianism the next, and Socinianism the next! To hear a man make Separation and Anabaptistry a great part of his business to men in preaching and to God in prayer for seven and seven years together; and at last confess that all this was his errour and his sin: (Or if he confess it not, it is so much the worse.) Is it not sad that ignorance and hasty rashness, should so much injure the Church and mens souls that so many well meaning people, should put evil for good, and good for evil, darkness for light, and light for darkness, *Isa.* 5. 20.

But because there is no hope that most should be judicious, there is no other remedy for such but this of Christs prescript which I have here set down.

First, Happy is he that chooseth a judicious faithful Guide and learneth of him till his own understanding be better illuminated ; And that escapeth the conduct of ignorant, erroneous, self-seeking, proud, dividing Teachers.

Seconly, Continue in the Communion of the *generality* of *agreeing* Christians: The generality of the godly are more unlikely to be forsaken of Christ, than a few odd self-conceited singular Professors. This is the way of peace to your selves and to the Church of Christ.

DIRECT. XLI.

Let not the bare Fervour of a Preacher, or the Lowdneſs of his voice, or affectionate manner of utterance, draw you too far to admire or follow him; without a proportionable degree of ſolid underſtanding and judiciouſneſs.

IT is pitty that any wiſe and judicious Miniſter ſhould want that fervour and ſeriouſneſs of ſpeech, which the weight of ſo great a buſineſs doth require. And it is greater pity, that any ſerious affectionate Miniſter, ſhould be ignorant and injudicious: And it is yet greater pity that in any good men, too much of their fervour ſhould be meerly affected, and ſeem to be what it is not; or at leaſt be raiſed by a ſelfiſh deſire to advance our ſelves in the hearers thoughts, and to exerciſe our parts upon their affections. But it is moſt pitiful that the Church hath any hypocrites who have no other but ſuch affected diſſembled fervency. And it is not the leaſt pity that ſo many good people, eſpecially youths and women, ſhould be ſo weak, as to value an affectionate tone of ſpeech, above a judicious opening of the Goſpel. I confeſs there is ſomething in an affectionate expreſſion, which will move the wiſeſt: And as light and *judgement* tend to generate *judgement*, ſo *heat* of affection tendeth to beget *affection.* And I never loved a ſenſeleſs delivery of matters of eternal conſeqeunce; As if we were asleep our selves, or would make the hearers to be so: Or would have them think by our cold expressions, that we believe not our selves when we set forth the great inestimable things of the life to come. But yet it grieveth my very soul to think, what pitiful, raw, and ignorant kind of preaching, is crowded most after in many places, for the meer affectionate manner of expression, and lowdness of the Preachers voice! How oft have I known the ablest Preachers undervalued, and an ignorant man by crouds applauded, when I that have been acquainted with the Preacher *ab incunabilis*, have known him to be unable well to answer most questions in the common Catechism. And I durst not tell them of his great insufficiency and ignorance, for fear of hindring the success of his labours, and being thought envious at other mens acceptance. I have known poor tradesmens boys have a great mind of the Ministry; and we that were the Ministry; and we that were the Ministers of the Countrey, contributed to maintain them while they got some learning and knowledge: But they had not patience to keep out of the Pulpit till they competently understood their business there: And yet many of the religious people valued these as the only men: And some of them shortly after turned to some whimsical Sect or other, and contemned the Ministers that instructed and maintained them: And all this while, understood not half so much as many of our sober Auditors understood. This prepareth the poor people to be hurried into any disorder or division, when they no better know how to choose their Guides.

DIRECT.

DIRECT. XLII.

Your belief of the necessary Articles of Faith, must be made your own, and not taken meerly upon the Authority of any: And in all points of Belief or Practice which are of necessity to Salvation, you must ever keep company with the Universal Church: for it were not the Church if it erred in these: And in matters of peace and concord, the greater part must be your guide; In matters of humane obedience, your Governours must be your guides: And in matters of high and difficult speculation, the judgement of one man of extraordinary understanding and clearness is to be preferred before both the Rulers and the major Vote.

IN several sorts of Controversies and Cases, you must prefer several sorts of Guides or Judges: It is a grand pernicious Error to think that the same mens judgements must be most followed in every Case. And it is of grand importance to know how to value and vary our Guides, as the Cases vary. And for the most part, every man is more to be regarded in his own way of study and profession, than wiser men in other matters, of other studies and professions: As a Lawyer is to be valued in the Law more than the ablest and most illuminated Divine: And a Philosopher

Various Guides in various Cases. 217

losopher in Philosophy, and a Linguist in the Tongues, and a Physician in Physick, &c. For instance,

First, Suppose it were a Controversie whether Christ be God, or whether there be a life to come, or a resurrection, &c. Here no man must be Judge, because if you are Christians indeed, it is past controversie with you: And you believe this upon the evidences of truth, which have convinced you: and herein the universal Church are your associates.

Secondly, Suppose it be made a Controversie whether you shall use this Translation or version in publick, or another, or whether you shall meet at this hour or that, at this place or that; what words of prayer shall be used in publick? what persons you shall communicate with in publick, and what not, &c. In all such, your lawful Pastors and Rulers are the Judges, and their judgements must be preferred before more learned men that are not related to you.

Thirdly, Suppose the question be among many associated Churches, whether *this Church* or *Pastor* be to be disowned as *Hereticall*, or owned by the rest as orthodox Christians. Here the judgement of the Pastors of those associated Churches in Councels, is to be preferred as of the proper Judges.

Fourthly, Suppose the question, were among a *free people*, that want a Pastor, whether this man or that or the other (being all sufficient) shall be the Pastor of that Church: Here the major Vote of the people of that Church should be preferred.

Fifthly, Suppose the question be, whether 1 *John* 5. 7. *e. g.* be Canonical Scripture; or the Doxology after the Lords Prayer, *&c.* here a few learned Antiquaries, are to be believed before a major Vote or Councel, unskilled in those things, who contradict them.

Sixthly, Suppose the question were of the Object of predestination, of the nature of the wills liberty, of the concourse of God, and determining way of grace, of the definition of justification, faith, *&c.* Here a few well studied judicious Divines must be preferred before Authority and majority of Votes: As one clear-sighted man seeth further and better than a thousand that have darker sight: So that you must in such cases vary your guides, according to their several capacities and the Case. *Obedience* hearkneth most to *Authority*, *Unity* and *Concord* must depend most on some majority of Votes: *Hard questions* must be decided by the best *studied Persons*, and the quickest clearest sights, and not by bare Commands or Votes.

DIRECT.

DIRECT. XLIII.

Take heed left you be tempted to reject a good Cause, because it is owned by some bad persons; or to like a bad cause when it is owned by men that are otherwise good: And that you judge not of the faith and cause by the persons, when you should judge of the persons rather by the faith and cause.

I Confess when we have no other reason to encline us to one opinion or to another, but only the reputation of them that hold it, *cæteris paribus*, in matters of meer godliness, the judgement of *godly men* is much to be preferred before theirs that are *ungodly*, and they are much liker to be in the right. But when God hath given us *other means* to know the truth, we must impartially make use of them.

It too oft falleth out that honest people are like straying sheep: If one leap over the hedge, the rest will croud and strive to follow him: And therefore errours are like Languages and Fashions, that follow the Country where they are bred. The religious people in *Sweden* and *Denmark* have one sort of errour; In *Holland* and *Helvetia* perhaps they have another: In *France*, and *Spain*, and *Italy* they have others: In *Greece*, and *Armenia*, and *Ethiopia* they have others. And it is an easier matter before we are aware, to fall into the common epidemical disease; and to think, This is best, because the best and strictest people are of this mind. And indeed sin doth seldom get so great an advantage in the world, as when it hath won the major vote among the most religious sort of people: If but a *Peter* separate, *Barnabas* and many more will follow.

And on the other side, sometimes the worser sort of men may hold fast the truth, and many ignorant persons are apt to reject it, because it is owned by men so bad. But if Truth be the Religion of their King and Country, or of their Ancestors in which they were brought up; or if their reputation or peace of conscience lie upon it; or if the defence of it shew their wit or learning; or if they can take an advantage by it, against better men, who err in that one point: It is no wonder in all these Cases, if the worser sort of men defend the truth.

For instance; If any Sect should rise in *England*, who should deny Christ, or the Scripture, or the Resurrection, or the Life to come, or the Lords day (for all that they cannot keep it holy, yet) the worser sort of the people would all rise up against such errours. Shall we therefore think that the people are in the wrong? So if any better persons deny *Infant Baptism*, or the use of the *Lords Prayer*, &c. the worser sort of people would be all against them; and yet be in the right.

And yet how many do take a form of prayer or Liturgy to be unlawful, meerly because the most of the worser sort are for it! As a Pharisee can gratifie his hypocrisie by *long Prayers*, which yet are good in themselves; so can an ungodly person gratifie his hypocrisie and sloth by Forms

and

and Liturhies: which yet doth not prove them to be unlawful.

DIRECT. XLVI.

Yea take the bad example of religious men, to be one of your most perilous temptations: And therefore labour to discover especially what are the sins of Professors in the age that you live in, that you may especially watch and fortifie your souls against them.

Sometimes the strictest sort run in a gang after one opinion, and sometimes after another: sometimes to overvalue free will with the *Pelagians*: sometimes to abuse the name and notion of free grace: sometimes they are drawn with *Peter* to lay about them with a private unwarranted Sword; or by Politicians tempted into unlawful tumults: sometimes they run together into unlawful Compliances and conformities to escape some censure or danger to the flesh: And most commonly they are hurried by Passion to follow some erronious Leader into Schisme and Divisions, which are contrary to Unity, Love, and Peace.

Studdy well what is the common errour of the *religious party* in the times and places where you live, that you may take a special care to escape them, (For some such or others it is too probable they have.) Like not their fault for their Religions

ons fake: But specially take heed lest the Devil draw you, to dislike their Religion for their faults. Joyn with them heartily in the one, but not in the other.

DIRECT. XLV.

Desire the highest degree of Holiness, and to be free from the corruption of the times: But affect not to be odd and singular, from ordinary Christians in lawful things.

AN affectation of *singularity* in indifferent things, doth either come from such ignorance as those were guilty of in *Rom.* 14. or most commonly from Pride, though you perceive it not your selves. If it be to go in a meaner garb than others, and as the Quakers, not to put off the hat; or with the Fryars, to go barefoot, or in a distinguishing habit, that all men may see and say, This is a singular person in Religion, it is easie to see how this gratifieth pride. Humility desireth not to be especially taken notice of: And therefore in all things lawful, to do as others do, doth gratifie humility very much. It's strange to observe how much stress some persons lay upon their singular habits, gestures, expressions and actions, when they have once taken them up? and how sharp they are against all that are contrary? For as the Masters of every Sect of Monks among the Papists had their several Rules of sin-
gula-

gularity in things indifferent; and yet presently desired to get disciples to take their names, and follow their rules; so is it with most that begin in singularity: they would have all to follow them, that it might grow common.

DIRECT. XLVI.

When you have to do only with stigmatized scandalous ones, to vindicate the honour of Christianity from their scandal, go as far from them as lawfully you can: But with the common sort of sinners, whose conversion you are bound to seek, go not as far from them as you can, but purposely study to come as near them, as lawfully you may, that you may have the better advantage to win them to the truth.

WHen it is our work to avoid persons that they may be ashamed, or that we may shew our detestation of their wickedness, then going from them is our duty; and we must do it; (To the excommunicate in publick, and to the notoriously wicked and impenitent after admonition in our private way of life.) But with most men, our duty is to labour their conversion, and in hope to seek the saving of their souls, till they prove as dogs and swine to their exhorters. It is a common question whether we should go as far as we may from wicked men, or come as near them as we may. And it is very great ignorance to say either the one or the other, without distinguishing of wicked men! Seeing our duty lyeth the clean contrary way, towards one sort of them and towards another.

And there is much difference also to be made of the *matter* in which our joyning with them, or going from them doth consist. For there are some things which though they are no sin, yet are so like sin, that our doing them is most like to be a snare, and to hinder mens repentance, and not to further it: And in this we must not come too near them. But there are other things in which our going too far from them is like to hinder their repentance.

The injudicious zeal of many young Christians, doth often carry them into this extream. Any fashion of apparel which the common people use, they will avoid as far as modesty will permit them. And any lawfull recreation which they use, they will fly the further from because they use it: And they think it a scandal, to shoot or bowl or use any such game which bad men use. And any form or *manner* of speech which is lawful in it self they think they must avoid because such use it. But especially any way of worshiping God, or any controvertible opinion in Religion, which is owned by bad men, they flye as far from as they can; By which means all this evil is committed.

First, Their own faith and practise is corrupted: For many an errour is taken up, by going too far from other mens faults. Many a one turneth Pelagian, by flying indiscreetly from Antinomianism, And many a one turneth Antinomian by avoiding Pelagianism. Many a one turneth Papist to shew his detestation of multitudes of sects: And many a one turneth to the giddiest sects, to avoid the things which are held and practised by the Papists; and are so zealous in avoiding the Papists ceremonies and forms and holidayes too far, that at last they renounce their Ordination and their Baptism, and some at last deny the Scriptures, the Creed, and the Christ, which the Papists own. Many a one turneth Separatist and Anabaptist and Quaker, to get far enough from Bishops and Liturgies: And many a one is ready to over-run his consideration, and abuse his conscience in the extent of his compliance with all impositions, through the indignation or contempt against the unreasonable humours of the Sectaries. And thus mens *own* judgement and practice is depraved, while they think more *from whence* to go, than whither.

Secondly, you lose your advantage of doing good to those you fly from: And therein disobey the will of God, and have a hand in the loss of the souls of men: *Paul* became a Jew to the Jews, and all things to all men to save some. 1 *Cor.* 9. 19, 20, 21, 22. I pray you mark his words: It had been no strange thing, if he had become *wise* to gain the *foolish*, and shewed himself *strong* to win the *weak*, &c. But to become a *Jew* (as when he circumcised *Timothy*, and shaved his head because he had a vow, &c.) and to be as under the Law to them that are under Law; and as without Law to them that withour Law; and to become as *weak* to them that are *weak*, to gain the weak, and to be *made all things to all men, to save some*, this is far from the Religion of the Separatists. What abundance of things do many now blame, and censure others as for temporizers, which they have nothing against (that may be called *Reason*) but only that their neighbours use them? If a man stand up at the profession of the Belief; or if he stand up when the Psalms and Hymns of Praise to God are uttered, they say, he conformeth to the gestures of the Congregation: and make that his dispraise which is his praise. And what! Is not *standing* a fit gesture to profess our Faith in? and a fit gesture to *praise God* in? Or is it praise-worthy to be *odd* and *singular* in the Church? and not to do as the rest of the Church doth? *Austin* professed his resolution, in all such gestures and lawful orders to do as the Church doth where he is: And *Paul* would have us with one *mouth* as well as with *one mind* to glorifie God. I entreat these men to mark whether it was Christ or the Pharisees that came nearest to their way, and whom they now imitate? Was it for going too far from sinners that the Pharisees did censure Christ? Or was it not for eating and drinking with Publicans and sinners (though he did it not to harden them in their sin, but as a Physician conversing with the sick to heal them) was it not for Sabbath-breaking and not being strict enough in such matters, that they were offended with Christ and his disciples? The case is plain: But corrupted nature more favoureth the *separating* zeal of the *Pharisees*, than the *Loving winning* zeal of *Christ*;

And

And will easilier suffer us to be imitators of the Pharisees than of Christ.

Thirdly, This going too far from those whom we should win, doth not only lose our advantage to do them good, but greatly tendeth to harden them in all their prejudices against a religious life; and to hinder their conversion and to undo their souls. When they hear and see us place any of our Religion, in avoiding a lawful recreation, or a lawful use of words, or a lawful fashion of apparrel, or a lawful gesture or circumstance in Gods worship, they will judge of the rest of our Religion by that part: And this is one thing that hath hardened thousands (especially of the rich who are enclined to excesses) in a scornful contempt of strictness in Religion, under the name of Puritans and Bigots and Precisians, and such like: They think they are but an ignorant humorous sort of people, who are almost mad with a pride of their singularity in Religion; And think that when you tell them of a Conversion, you would have them become such whimsical fanaticks: And that the difference between their Religion and yours, is but whether such a form of prayer, or such a gesture, or such a fashion of apparel, or such musick or other recreation, be lawful, or unlawful; In which they are confident that they are in the right? And what greater cruelty can you shew to souls, than thus to harden them in their sin and misery? Little do such persons think, how many be in Hell, through these scandals and snares which they have set before them? And yet they take on them, that is because they would not encourage men in fin, that they thus fly from them. When they do their worst to make all the world believe that strict religiousness, is but the whimsie of a giddy sort of people, who are almost out of their wits with pride. And what greater injury can men do to Christ and to Religion than this? To make it the scorn and contempt of the world?

I know they will say, that *Religion was ever scorned by the wicked, and ever will be*: But if it be *scorned* for its genuine nature, its heavenly wisdom, purity and goodness, this is the disgrace only of them that scorn it: Or if they maliciously and causelesly call *wisdom*, *folly*, or call *good*, evil, this will redound to the speakers shame, where true Reason hath but leave to work. But if you will therefore do as the Jews did, and cloath Christ in a fools Coat, and put a Reed in his hand for a Scepter, to expose him to the laughter and scorn of the beholders, it is you that will be found his deriders and crucifiers! If *you blind-fold him*, and others smite him, and say, Read who smote thee; his buffetting will prove to be caused by *you*: If you will *paint a Saint* in the garb of a *mad man*, the countreys hatred and abuse of Saints will be imputed unto you.

Fourthly, yea I may add, that you are the great cause of the *persecutions* of the *godly*, and of the damnation of the persecutors. While godly people appear in their own likeness, in wisdom and love and humility and meekness and sobriety, the world doth usually bear *some* reverence to *them*, though it hate them. But when you have made men believe that those that call themselves *Godly people*, are but a company of superstitious Pharisees, lees, that cry, *Touch not, taste not, handle not*; or a sort of melancholly humorists, who must sit because their neighbours stand, or must go out of the way, because their neighbours go in it; This maketh them justifie all their cruelties, to you and others, and think persecution to be their duty: and to say that, the *whip is for the fools back, and wanton children must be made wise by the rod*; and that it is no wrong to a mad man to lie in Bedlam.

If you say, that *Godliness hath been alwayes persecuted*, I answer, But if you are the *causers* of it, though it must needs be that scandal or offence come, yet wo to him by whom it cometh. *Matth.* 18. 7. *Luke* 17. 1, 2.

The way of heavenly wisdom is pure, but peaceable and gentle and easie to be entreated: The way that Christ and his Apostles have led us, is to draw as near to sinners as we can, by Love and all the offices of Love, neither following them in any sin, nor flying from them in any thing that is *lawful*; that they may be convinced that it is not *humour* and *disdain* and *pride*, but true *necessity* and *Gods commands*, which maketh us differ from them as we do. And that we may not be disabled by any contrary errors of our own from evincing and oppugning theirs,

DIRECT. XLVII.

When ever you are avoiding any error or sin, forget not that there is a contrary extream to be avoided, of which you are in danger as well as of that which you are opposing.

THe minds of most men are so narrow, that they cannot look many wayes at once. If they be intent on one thing, they forget another. But it is a narrow bridge betwixt dangerous gulfs, which Christian *faith* and *obedience* must pass over: And he that looketh on the one side, with the greatest fear and caution, is undone, if he look not also on the other.

    The common way of avoiding any error or vice, is to run into the contrary. And on those terms Satan himself will be Orthodox, and a reformer, and an enemy to vice. I gave you some instances even now. He is a rare person, that is so wise and happy, as to fly from every error and sin, with an impartial awakened fear of the contrary. And thence it is that the *most judicious old experienced* Christians are usually in controversies for a *middle way*; and in the croud of contentious sects, they commonly are the *reconcilers*: Not only because they are more calm and moderate, and peaceable than others; but especially because they have seen the errour on both extreams, when others see only the error on one side. Only in our *inclination* to our *ulti-*

mate

mate end, that is, in *our Love to God*, we never need to fear over-doing. But all the *means* may be perverted and turned into sin by extreams.

Many that observe the pollution of the Church by the great neglect of holy Discipline, avoid this error by turning to a sinful separation: And many that are offended at separation avoid it, by a gross neglect of Christian discipline, and taking it for a needless thing.

Many who observe how heartlesly and hypocritically prescribed forms of prayer are used by too many, do avoid it by denying the lawfulness of all forms: And many who see the error of this opinion, do escape it by turning to meer formality, and deriding all prayer which is not written in a book, or prescribed by another.

If any who see how those that were baptized in Infancy, are admitted to adult Communion without ever understanding or seriously owning the Covenant into which they were then entered; and seeing how the Church is corrupted hereby, do avoid this error by denying the baptism of Infants. And many that see the error of the Anabaptists, do avoid it by countenancing the aforesaid Church-corruption: and if Infants be but baptized, they never care whether they be called at years of discretion, to the solemn renewing and owning of their Covenant.

And many that see both these extreams do plead for *Confirmation*, as the middle way: But they turn it into a meer Ceremony, and defeat the ends of it, and never bring the baptized to a solemn renewall of their holy Vow. And many who

who see the Papists abuse of Confirmation, do wholly cast it off, and deny the healing use aforesaid.

Many who see the effects of Papal tyranny, dislike all *Generall Ministery*, which taketh the care of many Churches. And many who see the incoherence of Independent Churches, and the calamity of sects, do incline to Papal Usurpation.

Many who see the evils of Independency in respect of *Council and Concord*, are inclined to a *Regimental dependency* and *subordination* of one Church to one other, as of Divine appointment. And many who see that there is no proof that God ever appointed such a *Regimental dependency*, do turn to independency in point of *Council* and *Concord*.

Many who observe the grossness of their error, who would have the people have the power of the Keys, and govern the Church by the major Vote, do deny the people the liberty of choosing their Pastors, and being guided in spirituals as Volunteers. And many who see this error of denying the people liberty, do give them the foresaid power of the Keys, and make them Governours of themselves by Vote.

Many who hear the Papists talk so much of merits and of good works, do deny our own Faith, and Love, and Repentance, the place that God hath assigned them in order to pardon and salvation, in subordination to Christ: And many who hear the presumptuous boast of being Righteous by Christs imputed Righteousness, without any fulfilling of the Conditions of the Covenant of

Grace

Many who hear the Socinians make *faith* and *obedience* to be all one, do deny that the faith by which we are justified, is a giving up the soul in Covenant to Christ intirely in all his office, even as our Redeemer and Lord, and so an engagement to obedience by subjection. And many that hear men say, that faith justifieth us only as an instrument, apprehending Christ satisfaction and meritorious righteousness as their own, do confound our faith and obedience; and forget that the faith by which we are justified, is [*our becoming Christians*, or, *Assent and Consent to the Covenant which we made in Baptism*) nothing more or less;) and not our *living as Christians* in *after obedience*, which is the fruit or effect of faith.

And even in *civil things*, many who observe how Turkish, Tartarian, Japonian, China's, and other Heathenish and Infidel Tyranny, is the chief Resister of the Gospel, and Suppresser of Christianity to the damnation of millions of souls: And how Papal tyranny, and Muscovian, and Spanish cruelties, are the chief Maintainers of ignorance and unreformedness in the Churches, are ready hereupon to think dishonourably of Monarchy it self, and to murmure at the power of Christian Princes, and to rush into seditions and rebellions. And many that see the mischiefs of seditions, conspiracies and rebellions, are ready to forget the grand and heynous sin of Tyranny, and the calamity of Souls, and Churches, and

Kingdoms thereby: (As *Campenella* saith, *The abuse of the Potestative Primality is* Tyranny, *the abuse of the Intellective Primality is* Heresie, *and the abuse of the Volitive Primality is* Hypocrisie: Though indeed he should have mentioned both extreams.)

In a word, wo be to the Reformer, who feareth not running into the Extream, which is contrary to the Errour and Sin which he would reform.

DIRECT. XLVIII.

Think more and talk more of your faults and failings against others; especially against Princes, Magistrates, and Ministers, than of their fauls and failings against you.

THe Reason of this Councel is very obvious and past contradiction. Another mans sin as such is not yours: No mans sin shall damn you but your own; no nor bring any proper penalty on you. Our suffering by *other mens* sin, is the common way to Heaven, by which Christ and his Apostles went: But our own sin is that which must have the blood and Spirit of a Saviour for its cure, or it will undo us. He came to destroy the works of the Devil, and to save his people from their sins: *Matth.* 1. 21. 1 *John* 3. 8. But not to keep us from being persecuted by sinners: *Matth.* 5. 10, 11. without escaping persecution

we

we may be saved, (for every one that will live godly in Christ Jesus must suffer persecution, 2 *Tim.* 3. 12.) But except we repent of our own sin we shall perish, *Luke* 13. 3, 5. we must mourn for the sins of others *Ezek.* 9. 4.) but we properly *Repent* of none but our own.

Should we not most *fear* that which we are most in *danger* of? And most *lament* that, which we are most *guilty* of? And most *talk against* that which most concerneth us? And all this is not *other mens* faults, no not *Magistrates* or *Ministers* (though much to be bewailed) but our own.

Every one will confess, that the true spirit of Christianity is agreeable to what I say. And yet how contrary is the practise of no small number of the Religious? In all companies how forward are they to talk of the sins of Princes and Parliaments? of Countries and Nobility, and Gentry? especially of Ministers; And not only of the scandalous that are guilty indeed, but of the *innocent* that are not of their way; whose *faults* they rather *make* than *find?* But how seldom do you hear them tell any how bad they are themselves? (unless it be in formality to seem humble persons) yea, how impatient are they with any other that find fault with them? It would be much more acceptable to God and wise men, to hear you talk of your own infirmities, than of the Rulers or Ministers, or Neighbours? The one is a work of Repentance; and the other of detraction and backbiting. The one is a work which you are commanded by God (to judge your selves, and confess your faults one to another:) But the other is a work which we have seldomer a call
from

from God to do. One tendeth to your pardon; the other to your guilt: Therefore if you fall into the company of backbiters, that are dishonouring their Rulers or their Pastors, or telling how bad their neighbours are; labour to purifie these stinking waters, or turn the stream: say to them, [O friends how bad are we our selves! what pride is in our hearts! what ignorance in our minds! so wanting are we even in the lowest grace, Humility, that we have scarce enough to make us take patiently, such censures as now we are giving out upon others? so *selfish* as dishonoureth our profession with the brand of *contradictedness*, and *partiality*; so weak that all our *duties* are liable to greater censures than we can bear: And our inward graces weaker than our outward duties. Of such ungoverned thoughts, that *confusion* and *tumult* instead of *order*, and *fruitful improvement*, are the daily temper and employment of our imaginations: so passionate, impatient, and corrupt, that we are a trouble to our selves and others, and a dishonour to the Gospel, and a hinderance to the conversion of those whom our holy exemplary lives should win to God: so strange to Heaven, as if we had never well believed it: And to say all in one, so empty of Love to our dear Redeemer and the God of Love, that our Hearts lie vacant to entertain the love of worldly vanities; and draw back from the serious thoughts of God, which should be our daily work and pleasure; and flie from the face of Death, as if we should be worst, when we are nearest to our God. And when we are our selves no better, should we not rather complain of the sore that is so near us?
and

and marvel that our neighbours vilifie not us, and that the Church doth not judge us unworthy of its Communion! Nature teacheth or constraineth all men, to be more sensible of their own diseases, than of their neighbours; and to complain of them most as loving themselves best: Is it then because you love your neighbour better than your selves, that you speak more of their faults and infirmities than of your own? If not, take heed lest it prove not to be the voice of love! and then I need not tell you how bad it signifieth! God is Love, and he that dwelleth in love dwelleth in God, and God in him. The Devil is the *Love-killer*: And what way can you imagine so powerful to *kill love* to any others, as to make men think them to be very *bad*? Doth any man *love evil* that *knoweth* it to be evil? certainly therefore these speakings evil of others, are *love-killing* words (though to his face to make him know himself, they might be medicinal:) And therefore they are the service of the *love-killing* spirit.]

DIRECT. XLIX.

Take notice of all the good in others which appeareth, and rather talk of that behind their backs, than of their faults.

IF there were no *Good* in others, they were not to be *loved*: For it is contrary to mans nature, to will or love any thing, but *sub ratione boni*, as supposed to be good. The *good* of *nature*, is lovely in all men as *men*, even in the wicked and our enemies (And therefore let them that think they can never speak bad enough of nature take heed left they run into excess: And the *capacity* of the *good* of *holiness* and *happiness*, is part of the good of *nature*. The *good* of *gifts* and of a common Profession, with the possibility or probability of sincerity, is lovely in all the visible members of the Church. And truly the excellent gifts of Learning, judgement, utterance and memory, with the vertues of meekness, humility, patience, contentedness, and a loving disposition inclined to do good to all, are so amiable in some, who are yet too strange to a heavenly life, that he must be worse than a man who will not love them.

To vilifie all these gifts in others, favoureth of a malignant contempt of the gifts of the Spirit of God. And so it doth, to talk all of their faults, and say little or nothing of their gifts and virtues: yea, some have so unloving and unlovely a kind of Religiousness, that they backbite that *man* as a *defender* of the *prophane*, and a *commender* of the *ungodly*, who doth but contradict or reprehend their backbitings: And are ever gain-saying all the commendations which they hear of any whom they think ill of.

But if you would when you talk of others (.especially them who differ from you in opinions) be more in commendation of all the good, which indeed is in them. 1. You would shew your selves much liker to God who is love, and unliker to Satan the accuser. 2. You would
shew

shew an honest impartial ingenuity, which honoureth virtue where ever it is found. 3. You would shew an humble sense of your own frailty, who dare not proudly contemn your brethren. 4. You would shew more love to God himself, when you love all of God whensoever you discern it; and cannot abide to hear his gifts and mercies undervalued. 5. You would increase the grace of love to others, in your selves, by the daily exercise of it; when backbiting and detraction will increase the malignity from which they spring. 6. You would increase *Love* also in the *hearers*; which is the fulfilling of the Law; when detraction will breed or increase malice. 7. You will do much to the winning and conversion of them whom you commend, if they be unconverted. For when they are told that you speak lovingly of them behind their backs, it will much reconcile them to your persons, and consequently prepare them to hearken to the counsel which they need. But when they are told that you did backbite them, it will fill them with hatred of you, and violent prejudice against your counsel and profession.

Yet mistake me not: It is none of my meaning all this while, that you should speak any *falsehood* in commendation of others; nor make people believe, that a careless carnal sort of persons, are as good as those that are careful of their souls, or that their way is sufficient for salvation; Nor to commend ungodly men in such a manner, as tendeth to keep either them or their hearers from repentance; Nor to call evil, good, or put darkness for light, nor honour the works of the devil.

vil. But to shew Love and impartiality to all and to be much more in speaking of all the good which is in them, than of the evil: Especially if they be your *enemies*, or differ from you in opinions of Religion: *Tit. 3. 1. Put them in mind to be subject to principalities and powers; to obey Magistrates, to be ready to every good work, to speak evil of no man, to be no brawlers but gentle, shewing all meekness to all men. For we our selves were sometime foolish*, &c. Grace is clean contrary to this detracting vice.

DIRECT. L.

Study the Duty of instructing and exhorting, more than Reproof and finding fault.

I Deny not but that it is a duty to tell a *brother* of his *fault*, and to reprove and that with plainness too. Math. 18. 15. Lev. 19. 17. And it is but few that do this rightly, of many that will backbite and censure. But yet I have long observed, that many Christians are enquiring, How they must manage the duty of Reproof, who never enquired how to perform the duty of *Christian exhortation* or instructing of the ignorant. When as this latter is much more usually a duty than the former; And you are bound to *exhort* a multitude whom you are not bound to *reprove*. And *exhortation* to good is a duty which the hearer is usually less offended at; It doth not so much gall and exasperate his mind: It shameth him

him not so much, and yet is the greater part of our duty to him; as the possitives of Religion are before the negatives. Exhortation (rightly used) is the plain direct expression of Love, and an earnest desire of anothers good: When Reproof doth savour of a mixture of Love and displeasure; and the wrath doth often cloud the love.

And I must say, that I find many surly proud Professors, much proner to Reprove, than to Exhortation: Their pride and self-conceitedness makes them too forward to reprove their Governours, and the ignorant people are ready enough to reprove their Teachers, and the servant to reprove the Master or the Mistriss; but not to be reproved by them. Ministers must be wise and cautelous how they set such people on *reproving* and finding fault with others, when their own pride and passion and fond self-opinion, is ready to put them on too far.

DIRECT. LI.

The more you suffer by your Rulers (or any men) the more be watchful lest your sufferings tempt you to dishonour them. And the more you are wronged by your equals, the more be afraid lest you should be tempted to withdraw the Love which is their due.

THe Honouring of our superiours, is a Moral or Natural duty (of the fifth Commandment) which sufferings will not excuse us from: And so is the Love of all men, even of our enemies. And *selfishness* and *Passion* are things so powerful, that it is wonderful hard to escape their deceit; They will blind the mind, and change the judgement, and corrupt the affections, before you are aware, or believe that you are at all perverted.

Every man must watch most where his temptation is strongest. Do you not think that you have a far stronger temptation, to dishonour a persecuting Magistrate than a good one? And to hate an enemy than a friend? Therefore arm your selves, and one another against this snare. And when others are aggravating the fault and injury, do you in company remember each other in what danger you are now of losing your innocency, and of doing your selves more hurt by that, than any powers or enemies can do you. It is an easie thing to Love one that loveth you, and honour a Magistrate that doth good to you and all. But as the Apostle saith of servants, *Pet.* 2. 18, 19, 20. (*Be subject*——*Not only to the good and gentle, but also to the froward: For this is thank-worthy, if a man for conscience toward God endure grief, suffering wrongfully: For what glory is it, if when ye be buffeted for your faults you take it patiently? But if when ye do well and suffer for it, ye take it patiently, this is acceptable with God.*

DIRECT. LII.

Make conscience of heart-revenge, and tongue-revenge, as well as of hand-revenge.

IT is so notorious that Revenge is a usurpation of Gods prerogative, and a heinous sin, that Professors could not so frequently and easily commit it, if they did not first deceive themselves, and take that to be no revenge which is. To do any *open hurt* to another, they take notice of as sinful revenge. But is there no *secret wish* in your heart, that some evil may befall another? Nor no secret gladness that some evil hath befaln him? You will say, It is not in revenge, but in hope he may repent: But take heed what is in your heart. Its one thing to *Repent* of his *injury to you as such*, and to make you amends and repair your honour? And its another thing to repent of it as a sin against God, to the saving of his own soul. Is it not the former that you more desire than the later?

And are not your *Tongues* employed too often in revenge? What are all your secret reflections, and endeavours to dishonour those that have wronged you, but *revengeful speeches?* Railing, and backbiting, and nibling at anothers honour and good name, may be acts of revenge as truly as the actions of the hand.

DIRECT. LIII.

When you are exasperated at the hurt which you feel from Magistrates, remember the good which the Church receiveth by them, as well as the hurt.

IF you look all at the *evil* in *any man*, and overlook the good, you cannot choose but hate him: And if you think only of what *you suffer* by Magistrates, you may easily know what the effect must be. And the *sin* is so great, that it should not be made light of, by a tender conscience. The good of the Office and of the person is of *God*; and the evil is of Satan: And should you so look at *Satans* part, as to pass by all *Gods part?* What ingratitude is it, to take notice so deeply of your suffering, and to take no notice of your mercies. There are few *Heathen Magistrates*, from whom those Christians who live under them, receive not much more good than hurt. Much more *Christian Magistrates* are a blessing to believers. For if they *persecute some*, yet they usually *protect more*, from the fury of the
vulgar

vulgar rabble, who would quickly devour them, if Rulers did not restrain them. And the countenancing of the Christian Religion in the essentials, and defending Christian assemblies for Gods worship is an unvaluable mercy. If *Paul* said to the Romans [*Rulers are not a terror to good works, but to evil———Do that which is good, and thou shalt have praise of the same: for he is the Minister of God to thee for good.*] Rom. 13. 3, 4. How much may those say so who have Christian Magistrates! Or if some particular persons do suffer more under some such, than *Paul* or the Christians did under Heathens (*Acts* 28. *last*) yet every true Christian, must more regard the *publick* interest than his *own*; and must rejoyce that the Gospel hath any protection and furtherance, and the souls of the people any benefit, whatever his personal suffering be. Read *Phil.* 1. 12. to the 20.

DIRECT. LIV.

Learn to suffer by Ministers and Good people, and not only by Magistrates, nor only by the ungodly.

I Confess it is a thing most unnatural for one true Christian to afflict another; and especially for a Minister, who is the *father* of the flock, to be a hurter of them, and to do like an enemy; and to fleece them and devour them. But yet it is a thing which sometimes must be born. I have observed that Religious people when a *Magistrate* (though a usurper) persecuteth them, they can in some sort undergo it, as no strange thing. And they are not so forward to cast off the *office* and abhor the *persons* by whom they suffer. But if they suffer never so little by a *Minister*, they flye away from him, and are uncapable of comfortable communion with him, and the breach is hardly ever made up. I confess there is some more colour for this impatiency; (to be mentioned in another place.) But yet Gods servants have been tryed by this kind of suffering also, and therefore you must not be so tender of it, nor be driven by it into sinful separations, or into a contempt of the Ministers of the Gospel, as too many sects in these times have been. Read what at large is said of the afflicting Shepheards, *Ezek.* 34. & *Zech.* 10. & 11. And you will see that it is not a thing to be wondered at, to have *Shepheards which fleece and destroy the flocks, and tread down their pasture and muddy their waters, and feed themselves and not the flocks, and gather not that which goeth astray: Nay their own Shepheards pitied them not.* Zech. 11. 5. I know that it is the *Magistrates* that are often meant by *Shepheards* in the Prophets: but the Priests also are usually meant *with them*, and sometime distinctly by the same word. And their falshood and cruelty oft expressed, as in *Jer.* 2. 8, 26. & 5. 31. and 26. 7, 8, 11. & 32. 32. *Ezek.* 22. 26. *Hos.* 6. 9. *Mich.* 3. 11. *Zeph.* 3. 4. *Mal.* 1. 6. & 2. 1. &c. And remember that all the wickedness of these Priests, and their abuse of the people, did not warrant the

people

people to forsake the Jewish Church: Though the Ark was taken by the Philistines for the wickedness and violence of *Eli's* sons; and the people tempted to desire a King, by the sins of the sons of *Samuel*, yet none of their misdoings did warrant a separation from that Church. Yea, Christ who was persecuted by the Priests, did yet bid the cleansed Leper, go shew himself to the Priest, and offer according to the Law.

Therefore a true Christian must learn (though not to favour any mans sin, nor to be indifferent what Ministery he liveth under, yet) patiently to suffer much abuse and persecution, sometimes from Ministers themselves; and to see that it drive them not in peevish impatiency into any extream, or to any unlawful sect or separation, nor to a disdain of the sacred office which they abuse, nor to lose the benefit of it, or be unthankful for it.

And though it be sad that true Christians should abuse each other, yet this also must be born. Many can bear the scorn and cruelties of the openly profane, who can scarce bear to be neglected or set light by, much less to be hardly censured by the Religious. But observe first, that your *Pride* may notably appear in this: and it is no great sign of *humility* to suffer only from the *worst*. For you look on them as persons of *no honour*, and therefore not capable of *dishonouring you*: For a *dog* to bark at you, you take for no disgrace: Nay you take it for your honour to suffer by such persons, as supposing it a mark of Christs disciples. But the Religious you more reverence, and think their contempt is a great dishonour to you; and
there-

fore your pride will not suffer you to bear it patiently.

Secondly, And remember that different *opinions* and *interests* may possibly so far exasperate some that are otherwise religious, as to make them afflicters, or more plainly, *persecutors* of one another, though Godliness it self be applauded by them all. The experience of *England*, *Scotland* and *Ireland* within these 25 years, doth sadly tell us and the world, how far men can go in persecuting each other for different interests and opinions, who all profess a zeal for godliness.

And let it have your special remark, that one *reason why all men as Christians and Godly do more easily and commonly love one another, is because as Christians and Godly, they do not hurt or wrong each other: But as they are of various sects they hate and envy one another, because as they are sectaries they hurt and injure one another.* For the spirit and zeal of a sect as such is censorious, hurtful, unpeaceable and dividing: But the spirit and zeal of Godliness and Christianity, is kind and gentle and inclineth to do good to all.

Remember that you have never learnt the Christian art of suffering aright, till you can suffer not only by bad men, but by men that otherwise are good; nor only by enemies but by friends, nor only by them that bear the sword, but also by some who preach the word; and will not by oppression be made mad, nor driven from your innocency.

DIRECT.

DIRECT. LV.

When you complain of violence and persecution in others, take heed lest you shew the same inward sin, by Church-persecution and cruelty against them, or any others.

But because I know that guilt causeth impatience, and passion disposeth men to mistakes and false-reports, before I proceed, I must here foretell you, 1. That I mean not by *Separatists* all that are so called by interessed injudicious persons: But those 1. That account *true Churches* of Christ to be *no Churches*, 2. Or that account it *unlawful* to *hold Communion* with those Churches, whose communion is not *unlawful*; because they are *faulty*, or because they *differ from them* in some *opinions* or circumstances of worship: 3. Especially if they practise, and perswade others to practise according to these two opinions; of which the first is the higher sort of separation, and the second the lower.

And secondly, That by *Church-dividers*, I mean both these and all such whose principles and practises are against that love of a Christian as a Christian, and that forbearance of dissenters, which should be exercised to all the members of Christ; and who fly from the ancient simplicity and primitive terms of Church-communion, and add (as the Papists do) their own little novelties as necessary things.

And those that do *causlesly separate* from their
own

own *lawfully called Pastors*; For *ubi Episcopus, ibi Ecclesia*; *where the true Pastor is, there the Church is* (what ever place it be that they assemble in) (as *Cyprian* once said.)

And lastly, those that are of uncharitable, humerous, peevish, contentious and fiery spirits, and will stir up mutinies and sidings, and causeless divisions in any Church where they come. And truly they that think of the present state of *Hertford* and some other Churches in *New England*, (which I will not here make a Narritive of, me thinks should fear Separations, Schisms or Divisions, from or in the Churches called Independent, as much as those of a different Discipline do as to theirs: (if not somewhat more, on several accounts.)

Thirdly, And remember that I am not here speaking of any mens former faults, by way of uncharitable bitterness, insulting or reproach; but verily brethren, if we are not impartially willing to know the truth of every side, and of our own selves as well as others, we *choose* deceit, and resist the light, and provoke God to forsake our understandings. Do we not yet know where *Judgement* hath begun, after such plagues and flames, and Church convulsions? And do we not yet know where Repentance must begin? Enquire for good news whence you will, I will enquire whether we are awakned to a true *Repentance*; and by that I will fetch my prognosticks of our future state: Not whether you cry out against other mens sins, but against your own, and that particularrly with all their aggravations; and whether Professours of Religiousness do as heartily

tily lament their own notorious publick scandals, as they expect that drunkards and fornicators, and the friends of loosness, should lament theirs! Till we see this, what promise have we of the pardon of our dreadful temporal penalties? (to say nothing of the greater.)

Wo to the Land and People that can multiply sin and cannot Repent! And wo to them that pretend Repentance, and love to be flattered in their sin, and cannot endure to be admonished, but take all the discoveries of their sin to be injurious reproach? among the prophane we take this to be a deadly sign of impenitency? And is it so bad in them, and good in us? It is part of my office to cry with holy *Bradford*, REPENT O ENGLAND, and say after Christ, [*Except ye Repent, ye shall all Perish,*] And can I call men to Repent, when I must not dare to tell them of what? Nor to mention the sin which is most to be repented of? I use all this preface because I know that Guilt and Impenitency are touchy and tender, and galled, and querulous, and such will bestow the time in backbiting their Monitor, which they should bestow in lamenting their sin. But shall I therefore forbear, and betray their souls, and betray the Land through cowardly silence? Must I shew that I hate Professours by not admonishing them, (*Lev.* 19. 17.) when I must shew that I love the looser sort by my sharp reproofs? Must I not fear them that can kill the body? and must I fear to *displease* a professed Christian, By calling him to Repentance in a time of judgements.

Lord hide not my own miscarriages from my sight!

fight! and suffer me not to take any sin that I have committed to have been my innocency or duty, lest I should dare to father sin on God, and lest I should live and die without Repentance, and lest I should be one that continueth judgements and danger to the Land? stir up some faithful friend to tell me, with convincing evidence, where it is that I have miscarried, that Contrition may prepare me for the peace of remission? O save me from the plague of an impenitent heart, that cannot endure to be told of sin! and from that ungodly folly, which taketh the shame that Repentance casteth upon sin, to be cast upon God and Religion, which bind us to Repentance and Confession!

Nay in this place, I am not mentioning things past, so much to humble you, as necessarily to inform you, of the groundlesness of your present arguings, that you may see the truth.

Fourthly, Note also that I lay not any miscarriages on any whole parties, (Anabaptists or others;) For I have found that all parties of Christians indeed have some good, experienced, sober, charitable persons, and some self-conceited and contentious novices, (1 *Tim.* 3. 6.) But I speak only of the *persons* that were guilty and no more.

Fifthly, Lastly, remember that while I seem to compare the faults of one sort of persons, with anothers, it is none of my intent to *equal* them; much less to equal the state of the several sorts of Offenders as to the rest of their lives: But only to mention so much of the similitude, as is necessary to represent things truly and impartially to your view.

Read

Read on now with these *Memento*'s in your eye: And if after so plain a premonition you will venture to charge me with that which I disclaim, do it at your own peril; I stand or fall to the judgement of God, and look for a better reward than the hypocrites, which is to have the good opinion of men, be they professors of piety, or profane. And with me, by Gods grace, it shall hereafter be accounted a small thing (to the hindring of my fidelity to Christ and mens souls) to be judged of men, 1 *Cor.* 4. 3.

And if there should be any Pastors of the Churches, who instead of concurring, to heal the flocks of these dividing principles, shall rather joyn with back-biters, and encourage them in their misreports and slanders, because it tendeth to the supposed interest of their party or themselves. Let them prepare to answer such unfaithfulness to their consciences which will shortly be awakned, and to the great Shepherd of the Flock who is at the door, and who told even the Devils agents, that a House or Kingdom divided against it self, cannot stand, but is brought to naught! *Matb.* 12. If alas, alas, experience hath not yet, not yet, not yet, done enough to teach them this!)

For my part I have had humane applause enough: I'le value that Vanity as dying men do. And temptations to man pleasing from covetousness I have none: For I have nothing of worldly gain or expectations which I should fear to lose, to tempt me to betray my conscience or the truth by silence.

But (mark and remember brethren, what I say
to

to you,) *whosoever is of your mind at present,* Posterity will say as I have told you: And though *wrong wayes* seem fit or necessary for some *present exigence,* or *jobb*, yet nothing but *Truth*, and *Integrity*, and *Charity* and *Concord*, will do the main work, and hold out to the last.

The foresight of impatient guilt, and censure having caused me here to give you this premonition (besides what is in the Epistle) now Reader go on.

O the deceitfulness of the heart of man! Little do many real Separatists, who cry out against the spirit of persecution, suspect that the *same spirit* is in them! whence is *persecution*, but from *thinking* ill of others, and abhorring them, or not loving them? And do you not do so by those whom you causlesly separate from? you will say, that *though you think them not to be true Christians, yet you love them as men, and wish their good:* And so will those say by you, whom you call your *Persecutors*: Though they *think* you to be proud and humerous, and disobedient; yet they say they love you *as men*, and do but correct you to cure your self-willedness and humour, and to do you good, and to preserve the publick peace. They *think you* to be *bad*, and therefore *imprison* you: you *think* them to be *bad*, and therefore *avoid Communion* with them. They *think* you so bad as to be unworthy of *civil liberty*, and *priviledges*: you think them so bad as to be unworthy of *Church priviledges* and *liberties*. They think you unworthy to be suffered in the *land* perhaps. And you think them unworthy to be suffered in the *Churches*. They cry against you, Away with them they are schismatical or heretical: you cry against them,

Away

Away with them, they are prophane!

Obj. *But they who would not give us our bodily liberties, do more against us, than we would do against them.*

Answ. I pray you think on that again. First, Is not the priviledge of the Church, better than the priviledges of the Commonwealth? as the soul is better than the body? Secondly, is it not a deeper accusation to charge one to be *ungodly* and *prophane*, than to charge him only to be *schismatical*?

Obj. *But charity must not be blind: They are prophane: I charge them truly: But I am not schismatical or heretical, but they accuse me falsly.*

Answ. You say so, and they say the same of you. They say that *you are schismatical, but they are not prophane*. Now how shall a stander by know which of you is in the right? Doubtless by the witnesses and evidences: They *try* you in some *Court* or before some Magistrate before they punish *you*. You never *try* them, nor *hear* them speak for themselves, nor examine any witnesses publickly against them, nor allow them any Church-justice, but avoid their Communion upon reports or pretense of private knowledge. They judge you *personally one by one*: You condemn *whole Parishes* in the *lump*, *unheard*: They condemn you as for a *positive crime*: But you condemn them without charging any one crime upon them, because they have not yet given you a satisfying proof of their godliness; They say, *we prove you guilty*: You say, you have not sufficiently *proved your selves innocent*. If a man were robbed on the high way, and you and another were both charged with the robbery; and to the other it is said, *I prove by witness that thou didst rob me*; And to you it is said, *Do thou bring sufficient proof that thou didst not rob me?* Would you not think that you had the more injustice?

Obj. But of all men living no man can think that a persecutor is godly and fit for Church-communion.

Answ. Either of these answers may stop your mouths, First, What is that to the *whole Parishes* whose communion you avoid, who never persecuted you? Did all the Ministers and common people persecute you?

Secondly, Was it no persecution when many Anabaptists and Separatists made such work in *England, Scotland* and *Ireland* in *Cromwells* time and after as they did? When so many were turned out of the *Universities* for *not engaging?* and so many out of the *Ministry?* and so many out of the *Magistracy* and *Corporation priviledges?* And when an *Ordinance* was made to cast out *all Ministers* who would *not pray for the success of their Wars against Scotland*, or that would not *give God thanks* for their *Victories.* When I have heard them profess that they believed that there were many thousand godly men, that were killed at *Dunbar* (to instance in no other;) and yet *we* were all by *their Ordinance* to be *cast out*, that would not give God thanks for this? And the execution of it was much *threatned*, though they did it not. And what more harsh kind of persecution could there be, than to force men to go hypocritically to God against their consciences, and take on them to beg for the success of a war which they judged unlawful;

s have persecuted others.

:o return him a publick counterfeit
od-shed; yea for the blood of thou-
he blood of confessed godly men:
ime which they would have forced
e been so ductile as to obey them)
an *publick hypocrisie* and *owning* such
s; and the penalty no less than *se-*
our flocks and *publick maintenance*
silencing.)
t any of this to trample upon those
in justice hath cast down. (A thing
horred that I have avoided it to the
ure of others) But if you are of the
that Gods justice should not be ob-
stified; or that you should not be
entance; or that you should be suf-
to forget your sin, and die impeni-
hat the Nation should forget the ef-
ious pride and faction, and so lose
which they have had from God at so
nd be tempted again into the same sin
, for fear of offending the ears of
am in all this as far from your minds,
e acting of these crimes: And can no
t to you, than I should have done to
the Israelites murmurings, idolatry
; and the sins of *Noah, Lot, David,*
er, &c. forgotten. and the history of
mentioned in the Bible.
ray you mark it) *the way of God is to*
er, how good soever in other respects that
ave the greater shame, and Religion may
d as if it allowed men to sin, nor God the
ligion be dishonoured; nor others be with-

out the warning. But the way of the devil is, *To hide or justifie the sin, as if it were for fear of disparaging the goodness of the persons that committed it; that so he may thereby dishonour Religion and Godliness it self, and make men believe that it is but a cover for any wickedness,* and as consistent with it as a looser life is; and that he may keep the sinner from repenting, and blot out the memory of that warning which should have preserved after-ages from the like falls.

Scripture shameth the *Professors* (though a *David, Solomon, Peter, Noah,* or *Lot*) that the *Religion professed* may *not be shamed* but vindicated. Satan would preserve the *honour* of the *Professors,* that the Religion professed may bear the shame; and so it may fall on God himself. When God turneth *Lots* wife into a *Pillar of Salt,* Satan is willing to seem so tender of the honour of the godly, as to *take it down,* that it may be forgotten. God saith to the *Israelites,* that when those that pass by shall ask why hath God done all this great evil against this people, the posterity shall recount their ancestors sins, and say, Because they sinned against the Lord their God, *&c.* But Satan could find in his heart to pretend more tenderness of the names and honour of the Church, so he might but undo the present age by impenitency, and after ages by taking Gods publick warnings from before their eyes. On these terms he will be all for the honour of professors.

But God will make men more tender of *his honour* and less tender of *our own,* and more willing openly to take shame to *our selves* to vindicate the honour of *Religion,* before he will give us a full discharge. It *was my own doing: Religion is clear but I am guilty.*] Pardon this long excursion on this subject. And if you cannot bear it, I cannot help that. *I made not the sore, nor galled place* which is so *tender.* I only mind you, in answer to your objection, that *Faction* and *opinions* will raise *persecutions*, and have done, even by such as you, yet do not separate from. I know none of you that separate from the Anabaptists and Separatists who were the authors of these aforesaid persecutions, nor do I urge you to it. Therefore do but impartially judge of the sin.

Obj. But it is one thing to persecute for particular opinions and interests (as almost all parties have sometimes done) and another thing to persecute for Godliness it self.

Answ. I confess it is, and the difference between these two is very great. But I pray you consider, first, that they are *but few*, perhaps *not one*, of all that you separate from, that ever persecuted you any way at all: Nor can you prove that ever they so much as *allowed* of it.

Secondly, That they whom *you and I do suffer* by, do not *believe* that they *persecute us for Godliness*, but think that here the case is more defensible than *yours* was. For you had *no just authority over us:* When the Anabaptists did pull down the *Ministers* they pulled down the *Magistrates* too; And therefore it was a *persecution of equals without authority*; But those that *we Ministers* suffer

rent opinion joyned with difobedience. It is not *all men* whom they forbid to preach, but *us* who diffent and do not obey them: It is not *all men that are godly* whom they *imprifon*; but *thofe* that meet to worfhip God in a place and manner differing from theirs, and forbidden by them. So that how can you fay that this is not for *differing opinions.*

Ob. *But we forbid not them to hold their own Church-communion, though we feparate from them, we never denied them the liberty of their confciences.*

Anfw. Some of your judgement denied many of them much of that liberty which confifteth in worfhipping of God in their own way, when you were in power. But fuppofe they had not, it is but *another way of uncharitablenefs:* The *vice expreffed* feemeth to be the fame. For you condemn them as unfit for *Chriftian Communion*, and therefore you *exclude* them from yours: And you take their Church-communion among themfelves, to be but a prophanation of holy things: which maketh them the more impious, and therefore the more odious: And you tolerate it in them as you tolerate mens folly and madnefs, or leprofie or plague, becaufe you cannot cure it. And I pray you judge whether there be any more *Chriftian Love* in this kind of dealing, than there is in that which you call perfecution? Or at leaft, whether it proceed not from the fame uncharitablenefs? I fuppofe you to be fpiritual and not carnal persons, at least in profession and therefore that you are not so tender of the flesh, as to take its suffering to be any great matter to you, in comparison of any of the sufferings of the soul. When you refuse Communion with men, as judging them unfit for fellowship with the visible Churches of Christ, you judge them the visible members of the devil, and condemn them to the loss of the greatest priviledges on earth, and to be left out with the dogs, with Publicans and Heathens: Though you think that you have no more to do your selves in the execution of this sentence, but to separate from them, yet you declare that you think that all others should do the same: So that your tolerating their Communion among themselves, is no great signification of your charity.

The sum of all that I say to you is this: It is but one and the same sin in the *Persecutor* and the *Divider* or *Separatist*, which causeth the *one* to *smite* their brethren, and the other to *excommunicate them*: the one to cast them into *prison* as *Schismaticks*, and the other to cast them *out of the Church* as *prophane*: the one to account them *intollerable in the Land*, and the other to account them *intollerable in the Church*: the one to say, Away with them they are contumacious; and the other to say, Away with them they are ungodly. The inward thoughts of both is the same, that those whom they *smite* or *separate* from, are *bad* and *unlovely* and unfit for any better usage. When *Love* which thinketh no evil till it is necessitated, and believeth all things which are at all credible, and hopeth all things which are not desperate, and covereth sins instead of condemning without proof, would equally cure them both.

And let me yet conclude with this double protestation against the carping slanderer who useth to falsifie mens words. First, That I intend not in all this any flattery of the ungodly, or making them better than they are, or forbearing plain reproof or Church-discipline, nor any unlawful communion with the wicked, nor countenancing them in any of their sins, nor neglecting to call them to repentance.

Secondly, That while I here name *persecution*, my purpose is not to mark out any persons or party above others, or determine who they be that are the persecutors: But only to detect the deceitfulness of our hearts when we most complain of it; and to shew that wherever that sin is indeed, it cometh but from the same principle as sinful separation doth: even from the death of Love to others.

Thirdly, and I add, that though I here aggravate the persecution of unjust excommunications or separations, as robbing men of the priviledge of Christians, yet leaving them the common liberties of men and subjects; it is none of my purpose to equal this absolutely with that destroying cruelty, which leaveth them neither; and will not suffer them to enjoy so much liberty, as Heathens and Infidels may enjoy, or as *Paul* had under such. *Acts* 28. *ult.*

DIRECT. LVI.

Keep still in your thoughts, the state of all Christs Churches upon Earth: that you may know what a people they are through the world, whom Christ hath communion with; and may not be deceived by ignorance, to separate from almost all Christs Churches, while you think that you separate from none, but the few that are about you.

Thousands of well meaning people live as if *England* were almost all the world. And do boldly separate from their Neighbours here, which they durst not do, if they soberly considered that almost all the Christian world are worse than they. But narrow minds who can look but little further with their *Reason* than with their eye sight, do keep out at once both *Truth* and Love. It is a point that I have often had occasion to repeat, and yet will not forbear to repeat it here again: It is but about one sixth part of the known world: who make any profession of Christianity and are baptized: (besides how much peopled the unknown part of the world may be, we know not.) Of this sixth part the Ethiopians, Egyptians, Syrians, Armenians, the Greek Churches, the Muscovites, and all the Papists, are so great a body, that all the Protestants, or Reformed Churches are little more than a sixth part of this sixth: (The Papists being about a fourth or fifth part; and the other

the other half, which are supposed to be more Reformed, there is scarce any of so Reformed lives as these in *England* and *Scotland*: And among these, how great a number are they that you separate from? If you look to the Papists, their worship is by the Mass: If you look to the Muscovians, they have a Liturgy much more blameable than ours, and have a few Homilies instead of preaching? If you look to the Greek Church, to the Armenians, the Abassines, and all the Eastern and the Southern Churches, in *Asia* and *Africa*, they also worship God by Liturgies, much more lyable to blame than ours, and have but little preaching among them, besides Homilies; and the Members of their Churches are commonly far more ignorant than the worst of ours, even than the rudest part of *Wales*. If you look to the Lutherans, they have Liturgies, and Ceremonies, and Images in their Churches, though not adored; and have far worse Preachers, and of worse lives, and more unprofitable preaching than is usually found with us; and the people more ignorant and vicious. If you look to the remnant, called the *more Reformed Churches*, in *Holland*, *France*, *Helvetia*, *Germany*, though they have much less of Liturgy, or Ceremonies, yet are their Church-members usually as ignorant as ours, and more addicted to intemperance, and there is no less scandal in their lives, than among ours. Now this being the true state of the world, and though

we

Queries about Separation. 265

we daily pray that it may be better, yet it is no better, I would only intreat you but to think of it as it is, and that to answer me deliberately these few Questions.

Quest. 1. Do you believe that all baptized professed Christians, (not denying any essential part of Christianity) are Christs Universal Visible Church?

Qu. 2. Do you not believe that this Church is only *One*; and that every particular Church, and every Christian is a part of it?

Qu. 3. Do you not believe that it is unlawful in any case whatsoever to separate from it? And that to separate from the Universal Visible Church, is visibly to separate from Christ?

Qu. 4. Do you not believe that to give a Bill of Divorse to the Universal Church, or to many hundred parts of it, or to any one part, and to declare that they are none of the Church of Christ, is not great arrogancy, and injury to men, and unto Christ himself?

Qu. 5. Dare you say before God, Let me have no part in any of the prayers of all these Churches on earth who use a Liturgy as culpable as ours? because I will have no Communion with them? Do you set so light by your part in their prayers?

Qu. 6. If you travelled or lived in *Abassia*, *Armenia*, *Greece*, or any Christian · Country, (where their worship is not Idolatry nor substantially wicked, nor they force not the worshippers to any false Oaths, subscriptions or other actual sin) would you refuse all communion with them, and all publick worshipping of God? Or would

would you not rather joyn with them, than with no Church at all?

Qu. 7. When you remember on the Lords days, that now all the Christian world are congregate, and are calling upon God and praising him, in the name of one Christ, and in the profession of one Faith, dare you think of being a Body separated from them all? And can you think that Christ disowneth them all, save you?

Qu. 8. Can you think it agreeable to the gracious nature, design and office of Jesus Christ, to cast off and condemn so many hundred parts of the Church-universal, and to accept that one part only which you joyn with? Judge by his actions and expressions in the Scriptures.

Qu. 9. If there were but ten persons of your mind in all the world, would you believe that God would save none but those ten, or accept the worship of no more, or that it were lawful to have communion with none but those ten? If not, how can you think so in a case so near it?

Qu. 10. Can you prove that Christ doth separate from all the Christians of the world which you separate from? or that they have no visible Communion with him? or that he taketh them for no Churches, and disowneth the administration of all the Ministers in the world whom you disown? or yet that it is safe, to separate where Christ doth not separate, and to be gone from his House while he there abideth? and to condemn those whom he condemneth not? nor yet commandeth you to forsake or to condemn?

Obj.

Obj. *The Church of Christ is a little flock, and not to be estimated by number: And if he confine his grace to never so few, I will confine my Communion to as few.*

Answ. First, Grace is not visible to you, but the *Profession* of it only: Therefore your Communion must be extended according to *mens profession*, and not according to sincerity which you know not? when the question is, *who hath grace, and who hath not,* God hath not made you a heart-searching Judge, but hath made *profession* the sign which you must judge by. And he that *professeth Christianity, professeth* all that is of necessity to salvation.

Secondly, If Christs flock was little when he spake those words, it is much greater now. And if it be *little still* (as it is in comparison of the world of Heathens, Infidels, and Hyppocrites) will he give them thanks that will make it less, yea a thousand times less than it is indeed? Hath he so few? and will you take from him almost all those few? If you had but a hundred sheep when your neighbour had a thousand, would you thank him that would rob you of all save one?

Thirdly, So far as God hath revealed the fewness of the saved, we reverence his Counsels, and believe his word: But if you will make it so much less a number, while you *falsifie* Gods word, you will tempt your selves at last, not to *believe* it, because you have *made it false* and *incredible* by making it your own. Brethren, I beseech you be not angry with us while we pity you, and would save your souls from your own snares and delusions. You know not how fast you are hastening to *infidelity*, and to the renouncing of Christ himself? you little suspect that your extraordinary strictness, for the purity of the Church doth tend to your turning *heathens*, and denying the *whole Church*? But remember, that the nature of God is so *infinitely Good*, as well as *Just*, and the *Gospel* is such *glad tidings to all the world*, and Christ called, the *Saviour of the world*, and God is said *so to love the world in giving him*, Joh. 3. 16. that if you should say God would save but *one man* in the world, or *ten*, or a *thousand*, and damn all the rest, if you did in your bravado believe your selves *this year*, by the *next* you might be like enough to believe that the Gospel is but a fable. I have much ado to forbear naming some high Professours (known lately at *Worcester*, *Exeter* and other parts) who died Apostate-infidels, deriding Christianity and the immortality of the soul, who once were Separatists. And I must profess to you that for my own part, if I did believe that Christs Church were no more numerous than all the Separatists on earth, it would make the work of faith more difficult: For as he is no King that hath no Kingdom; so he is next to no King, whose Kingdom is next to none: He that would prove that our King is only King of *Islington*, or *Hackney* and no more, would by deriding him to day, prepare for the deposing him to morrow. They are glorious things that are spoken of the Kingdom of Christ; even that the Kingdoms of the world are become his Kingdoms. And if you will take from him all save two or three Cottages, I mean the separated Churches only, it is but a little addittion to your treason to take the rest,

rest, and to Crucifie Christ afresh and write over him in derision, the title of a King. You do not discern the design of Satan. He that cannot entice an Apple from a Child, if he can get him to let him eat all the rest till it come to a little of the Core, will then easily get him to throw away that worthless relict. If to day you will needs believe that Christ will reject all the world, and all the Churches, save only a few persons who have pride enough to condemn all the rest, by too morrow or ere long you are like enough to add one other degree to your derision, and to deny him to be Christ.

Obj. But we are more than were in the Ark of Noah.

Answ. First, You never yet proved that all that were out of the Ark were damned, and no more saved from Hell, than were saved from the Deluge. Secondly, If you had; yet the Scripture speaketh such great things of the Universal Gospel Church, as that which maketh up the former diminutions and losses, and helpeth Faith against such difficulties.

. DIRECT.

DIRECT. LVII.

Yet let not any here cheat you by overdoing, nor meer names and titles of Unity deceive you instead of the thing it self: Nor must you ever dream of any Head and Center of the Unity of the Catholick Church, but Christ himself.

THere is no part of Religion which Satan doth not endeavour to *destroy*, under pretense of promoting it: And his way is to overgo Christ and his Apostles, and to seem more zealous than ever they were, and to mend their Work by doing it better or doing more. Christ was not strict enough for the Pharisees, in keeping the Sabbath, nor in his company, nor in his diet. Satan hath alwayes two wayes to destroy both *truth and duty*; The first is by direct opposing it; But when that will not do, the next is by overdoing and pretending to defend it. If he cannot destroy *zeal*, by scorning it, and quenching it; he will try to do it by overheating and distempering it. If he cannot destroy *knowledge*, by the way of gross *ignorance*, he will try to spin it out into the finer threds of vain and innumerable questions and speculations, and to crumble it into such invisible atomes, that it shall be reduced to scepticism or nothing. If he cannot destroy faith by open *infidelity*, he will try to make them believe too much, by making the objects of their own belief, and calling that a *particular faith*, and altering Gods

word

ons, and put out their eyes in honour of the sun, and of their Physician, left either of them should be accused as insufficient.

Even so when Satan findeth that he cannot directly destroy the *Unity* of the Church, and bring division into credit, he will be more zealous for unity than Christ himself: He will then endure no disagreement among Christians, no not in an opinion, nor a form, or ceremony; not in meats or drinks or keeping of dayes; or in judging of things lawful or unlawful, which are not of necessity to the Churches concord. He is either for Tolerating all propagation of Heresie and practise of wickedness, or else he is so much for *Unity*, that no difference almost is to be tolerated. For he well knoweth that while men are imperfect such differences *will still be*: And then if he can but perswade the world, that for Concord sake they must not be endured, what followeth but that the dissenters must be fined, imprisoned or banished to bring them (or the rest) *to unity*. And so he will set all the world together by the ears, in cruelties and blood-shed, and in hating one another, and all under pretense of making them one. You may think that till mankind be all turned Bedlams, they can never be so cheated by such a gross deceit, nor ever guilty of so mad a work. But what will you say if this be the common case, of the far greatest

part

part of the Christian world? And what will you say further, if after above a thousand years universal experience of the unhappy success, they continue it still as the only way to unity and peace? Look but about you with opened eyes, and see whether it be not so.

Were not he a gracious promoter of Unity in the world, that would say [Unity is so excellent a thing, that it is meet we should be all of one complexion, or at least that the world should speak but one language; and therefore no other but one should be tolerated] And here how easie it is to dilate of the great inconveniences of many languages: I could write a volume in folio of it my self; and all true and evident. Methinks I see hereupon how these Books are scattered and read, and how those called Learned men and politicians applaud them, and shake their heads and gnash their teeth at those that would have so great a mischief tolerated: And hereupon they set about the business, and desire a Law that upon pain of imprisonment and banishment (I know not whether) no one in the world shall speak any other language but one. And now I hope Unity will be promoted indeed; when all the world is thus engaged in a war to perfect nature and make men one.

But me-thinks I hear one man that is awake thus bespeak the promoters of this Concord [*Unity* and *Concord* in those points where God hath made them necessary, cannot be over-valued: But yet it is visible that there is a marvellous diversity which nature is delighted in: when of all faces and of all voices, and of all the sorts of animals

Overdoing for Unity is undoing. 273

mals and plants; there is so discernable a difference: yea of all the millions of stones in the field, no two is perfectly like each other. And where greater Unity is most desirable, it must first be considered how much of it is possible, or to be hoped for, and next, what are the proper means to attain it. For first, the medicining of an incurable disease, especially with violent Physick, is not the way to make it better, but to exasperate it and hasten death, when a palliate and patience might do better. It is very desirable, that all the Kings subjects were *strong*, and *beautiful* and ingenuous and Learned; but it is not to be hoped: But that they may be all *Loyal*, and *honest* in their dealings with others, may be well endeavoured. And secondly, a wrong kind of medicine will much more hasten and ascertain death, than to let the disease alone to nature: It is desirable that all the Kings subjects be as is said, both *wise* and *Learned*, yea and *perfect in honesty* and *piety* without fault: But if you make a Law that for the honour of *Unity*, all that are not *Learned* and *perfect in vertue* shall be *fined, imprisoned* or *banished*, the King nor his subjects will be but little beholden to you for their Unity. So *one Language* is very desirable to the world: But first it is not attainable, and secondly a Law to punish all that speak *another* Language is not *the way to procure it*; but to set them together by the ears: You must appoint *Parents* and *School-masters* to *teach* them all one language by degrees, and keep them to their duties; and remove impediments, and thus stay the time; and what cannot this way be attained must not be expected in this world.]

It is very desirable that all Christians were perfect in *knowledge, gifts* and *graces*, and consequently that there were no different opinions, nor no different forms or modes of worship; but that all were equal to the wisest, and to the most sober, pious, zealous and sincere. But if a Law be made that none shall be endured in any Kingdom, that are not of this temperament and stature, the subjects of all Princes may soon be numbered. Set *Parents, Schoolmasters and Ministers at work, to make men wiser, and drive them on to diligence in their duty, and restrain men from hindering them, and from intollerable wickedness and sin, and patiently expect the success of this: And what this will not do expect not.*

And I intreat the Separatists who will think this doctrine of forbearance gratifieth them, to observe that I speak all this to them as well as to Magistrates. I told you that there is a *Church-persecution* and a *Church-forbearance*, as well as a *Civil*. If Christ will have *Magistrates forbear the weak*, he will have *you forbear them*: and not say, *We will have no Communion with those that pray by such Forms and Liturgies, or that use such a Ceremony, or are not of our own opinions:* Read Rom. 14. and 15. and you will see that it was a *Church-forbearance* towards one another, and a *Receiving dissenters* to Christian communion (even as Christ receiveth us for all our weaknesses) which *Paul* there pleadeth for, and not only a forbearance of *smiting* them with the sword. What a wonder and what a lamentation is it, that those men that cry out so much for forbearance to the Magistrate, should themselves be as rigid and more by *Church-severities*, and less *forbear* dissenters, even in a form or ceremony, as to communion, and yet never see the same sin in themselves, which they so much complain of.

And here my principal business is to warn you of the Papal way of *Unity*: They are so great enemies to divisions and sects, that they must have all the Christian world, united not only in one *Christ*, but one profession and baptism, but also in one *mortal Monarch* as his Vicar, that men may know at the Antipodes when they understand not the Scripture, or differ in opinions, who to step to for the ending of their controversies, and to give them an infallible commentary on the Bible, and to tell them with whom they must hold communion. And all their differences may thus have a speedy dispatch: If it be doubted whether one in *Abassia* or much further off, be a Heretick, or an impenitent sinner and to be excommunicated or not; and the Church where he liveth is divied about it, if the matter be but referred to the Pope, as the supream Judge, it is but going to *Rome*, and sending thither all the parties and witnesses on both sides, and the Pope can decide it much more judiciously than those that are on the place and know the persons and all the circumstances. And all this may be done in three years time or less, if wind and weather and all things serve: And if all the persons die by the way, the controversie is ended: If one part only die, let the longer liver have the better, and be juſtified. Or if the Pope will rather ſend Governours to the place to decide the controverſie, whether the next Lords day you ſhall hold communion with ſuch a man, or not, and ſo forward, its like in a few years time ſome of them may live to come thither. And if you muſt ſtill appeal to the Pope himſelf for fear leſt a Prieſt be not the infallible or final Judge (and can do no better than other folks Prieſts,) you may after all, have the liberty of the voyage: And if you cannot in that age get the caſe diſpatched, yet you muſt believe that you have appeared to the only center of Unity.

The cheating noiſe and name of *Unity*, hath been the great divider of the Chriſtian world. And under pretence of ſuppreſſing Hereſie and Schiſm, and bringing a bleſſed peace and harmony amongſt all Chriſtians, the Churches have been ſet all together by the ears, condemning and unchurching one another, and millions have been murthered in the flames, inquiſition and other kinds of death, and thoſe are Martyrs with the one part, who are burnt as Hereticks by the other; And more millions have been murdered by wars. And *hatred* and *confuſion* is become the mark and temperament of thoſe, who have moſt loudly cryed *up Unity*, and *Concord*, *Order* and *Peace*.

It is a common way to ſet up a ſect or faction, by crying down ſchiſm, ſects and factions. And a common way to deſtroy both *Unity* and *Peace*, by crying up *Unity* and *Peace*. Therefore let not bare *Names* deceive you.

Remem-

Remember that one of the old sects or factions of carnal Christians, cryed up *Cephas*, that is, *Peter*, and said we are of *Cephas*; which I know not how they could be blamed for, if he was the Churches *Constitutive* or *Governing* Head. 1 Cor. 1. 12. and 3. 22. And remember that the Church is not the *body of any Apostle*, but of *Christ*, and that all the Apostles are but the nobler sort of members, and none of them the Head. 1 Cor. 12. 27, 28. *Now ye are the body of Christ, and members in particular: and God hath set some in the Church, first Apostles, secundarily Prophets, thirdly Teachers,* &c. But *Bellarmine* (aware of this) hath devised this shift, that the Pope succeedeth *Peter*, in more than his Apostle-ship, even his Head-ship: But when he hath proved *Peter* more than an Apostle, and the Pope his successor, he will do the business: Till then we must say, that if the Pope were but a good Priest or Bishop, below an Apostle, we should give him more honour, than his treasonable usurpation of Christs prerogatives is like to procure him. For he that will needs have all, shall have none, and he that exhalteth himself, shall be brought low; and he that will be more than a man, shall be less than a man.

DIRECT.

DIRECT. LVIII.

Take heed of Superstition, and observe well the circular course of zealous superstition, malignity, formality, and peevish singularity and schism, that you may not be misled by respect of persons. I mean, that First, Indiscreet zeal and devotion hath been the usual beginner of Superstition; Secondly, Malignity in that age hath opposed it for the Authors sake; Thirdly, In the next age the same kind of men have adored the Authors and made themselves a Religion, of the formal part of that superstition, and persecuted those that would not own it. Fourthly, And then the same kind of men that first made it, do oppose it in enmity to those who impose and own it, and suffer and divide the Church in dislike of that which was their own invention.

IT is marvellous to observe this partial dance: But Church-History may convince the understanding Reader, that so it hath been, and so it is; First, the zeal of some holy persons doth at first break forth in some *lawful*, and in some *indiscreet and unwarrantable* expressions. Secondly, the *malignant* enemies of Godliness, hate and oppose these *expressions*, for the sake of the persons and the zeal exprest. 3. When they are dead, God per-

their fore-fathers hated and murthered. *Matth.* 23. 29, 30. *Wo to you Scribes and Pharisees, hypocrites, because ye build the tombs of the Prophets, and garnish the sepulchres of the righteous, and say, If we had been in the dayes of our Fathers, we would not have been partakers with them in the blood of the Prophets: Wherefore ye be witnesses to your selves, that ye are the children of them which killed the Prophets: Fill you up then the measure of your fathers.* The wicked of one generation kill Gods servants, and the wicked of the next Generation do honour their names, and celebrate their memorial: The reason is, because it is the *Life of Godliness*, which the sinner is troubled with and hateth: And therefore it is the *living Saint* whom he abhorreth. But the *name* and *form* of *Godliness* is less troublesome to him, yea and may be *usefull* to make him a Religion of, to quiet his conscience in his sin: And therefore the *name* of *dead Saints* he can honour, and the *form* of their worship, and *corps* of piety he can own. And having become so *Religious*, both his former enmity to *living holiness*; and his carnal zeal for his *Image* of Religion, engage him to make a stir for it: and persecute those that are not of his way. And when the *zealous* and devout people of that age see this; they loath that carkass or Image which the formalist contendeth for, and many flye from it with too great abhorrence for the persons sake who now esteem it; forgetting its original, and that it was *such as they*, that set it up, and were the first inventers.

For instance: The most of the persons whom the Papists now keep holy dayes for, were very religious godly people: And the zealous Religious people of that age, did think that the honouring of the memories of the Martyrs, was a great means to invite the Infidels to Christianity, and to encourage the weak to stick to Christ: And therefore they kept the dayes of their martyrdom, in thanksgiving to God, and in honour of them. The wicked of that age hated and persecuted both the Martyrs and them that honoured them. In the next age Religion being uppermost in the world, the wicked did turn Hypocrites, and keep Holy dayes for the honour of their names whom their fore-fathers murthered. At last when it was observed that the Papists who burned the living Saints, were the greatest honourers of the dead, the most religious people turned quite to dislike and reject those very dayes, which their predecessors had set up in thanskgiving to God, for the doctrine, example and constancy of the Martyrs.

The same all along I may say about the Relicts of Martyrs, and pilgrimages to their shrines, which the Religious sort *begun* at first, and *loathe* at last.

So also those *forms* of Liturgy which now are most distasted, were brought in by the most zealous religious people at the first: The many short invocations, versicles and responses which the people use, were brought in when the souls of the faithful did abound with zeal, and in holy favours break out into such expressions, and could not well endure to be bare auditors, and not vocally

cally to bear their part in the praises of God and prayers of the Church. And in time those very words which signified their raptures, were used by formal hypocrites without their zeal who first exprest them; and so being mortified, and made dead Images and used but by rote, in a senseless canting among the Papists, and also forced upon others; it is now become a point of *zeal* to *avoid* them, and take them as *unlawful*, and it is a great reason, because they are in the Mass-book: when the Mass-book received them from the predecessors of many of *those men* that now refuse them: But though indeed the highest expressions of zeal and rapture, are most lothsome when they are counterfeited and turned into a meer lifeless form: Yet it is the privation of life which is the fault of the Image, and not the thing as in it self. Restore the same spirit to those words, and they will be as good as they were at the beginning.

I might instance in most of the Popish superstitions, and shew you, that for the most part, it was the godliest sort of people of that age, who at first did either set them up, or that which did occasion them; and that the hypocrite after made them his Religion, taking up the form without the life, and that upon this the godly of after ages did abhor them.

But what is my inference from all this? Why first, I would advise you, to look more to the *nature* of the things themselves, and less to the *persons*; and regard the honour of humanity, if you regard not the honour of Religion; and make not the Infidel world deride you, while they see

you

you alter your opinions and practise in meer opposition to one another: and to take up and lay down as the two ends of the ballance move, which must be contrary to each other. Secondly, that you truly understand what interest such zealous persons as your selves had in those opinions, forms and practises at the first, that if you will avoid them for *some mens* sake, you may think the better of them for *other* mens: so far as to bring you to some impartiality. Thirdly that you suspect that zeal in your selves, which you think so much miscarried in your ancestors.

I do not take all that I have mentioned for *superstition*, but I shew you the circulation which zeal, and *formality* and *malignity* make, both in things warrantable and unwarrantable.

But especially take heed of that which is true *superstition*, indeed: By which here I mean, the *making of any new parts of Religion to our selves, and fathering them upon God*, who never made them. Of this there are two sorts, *Positive* and *Negative*: When we falsely say, *This is a Duty commanded by God*; or when we falsly say, *This is a sin forbidden by God*. Take heed of both. I do not speak here of *doing* or *not-doing* the same things upon any other account (as humane duties, or meer conveniences or the like) but as they are falsly pretended to be *Divine*.

For first, this is properly a *belying* of God, and that *adding* to his word (whether *precepts* or *prohibitions*) which he hath so strictly forbidden us, *Jer.* 15. 12. *Deut.* 12. 32.

Secondly, it *debaseth* Religion objectively con-

considered as mixture of base mettals debaseth the Kings coyn: To joyn things humane with things *divine*, and say they are *Divine* when they are not, is putting of dung into the treasuries of God. Nothing will be found fit for Divine reverence and honour, which is not Divine indeed.

Thirdly, it corrupteth Religion in the *minds of men*; and causeth them to fear where no fear is, and to be devout erroneously: As if one should mistake the person of the King, and give his honour to another who is like him: or should run into a play-house to do his devotion, and think that he is in the Church. *Ye worship ye know not what: we know what we worship. John* 4. 22.

Fourthly, This *superstition* tendeth to *destroy* true Religion, by gratifying and increasing aversation and opposition, by making it seem an unlovely tiresome thing. All that is truly of God is *Rational* and *amiable*, and wisely contrived for our good: And the enemies of Godliness, have not a word of solid Reason, to say against it: But that which is brought in by *corrupters* may be confuted: And *unnecessary* things become a *burthen*, *Acts* 15. 28. What a toilsome task doth Popery contain? of positives and negatives? ceremonies, and austerities, and useless labours? And then they that take their pilgrimages, and penances, and night-risings, and multiplied formalities to be a *burthen*, and hear them called by the name of *Religion*, do account *Religion it self* a burthen, as taking this to be a part of it: And when Religion is not *loved* it is *lost*. To make it seem *bad* and *unlovely*, is the way by which the devil destroyeth it in the world.

Fifthly,

Fifthly, *Superstition* is the great dividing engine, which Satan useth to cut the Churches of Christ into Sects and pieces; and consequently to stir up party against party, to the hating and persecuting of one another: For while some take that for Religion which is none; others will see their errour and avoid it: And thus the division will lay the foundation of disputes and quarrels, of enmity and opposition. For who can think that all the Churches should ever be so blind and slavish, as to take up that as a part of Religion, and a divine institution, which was forged by the private spirit of some erroneous person of an overheated brain.

Sixthly, Lastly, *Superstition* much displeaseth God, and maketh us *sinners*, even in that, in which we think especially to honour him. *Math.* 15. 9. *In vain do they worship me, teaching for doctrines the commandements of men:* Though God in mercy can distinguish between his own and ours, and doth not count *the whole* worship to be *in vain*, where *any degree* of superstition is mixed (For then most zealous persons were undone;) yet the *superstitious part* of worship is alwayes *in vain*; and all the rest is made as vain, where that is the predominant and denominating part. Thus *overdoing* is *undoing*, and thus the superstitious are (materially) *righteous overmuch.* And not only much cost and pains is lost, but the soul corrupted, the Church divided, Religion debased and endangered and God displeased, by ignorant zeal.

Here note to prevent mistakes; First, that as God is related to our actions, either as the *efficient*

other when we feign him *finaly* to be *pleased* with a Religious worship of our own invention, though we confess it to have no higher an original than our selves.

Secondly, that the matter of this latter sort of superstition is either that which God *forbiddeth* and so is *displeased with*; or that which he hath made and holdeth *indifferent*; and so is neither pleased or displeased with, in any moral consideration, in it self considered. He that offereth God a *sacrifice* of *sin* (or things prohibited) or of a worthless and indifferent thing, and taketh God to be *pleased* with the latter, or *not displeased* with the former, doth indeed displease him by either of these conceits. And the *general prohibition* of not *adding* or *diminishing*, rightly understood, may notifie things as under the former head.

Thirdly, But it is no superstition to hold a good thing to be good; a bad thing to be bad; or an indifferent thing to be indifferent.

Fourthly, Nor yet to determine of those circumstances of worship which God hath left to humane determination; being made necessary *in genere* by nature or scripture: Nor yet to judge that God is pleased with such a prudent determination.

Fifthly, it is not superstition to do the same material thing, which another doth superstitiously,

ously; if we have not the same superstitious conceit of it as he hath. If a Papist should annoint the sick, as a Sacrament, and a Protestant do it as a medicine, the former is superstition, and not the later. And so in other things.

Sixthly, Whether that indifferent thing remain indifferent to our use, which others use to superstition, is a case which a judicious collation of circumstances must determine. His superstitious use doth not make it simply a sin in any other, who hath none of his false conceits and ends: (else some superstitious persons so abusing meat and drink and cloaths, and all things in the world might make all things become unlawful to us: or at least deprive us of all our liberty in things indifferent.)

Seventhly, If we avoid *anothers superstition* as to the *form* or *intention* which maketh it superstition, and this as a sin, we do well: If we avoid the *matter* it self which he useth superstitiously, because it is by him made *scandalous*, we do our duty when it is *scandalous indeed*, and no contrary greater accident maketh it *our duty*. But if we take it to be *simply superstition* or *sin*, to do materially the same action, which a superstitious person doth, we are *superstitious* in avoiding his *superstitious* act.

For instance, a Papist visiteth the Lady of *Lauretto* as a divine duty: This is superstition: A Protestant goeth thither upon lawful and necessary business: This is no superstition: Another Protestant who hath no necessary business there, avoideth it that he may not be *scandalous* and encourage others to it, This is well done. A Sectary thinketh it *superstition* or other sin, simply to

go

testant fasteth the same day, because an Act of Parliament commandeth it, which renounceth the Papists religious end; Or because his Physician prescribeth it as necessary for his health. This is not superstition. Another Protestant avoideth it through necessity for his health: And another in Popish Countries avoideth it only as *scandalous*: Neither of these are superstitious. Another fasteth on a Fryday for his own necessity or convenience, as a time which he may lawfully choose. And another fasteth on a Friday; because the Master of the family, or the Pastors of the Church, have appointed a fast on that day. This is no superstition. A Sectary thinketh that it is superstition, or some other sin to fast the same day that the Papists do, because the Papists do it superstitiously. This is superstition (unless in the case of scandal as aforesaid.)

The multitudes of superstitions by which the *Papists* or *any others*, have corrupted and debased the *Christian Religion*, I shall not now digress to mention; But only touch upon a few instances, of the *superstitions* of *those godly persons* of *this age*, to whom I am now writing: To shew them, that it is the *Religious sort*, that are the common beginners of superstition, by *over-doing*, out of a mistaken zeal, or fear of sinning.

I refer the Reader to *Bilson* for full proof.

But here again I must first crave the patience
of

of those that love not errour better than information; and desire them not to be too angry with me for telling them what I confidently hold, though it differ from the opinions of many whom I greatly reverence and honour; while I profess withall that I do it not in a Majesterical imposing way, nor as slighting the persons from whom I differ, but as offering my brethen that Light which I think needful to their own and to the Churches cure: And I will thank them if they will do the like by me, if I be guilty of any superstitious errour.

First, the Scripture telleth us of no *Church-Elders* but what were *ordained*; and of none but such as were of the same *Office* with the preaching Pastors or Elders: of none that had not authority to baptize and administer the Lords supper: Nor doth Church-history tell us of any other as a Divine office. But when one Assembly had many Elders or Pastors, those that were best gifted for publick Sermons did preach; and the rest did help to rule the Church, and to catechize, and instruct and visit particular families and persons, and other parts of the office, as there was cause. But now we have concluded that there is a *distinct office* of Ruling-Elders, who need *not be ordained*, and who have no *power to baptize* or to administer the *Lords Supper*. This I think is *a superstition*: For we feign God to have made a *Church-office* which he never made. And though we must *honour* and *hold Communion* with the Churches which have this blemish; yet still it cannot be freed from *superstition*.

Secondly; God hath required nothing but *profession*

by some Religious people. 289

session of the Baptismal Covenant, to prove a mans title to his entrance and priviledge in the *Universal Church*: And a consent to our *Relation* to the *particular Churches*, to our membership in *them*. But mistaking-zeal hath accounted this too loose a way, and hath devised stricter terms: Many must have other proofs of Godliness, besides the *understanding*, *voluntary assent and consent to the Baptismal Covenant*: Yea of those that are in the *Universal Church already*; before they can be admitted to its priviledges, or to a *particular Church*. And which is worse, they here give the Church no *certain rule*. instead of Christs rule, which they cast by: But one man requireth one account, and another requireth another; and the rule and test doth vary as the charity or prudence of men do vary. This is a Superstition, which hath already torn the Churches in pieces, and is going on still to do worse: And its raised by mistaking-zeal.

Thirdly, that none that at the same time or before are not entred members of some *particular Church*, may by *Baptism* be entred into the *Universal Church*; is a *superstition*, which some good men have taken up.

Fourthly, that he who is a member only of the *Universa Church*, may not *in transitu* be admitted to communio with *particular Churches*, unless he bring a Certificate from a *particular Church* of which he sometime was a Member.

Fifthly, that the Pastor may not lawfully receive any member into a particular Church without the consent of the *major Vote* of the people.

Y   Sixthly,

Sixthly, that a Minister of Christ may not by *Baptism* receive any into the *universal Church*, but by the *consent* of the *Major Vote* of some *particular Church*.

Seventhly, that no man is a Minister or Commissioned Officer of Christ, for the discipling and baptizing of those *without* the Church, unless he be also the Pastor of some particular Church (or at least have been such.)

Eighthly, that the people do not onely *choose* the persons who shall be *their Pastors*, but also give them their *office* or *power*.

Ninthly, that the people have the power of the Keyes, or of Church-Government, by Vote.

Tenthly, that the *people* of a *particular Church*, do give authority to men to be *Ministers* in the *universal Church*, and to *preach* and *baptize* among those that are *without*.

Eleventhly, that he that is a member of *one Church*, may not *communicate* with *any other* but by the consent of the *Pastor* and *people* of that *one*.

Twelfthly, That he that is a member of a Church, may not *remove* his *relation* to another Church, (when his occasions and personal benefit require it, and the publick good of many is not hurt by it) without the consent of the Pastor and people of that Church.

Thirteenthly, that it is simply unlawful to use a form of prayer, or to read a prayer on a book.

Fourteenthly, That if a School-master *impose* a form upon a schollar, or a parent on a child, it maketh it become unlawful.

Fifteenth

Fifteenth, that our *presence* maketh us guilty of all the errours or unmeet expressions of the Minister in publick worship: At least if we before know of them. And therefore that we must joyn with none whose errours or mis-expressions, we know of before.

Sixteenth, that as oft as a Minister is removed from his particular flock, he becometh but a private man, and is no longer a Minister and Officer of Christ.

Seventeenth, that we are guilty of the sins of all unworthy or scandalous Communicants if we communicate with them: Though their admission is not by our fault.

Eighteenth, that he whose judgement is against a *Diocesan Church*, may not lawfully joyn with a *Parish Church*; if the Minister be but subject to the *Diocesan*.

Nineteenth, that whosoever is unlawfully commanded is not lawful to be obeyed.

Twenty, that it is unlawful to do any thing in the worship of God which is imposed by men, and is not commanded it self in the Scripture (As what Translation of the Scripture shall be read; what meetre and what Tune of Psalms shall be in use; what hour and at what place the Church shall meet; Pulpits, Tables, Fonts, &c. Printing the Bible, &c. dividing it into Chapters, verses, &c.

These and more such as these are Superstitions which some Religious people have brought up.

And among those who are of another opinion, & will speak against all the fore-mentioned superstitions,

stitions, there are too many introduced, which they are as fond of, because they are their own.

☞ As that all the Pastors of the Protestant Churches abroad, who had only the election of the people and the Ordination of Parochial Pastours, and not of Diocesan Bishops, are no true Ministers of Christ, but Lay-men.

That therefore those Churches are no true Churches (in a political sense, and as Organized.)

That therefore their Baptism is unlawful, and a nullity, and all those nations are no baptized Christians. (Though the Papists who hold the validity of Lay-mens baptizing, do here censure more easily.)

That it is not lawful to communicate in such Churches, and receive the Sacrament of the Lords Supper from such Ministers.

That those Countries which are baptized by such, should be rebaptized.

That those Ministers who are ordained by such, should be re-ordained.

That it is unlawful to joyn with those Churches, where the Minister prayeth only from a *Habit* of prayer (called *extemporary*) without a fore-known form; because they know not but he may put somewhat unlawful into his prayers; and because the mind cannot so readily try and approve and consent to words, which are hastily uttered, and not known to the hearers before.

These and abundance other Superstitions some men would introduce on the other side. And by all such inventions fathered upon God, and made a part of Religion, the minds of men are corrupted and disquieted, and the Churches disturbed and divided; by departing from primitive simplicity.

I shall only now propose this to the consideration of those of the first sort.

Whether they are sure that these superstitions of theirs may not run the round as other superstitions have done before them? Or some of them at least? What if the next age should turn them into a dead formality? And what if the next age after that should make Lawes to enforce them? And then Godly people first scruple them? and then flye from them as discerned superstition? And then the worst men be glad of that advantage to persecute those that would not submit to them? By this circulation, if the same men who invented *un-ordained Elders, new and needless Church-Covenants,* &c. could but live two or 300. years, they might come to be among the number of those who cry out of them as *superstitions,* and suffer persecution because they will not use them.

Yea there are among you now many things of a lower nature, which some dare scarce plainly say, God commandeth or forbiddeth, and yet they are censorious enough about them; As heretofore many were against wearing the hair of any considerable length; Against wearing cuffs upon a day of humiliation: Against dressing meat or feasting at least, on the Lords day (which is a day of Thanksgiving of divine institution)and held: That it is necessary to feast twice at least, upon a day of Thanksgiving (of mans appointment:) That a Minister should not lift up his eyes, much less kneel down to signifie his
private

private prayer, when he goeth into the Pulpit. Nor any other when they enter into the Church; That no prayer may be used, and no Psalm sung in our common mixt Assemblies, which have any expressions, which all both good and bad may not fitly use as for themselves: That no Minister may use notes in preaching to help his memory: That the Sacramental bread and wine must not (say some) or must (say others) be delivered by the Minister into each mans hand. That no gesture but sitting is lawful at the sacrament. That it is unlawful to wear a Gown in divine worship, if it be commanded: That it is unlawful to keep any aniversary day of humiliation or thanksgiving of mans appointment: That just such and such hours for family worship must be observed by all: Or others say, that no set times or number of family prayers are to be observed. That it is not lawful to preach or hear a sermon upon a humane holiday. With abundance more such, (about phrases, and gestures, and fashions of apparel, and customes, &c. I am not at all now accusing these opinions of superstition, nor telling you whether I take them to be right or wrong; Much less would I perswade any to make no conscience how they order these or any other the smallest circumstances of their *lives:* Obedience must extend to the smallest parts of the lawes of God. But I am shewing you the circular course of many religious people in the world. Suppose now that the next age should make strict lawes for every one of your own opinions in all these points.. And that the Religious people should then scruple them, because they are

impo-

imposed: And that the Rulers then should make their Laws more strict, and that all the common people should take up these opinions, and all that sort of men that first were zealous for them, should turn against them, because the common people are for them; and should call them Popish superstitions, and should suffer imprisonment rather than conform to them; I pray you tell me, if you fore-saw all this, what is it you vvould advise a sober Christian to do in such a time and case as that? Would you have the same men that now are for these opinions, cry out against them, and censure all as superstitious who are for them; and separate from them; and rejoyce in their sufferings on that account? Why I tell you that many of the customs and practises in the Church, which you now thus avoid as superstition, were brought in at the first thus, by the most Religious sort of people: And yet it is now accounted by many a necessary point of Religion to avoid them: And all because that men take up their opinions in such matters of Religion, from the estimation of the persons that are for them; and avoid those things with prejudice and scrupulosity, which are liked, or practised or commanded by those whom they think ill of, and take for the adversaries of Religion.

DIRECT. LIX.

If through the faults of either side or both, you cannot meet together in the same particular Church or place, yet preserve that unity in Faith, Love and practise, which all neighbour Churches should maintain with one another, and use not your different Assemblies to revile each other, and kill your Love.

ALL distances are undesirable and tend to more: But yet our *Unity* lyeth not so much in *meeting in one place*, as in being of one *Mind*, and *Heart* and *Life*: Many occasions may warrant our corporal distance; but *Heart-divisions* should be most avoided. It is the *principles* and *motives* upon which you withdraw which are more considerable than the local distance.

Therefore on one side let us take heed how we *unchurch* and *unchristen* any with whom we do not corporally joyn: And on the other side, let us take heed how we revile them all as Sectaries and Separatists, who do not joyn with our assemblies: But let us know the reason of their practise before we peremptorily judge them.

I. Perhaps you think that such or such a Church-government, or Forms, or Ceremonies, are unwarrantable, and such and such oaths and subscriptions are unlawful, and therefore you cannot have local Communion with the Churches that impose them. If it were so, yet take heed of accounting these no Churches of Christ, or pretending

tending that Chriſt diſowneth and rejecteth them. If they caſt out you by impoſing any thing which you think is ſin, yet take heed that you excommunicate not them. If there be a difference between a weak and culpable Chriſtian, and no Chriſtian, there is a difference between a weak and culpable Church and no Church; And as there are innumerable degrees of good or evil, ſtrength or weakneſs in particular Chriſtians, ſo there is in Churches alſo.

You may perhaps find that another Miniſter is more profitable to you, and another Churches principles more pleaſing to you, and their diſcipline better in your account: And therefore you think that you are bound, to chooſe the beſt for your perſonal Communion. Be it ſo: There is yet ſome modeſty in theſe termes: But do not therefore conclude that Communion with that Church which you turn from is *ſimply unlawfu.*; or that *another* may not uſe it who can have no better! Or that you your ſelves ſhould not rather joyn with that than with *none*? Or that you may not occaſionally ſometimes communicate with them, though your more ordinary communion be elſewhere. Nor do not diſown all *ſpiritual* communion with them, though in body you are abſent. But when ever you pray to God, go to him as a member of the Univerſal Church, and not of a Sect only: Pray for the whole Church, and deſire a part in the prayers of the whole. Own them and their worſhip ſo far as Chriſt owneth them. While you diſown their errours and failings, yet own their faith, and all that is found in their prayers and worſhip; And

ſee

see that you love them as members of Christ, who if weak are yet Christians, and perhaps in other respects better than you. (To say nothing whether it be they or you that are in the right.) You like not all that is done in the *Lutherans* Churches, much less in the *Greek* and *Ethiopian:* And yet I hope you disown not their spiritual communion as Churches though faulty, and as members of the same body. But if you are not content to choose an ordinary communion most suitable to your self, but you must conclude that such are no Ministers or no Churches of Christ: their worship is not accepted by him, it is not lawful to have communion with them, but rather to joyn with no Church, than with them; and will accordingly contemn them and irritate and alienate mens minds against them; Be sure that you prove well what you say, or wonder not if all wise and sober men do take this for downright odious schism, and one of the worst of the works of the flesh. *Gal.* 5. 20, 21. 1 *Cor.* 3. 1, 2, 3, 4.

II. On the other side, if any withdraw from our Communion, let us not too hastily accuse them of schism: And when we do let us well distinguish of schism, and not go further from them than they have gone from us, and to become our selves the Schismaticks while we oppose it.

There are many cases in which *local separation* may be lawful. First, As if our callings justly remove us to another place or Country. Secondly, If our spiritual advantage bind us to remove to a better Minister and more suitable society

ciety when we are free. Thirdly, if our lawful Pastors be turned out of the place, and we follow them, and turn away but from Usurpers. Fourthly, If the Pastors turn Hereticks or Wolves. Fifthly, If the publick good of the Churches require my removal. Sixthly, If any sin be imposed on me, and I be refused by the Church unless I will commit it. In these and some other such cases a remove is lawful.

And when it is *not lawful*, yet it may be but such a blemish in the departers, as the departers find in the Church which they depart from; which will on neither side dis-oblige them from Christian Love, and such Communion as is due with neighbour Churches.

There is a schism *from* the *Church*, and a schism *in* the Church: There is a schism from *almost all* the Churches in the world, and a schism from *some one* or *few* particular Churches. There is a separation upon *desperate intollerable principles* and *reasons*, and a separation upon some *weak* but *tollerable* ones. These must not be confounded. The Novations were tolerated and loved by the sober Catholicks, Emperours and others; when many others were otherwise dealt with.

If any good Christians in zeal against sin, do erroneously think that an undisciplin'd Church should be forsaken, that they may exercise the discipline among themselves which Christ hath appointed; It is the duty of that Church to take this warning to repent of her neglect of discipline, and then to *love* and *honour* those that have (though upon mistake perhaps) withdrawn. But if when they have occasioned the withdrawing by their

their corruption, they will profecute the perfons with hatred, reviling, flanders, contempt or perfecution, and continue impenitent in their own corruption, they will be the far greater Schifmaticks and err a more pernicious error.

DIRECT. LX.

When the Love-killing spirit, either cruel or Dividing is abroad among Christians, be not idle nor discouraged spectators, nor betray the Churches Peace by a few lazy wishes; but make it a great part of your labour and Religion, to revive Love and Peace, and to destroy their contraries: And let no censures or contempts of any Sect or party take you off: But account it an honour to be a Martyr for Love and Peace, as well as for the Faith.

OF all parts of Religion, (I know not how unhappily it comes to pass) men think that *Negatives* are sufficient for the service of *Peace*: If a man live *not unpeaceably* and do no man wrong, nor provoke any to wrath, this is thought a sufficient friend to peace. And therefore it is no wonder that *Love and Peace* so little profper. When Satan and his inftruments do all that they can by fraud and force againft it, and we think it enough to ftand by and do no harm. It is the *Peace-makers* that Chrift pronounceth *bleffed*, for

theirs

theirs is the Kingdome of Heaven. Mat. 5. 9. Here he that is not with Christ and the Church is against it. Why should we think that so much actual diligence, in hearing, reading, praying, *&c.* is necessary to the promoting of other parts of holiness, and nothing necessary to Love and Peace, but to do no hurt, but be quiet patients! Is it not worthy of our labour? And is not our labour as *needful* here as any where? Judge by the multitude and quality of the adversaries: and by their power and success. It is a mark of hypocrisie to go no further in duties of *Godliness,* than the safety of our reputation will give as leave? And is it not so in the duties of *Love* and *Peace?* If the Kingdom of God be in Righteousness and *Peace* then what we would do to promote Gods Kingdom, we must do for them. *Rom.* 14. 17. And if dividing Christs Kingdom is the way to destroy it (and Satan himself is wiser than to divide his own Kingdom, *Mat.* 12.) then whatever we would do to save the Kingdom of Christ, all that we must do to preserve and restore the peace of it, and to heal its wounds.

 I know if you set your selves in good earnest to this work, both parties who are guilty will fall upon you, with their censures at least; One side will say of you that you are a favourer of the Schismaticks and Sectaries, because you oppose them not with their unhappy weapons, & love them not as little as they. (As they say of *Socrates* and *Sozomen* the Historians, that they were Novatians because they spake truth of them & called them honest men; And as they said of *Martin* and *Sulpitius Severus,* that they were favourers of unlearned

Fana-

Fanaticks, and of the Priscillian Gnosticks, because they were not as hot against them as *Ithacius* and *Idacius*, but refused to be of their Councels, or communicate with them, for inviting the Emperour to the way of blood and corporal violence.

And the other side will say that you are a temporizer, and a man of too large principles, because you separate not as they do; And perhaps that you are wise in your own eyes, because you fall in with neither Sect of the extreams: But these are small things to be undergone for so great a duty. And he that will not be a peace-maker upon harder terms than these, I fear will scarce be meet for the reward. I again repeat *Jam.* 3. 17. *The wisedome from above is first pure and then peaceable, gentle and easie to be intreated, full of mercy and good fruits, without partiality, without hypocrisie: and the fruit of righteousness is sown in peace of them that make peace.* Rom. 12. 18. *If it be possible, as much as in you lyeth live peaceably with all men.* Heb. 12. 14 *Follow peace with all men, and holiness.*

Obj. *But is it not as good sit still as labour to no purpose. What good have ever any peacemakers done, among differing Divines.*

Answ. A grievous charge upon Divines and Christians: Are they the only Bedlams or drunken men in the world? If *Princes* fall out, or if *neighbours* fall out, arbitrators and peace-makers labour not alwayes in vain: But I answer you, It is not in vain: Peace-breakers would have yet prevailed more and made the Church unhappier than it is, if some Peace-makers had not hindered them

them. The minds of thousands are seasoned with the Love of Peace, and kept from cruelties and Schisms, by the wholesome instructions and examples of Peace-makers. And it is worth our labour to honour so holy and sweet a thing as Love and Peace; and to bear our testimony for it in the world. And Gods promise of reward doth tell you that you labour not in vain. Is that in vain which *Heaven* is promised to?

Quest. *But what is it that you would have us do for Love and Peace, and against the contraries?*

Answ. First, *Preach* and *write*, if it be your calling.

Secondly, Let the cause of Love and Peace, be much in your secret and open prayers to God.

Thirdly, Instruct all that learn of you with principles of Love and Peace, and labour to plant them deep in their minds, and make them as sensible of the evil of the contraries, as they are of any other sin. Unless Divines and Parents do take the way to bring up the people, and children under this kind of doctrine, that Love and peace may become their Religion, the Church is never like to be recovered.

Fourthly, In all your conference, labour (seasonably and prudently) to inculcate these matters on the hearers minds, and to bear your testimony against *cruelty*, and *division*.

Fifthly, Put such books into peoples hands as plead best the cause of Love and Peace. Among others get men to read these: Bishop *Usher's* Sermon on *Eph.* 4. 3. at *Wansted* before King *James*, Bishop *Hall's* Peace-maker: Mr. *Jeremiah*

miah Burroughs of Heart-divisions; and Mr. *Stillingfleet's Irenichon*; and all Mr. *Daries*.

Sixthly, Disgrace not your Doctrine by the badness of your own lives; but be as much more *Holy* than them as you are more *Peaceable*, that they may see that it is not a *carnal unholy Peace* that you desire. But these things belong to the following Directions.

Finally, Brethren, farewel; Be perfect; be of good comfort: Be of one mind: Live in Peace: And the G d of Love and Peace shall be with you. 1 Cor. 13. 11. Phil. 4. 9. 1 Thes. 5. 23. *And the God of Peace shall bruise Satan under your feet shortly.* Rom. 16. 20. *Now the God of Peace be with you all. Amen.* Rom. 15. 33.

Martyrdom for Love and Peace is as honourable and gainful, as Martyrdom for the Faith.

Part

Part II.
DIRECTIONS TO THE PASTORS,
HOW TO
Esteem and use Chrifts Flock.

EVEN
The weak ones and the quarrelsome Children: And what muft be done by themselves in the firft place, both to prevent and heal
DIVISIONS.

THE Practice of which, the Author doth humbly and earneftly beg of them, as with tears upon his knees, for the fake of Chrift, that purchafed the weakeft with his blood; for the fake of thofe that muft live in peace with Chrift for ever; for the fake of thofe who are in danger of turning to Popery or contemning Godliness, through the scandal of our Divisions, to their own damnation: for the sake of these poor distracted Churches; for the sake of the King, that he may have the comfort of Governing a quiet and united people: and for their own sakes, that they may give up their account with joy, to the chief Shepheard and Bishop of our souls, and not with terrour, for the consuming and scattering of his flock.

And (that he may both begin and end with Divine Authority) the Author humbly beggeth of them all, that *England* may but SEE and FEEL, that the PASTORS do UNDERSTAND, BELIEVE, CONSIDER and OBEY that will of God, which these following Texts of Scripture do express.

Psal. 15. 4. *In whose eyes a vile person is contemned, but he honoureth them that fear the Lord.*

Math. 25. 40, 45. *Verily I say unto you, in as much as ye did it not, to one of the least of these (my Brethren) ye did it not to me.*

Math. 18. 6, 10. *But whoso shall offend one of these little ones which believe in me, it were better for him that a milstone were hanged about his neck, and that he were drowned in the depth of the Sea —— Take heed that ye despise not one of these little ones: for I say unto you, that in Heaven their Angels do always behold the face of my Father which is in heaven.* 11 *For the Son of man is come to save that which was lost.*

2 Cor. 4. 3. *But if our Gospel be hid, it is hid to them that are lost.*

1 Cor. 9. 16. *For necessity is laid upon me, yea*

how to esteem and use Christs flock.

wo is unto me if I preach not the Gospel.

Act.20.20,24,28,33. *I have taught you publickly and from house to house — But none of these things move me, neither count I my life dear unto my self, so that I might finish my course with joy, and the ministry which I have received of the Lord Jesus — Take heed therefore to your selves and to all the flock over which the Holy Ghost hath made you overseers, to feed the Church of God, which he hath purchased with his own blood — I have coveted no mans silver or gold or apparel —*

1 Pet. 5. 2, 3. *Feed the flock of God which is among you, taking the oversight thereof, not by constraint, but willingly; nor for filthy lucre, but of a ready mind; neither as being Lords over Gods heritage, but being ensamples to the flock. And when the chief Shepherd shall appear ye shall receive a Crown of Glory that fadeth not away.*

Luk. 22. 24, 25. *And there was a strife among them, which of them should be accounted the Greatest: And he said unto them; The Kings of the Gentiles exercise Lordship over them, and they that exercise authority upon them are called Benefactors; But ye shall not be so: but he that is greatest among you let him be as the younger; and he that is chief, as he that doth serve — I am among you as be that serveth.*

1 Thes. 5. 12,13. *Know them which* LABOUR AMONG *you, and are over you in the Lord, and admonish you, and esteem them very highly in Love, for their* WORK *sake, and be at peace among your selves.*

1 Tim. 5. 17. *Let the Elders that Rule well be coun-*

...ted worthy of double honour: Especially they who labour in the WORD and DOCTRINE.

Phil. 1. 15, 16, 17, 18. *Some indeed preach Christ even of envy and strife, and some also of good will: The one preach Christ of contention, not sincerely, supposing to add affliction to my bonds: What then! Notwithstanding every way, whether in pretence or in truth, Christ is preached, and I do therein rejoyce, yea, and will rejoyce.*

Act. 28. 30, 31. *And* Paul *dwelt two whole years in his own hired house, and received all that came in unto him; preaching the Kingdom of God, and teaching those things which concern the Lord Jesus Christ, with all confidence no man forbidding him.*

Rom. 14. 1, 2, 3, 4. *Him that is weak in the faith receive ye; but not to doubtful disputations: For one believeth that he may eat all things: Another who is weak, eateth herbs: Let not him that eateth despise him that eateth not; And let not him which eateth not judge him that eateth: For God hath received him: Who art thou that judgest another mans servant? To his own Master he standeth or falleth: yea he shall be holden up: For God is able to make him stand. One man esteemeth one day above another: Another esteemeth every day alike. Let every man be fully perswaded in his own mind.*

Rom. 15. 1, 2, 3, 4, 5, 6, 7. *We then that are strong, ought to bear the infirmities of the weak, and not to please our selves: Let every one of us please his neighbour for his good to edification. For even Christ pleased not himself —— Now the God of Patience, and Consolation grant you to be* like minded one towards another, according to *Christ Jesus: That ye may with one mind and one mouth glorifie God — Wherefore* RECEIVE *ye one another, as Christ also received us to the Glory of God.*

Rom. 14. 17, 18, 19, 20. *For the Kingdome of God is not meat and drink, but* Righteousness *and* PEACE *and Joy in the Holy Ghost: For he that in* THESE THINGS *serveth Christ, is* Acceptable to God, *and* APPROVED *of* MEN. *Let us therefore follow after the things which make for* PEACE, *and things wherewith one may* Edifie *another —— For meat destroy not the work of God — Happy is he that condemneth not himself in the thing which he alloweth (that is acknowledgeth to be indifferent or lawful.) And he that doubteth is damned if he eat.*

The rest, and some of the same again you shall have in the Conclusion, and I shall not accuse my self of vain repetition; but account my self and *England* happy if twice or ten times warning you of your undoubted duty, in the plain words of God which you cannot without professed Infidelity deny; will but perswade you to heal our grievous wounds, at so cheap a rate, as the doing of that good and blessed work, which NONE may so EASILY do as YOU, and none are more OBLIGED to do, nor shall suffer more everlastingly for *not doing* it, if no Scripture, no reasons, no experience, no petitions, no groans and tears of the distressed Church of Christ can intreat you to it.

But alas,

Rom. 3. 16, 17, 18. *Destruction and misery are in their wayes: The way of PEACE they have not known: There is no fear of God before their eyes.* ——

Ecclef. 7. 7. *SURELY OPPRESSION MAKETH A WISE MAN MAD.*

Rev. 6. 10. *QUAM DIU DOMINE, SANCTE, VERAX.*

Psal. 120. 6. *DIU HABITAVIT ANIMA MEA, INTER OSORES PACIS.*

The Preface.

THE Reason why I think it needful, to adjoyn these few Directions to the Pastors, are, first, Because I think that the rest will do but little good without them. Though the people are more inclined to separations than the Pastors, yet are the Pastors the greater causes of most of the Divisions in the Church; And therefore must be the chiefest in the Cure: Because the advantage of their parts and place, doth make them most significant in both: (And their office obligeth them to be the most skilful and forward in the Cure.)

Secondly, Because I should be chargeable with such partiality as beseemeth not a Minister of Christ; if I should fall upon the miscarriages of the people only, and say nothing to my self and brethren, who are as deeply concerned in the matter in hand.

Yet I must here premise, that as I have done this part with greater brevity, so also with submissive tenderness and respect: And that I do not at all intend any of the Directions following, as a Magisterial Dictator to those in authority; nor any of the admonitions, as factious reflections upon superiors or inferiors; or as pleading for or against any party now among us.

To the reasons after given for tenderness to Religious dissenters, though too much inclined to separations, I shall here only add First, That the general weakness, even of the Pastors through most of the Churches upon earth, should make us rather pity the weakness of the people, than angrily revile them: And so think of *Christs* words, *Let him that is without sin cast the first stone.* Alas our preaching, our praying, our conference, our living, tell all the world too loudly that we are weak! How few are there that be not either ignorant, or injudicious, or imprudent, or dull and livelefs, or dry and barren, or of a stammering tongue, in our *Ministerial* work? And in so high a business any one of these is a loathsome blemish. If we are put to defend our Religion, or any necessary part thereof, how weakly and injudiciously is it usually done? In a word, Our great divisions among our selves, with our censures and usage of one another, do tell all the world not only that we are weak, but that too many of us account one another to be worse than weak, even intollerable, and unworthy of our sacred office. And shall we by our weakness and faultiness become the peoples scandal, and tempt them to undue separations; and when we have done be impatient with their weakness, while we overlook our own?

Secondly, Let us be so impartial as to remember, how far some have spoken to their sense, who have been of most veneration in the Church. I instance but in two: *First,* The wise and ancient *Britain,* Gildas, who saith no less, than, Apparet ergo eum qui vos sacerdotes sciens ex corde dicit, non esse eximium Christianum: Sane quod sentio proferam — O inimici Dei & non sacerdotes! O licitatores malorum, & non pontifices! traditores, & non sanctorum Apostolorum successores! impugnatores, & non Christi ministri! — Sed quomodo vos aliquid solvetis, ut fit solutum & in cœlis, a cœlo ob scelera adempti, & immanium um peccatorum funibus competiti? &c. If the Autour of these words be Venerable, account not the Speakers of such like now, to be utterly intollerable.

The second is St. Martin, whose Story out of Sulpitius Severus, I have afterwards abbreviated. If a Sainted Bishop must famous for miracles, p e end to Angelical Revelation for so much as is there mentioned; let us be charitable and patient to those tender conscionable Christians, who mistakingly go in such like wayes.

I am my self so sensible of the evil and danger of Dividing separating principles and wayes, that it is much of my labour to cure them withall! And therefore I have written what I have here done, th u h I am sure I shall displease the guilty: But overdoing and ill doing will prove but undoing.

The Lord give more Wisedome, Holiness and Love, to Pastors and People; and open our ears to Healing Counsels, before we are incurable!

Dire-

Directions to Pastors how to deal with those weak Christians who are inclined to Divisions.

WHen the young and ungrounded sort of Christians, do by their errors, pride or passions disturb the Churches peace and order, it is the *Pastor* usually that are first and most assaulted by their abuses, and therefore are most impatient and exasperated against them: And it were well if we were so innocent our selves, as that our consciences need not call us to enquire; whether all this be not partly the fruit of our own miscarriages. However seeing that both the eminency of our *place* and the nature of our *office*, should make us more sensible of the Churches dangers, and more solicitous of its safety, than the private members are, I think that the chief part of the *Duty*, is incumbent upon us, which must be done in order to the prevention of these maladies, and to the cure. And therefore I think that the principal work of a Director or Counsellor in this case, must be with the Ministers of Christ themselves; The Churches Peace lieth most upon our hands: And if we miscarry, and will not understand instruction, nor bear admonition, nor do our parts, how little hope will be left of our tranquility? The Body must needs languish, when the Physician is as bad as the disease.

DIRECT.

DIRECT. I.

Let it be our first care to know and do our own duty, for the strengthening and uniting of the people: And when we see their weakness and divisions, let us first examine and judge our selves, and lament and reform our own neglects.

THat the state of the flocks doth usually follow the state of the Pastors, is known by the experience of all the Churches, in all ages and places of the world. Where there is a *holy, faithfull, able, diligent, concordant* Ministery, there is usually a reformed and agreeing people. And where there is an ignorant, lazy, formal, ungodly and contentious Ministery, there is either a people divided, or else agreeing in ignorance, formality and ungodliness. At least if such a Ministery have been long among them.

And we need no other proof of this, and of the chief cause of the peoples divisions and mistakes, than the accusations and charges of the Ministers against each other. On every side it is the Pastors of the flocks that are accused, by those of the adverse party, as the chief offenders. One side saith, it is you that teach the people errours, and put scruples into their minds, and lead them into contempt of order and authority! And the other side saith, It is you that proudly usurp

usurp authority which Christ never gave you, and lord it over Gods heritage, and by your own inventions lay snares before the people to divide them, and will not suffer them to unite in their proper center, and agree in the primitive simplicity. And that bring the Ministery into hatred and contempt by your cruelty and vicious lives.] And whilest each side is thus accused by the other, they have all the greater cause to suspect themselves: Because it seemeth to be agreed on all hands, that it is the Pastors who are principally in the fault, though it be not agreed what the fault is, nor which party of the Pastors must bear the blame.

And indeed where are there any sects or factions, but there are Ministers that bred them, and that caused them at first, and keep them up? Is it not the Bishops that have caused the long division, between the Greek and Latin Churches? Was it not principally a contention for their interests, which of them should be the greatest (so little doth Christs own decision of that controversie among his Apostles, signifie with those men, who are contending about a successive infallible Judge.) Is it not their Councils and their contentious writings and practises, which have been the grand causes of this woful schism? And are not the dividing snares which cause most of the rest of the Schisms of Christendome, the meer usurpations, and impositions of the Roman Prelates? It was the Bishops of each party, with their Presbyters, who headed the division in the second Council of *Ephesus*, and in the Council of *Ariminum*, and many others: And

by

by them the Heresies of the Arrians, the Nestorians, the Eutychians, &c. with the schisms of the Novarians, Donatists and most others, have been maintained. And among our selves, most parties have their *Leaders*, who first made the *breach* and still *keep it* open. It is therefore but reasonable that we all suspect and search our selves: And perhaps the lot may find out that *Achan* who is thought most innocent, and *Jonah* who is not the worst in the ship, may be the man; and he may be the *Judas* who is last in asking, Master is it I? And it is ten to one but the leaders of every party will be found blame-worthy in part, though not in equality.

Besides all that shall be intimated in the following Directions, these causes of the peoples *weakness* and *Divisions* are so openly manifest in too many Pastors, that they cannot be concealed or excused.

First, there is so much *Ignorance* in many that they are not able judiciously to edifie the flocks; nor to teach sound principles in a suitable manner and method to their hearers. Who can teach others that which they never learned themselves?

Secondly, Too many are strangers to the people whom they teach, and know not the weaknesses of the vulgar, and therefore neither justly resolve their doubts, nor answer their objections, nor indeed speak that language which the people understand. They have been bred from their childhood in the Universities among Schollars, and have little conversed with Plow-men and poor people and ignorant persons, who have
quite

quite other conceptions and expressions than schollars have. Their accurate stiles and well-couched words, and elegant phrases, are most of them like an unknown tongue, to the greatest number of their Auditors. And that which they use as congruous to the matter, is so incongruous to their hearers, that it's little to their benefit.

Thirdly, And some in avoiding this extream, do fall into the contrary; and never go beyond the present understanding of the people, and teach them nothing but what they know already; And hereby they bring themselves into contempt entising the hearers to think that their Teachers, are as ignorant as they, and know no more than they teach: And they tempt the people to be puffed up, and think themselves worthy to be Preachers, because they can do as much and as well as their Teachers use to do.

Fourthly, And how cold and unskilful are many in the application of that Doctrine which they have tolerably opened? And speak the truths of the living God, without any effecting reverence or gravity. And talk as drowsily of the evil of sin, the need of grace, the love of God in Jesus Christ, yea of Death and Judgement, Heaven and Hell, as if it were their design to rock the Auditors asleep, or to make them believe that it is but an histrionical fiction which they act, and that nothing which they say is to be believed! There is no need of any more forcible means to entice men to sin, than to hear it preacht against so coldly: Nor is there need of any more to teach men to set light by Christ and Grace and Heaven it self, than to hear them so heartlesly
commend-

commended: We speak a few good words to the people in a reading tone, like a child that is saying his lesson, as if we believed not our selves; and then we blame the people for their being no more edified by us; and we look they should be much affected with that which never much affected the speakers. If Christ himself, who preached with authority, and used to awaken them, with an [*He that hath ears to hear let him hear*] did yet convert no more than he did, what can we expect upon our drowsie and dry discourses, but drowsiness in the hearers, if not contempt.

Fifthly, And alas the *private work* of the Ministery is done as poorly by too many who do pretty well in publick, as if they knew not that it is any considerable part of their employment; or as if indeed they believed not the immortality and preciousness of souls! And if the praise of men constrained them not to do the publick part somewhat better, they would become contemptible burthens of the Church.

Sixthly, the great duty of Catechizing is so much neglected, that few of the people understand the great fundamental truths; and few are instructed in the true method of the Christian doctrines, who know somewhat of the matter of them. And such defects and languor in the Vital parts, will one time or other appear in the externals.

Seventhly, Formality and imagery choaketh or excludeth the sense, life and power of the most necessary truths. They that teach youth the *words* of the Catechism, do oft content themselves

selves with that much, as if they had made them understanding Christians; and leave them as ignorant and senslefs of the importance of those words, as they were before ever they learnt them. The foresaid unacquaintedness with the people and their weaknesses, doth make many teachers lose their labour; while they measure the common people by themselves, and think that they can understand such words as they themselves can understand: When they little know how utterly ignorant abundance are of the m*t·er, when they have learned to speak all the w rds by rote. Therefore experience hath oft constrained me to say, that after all their study and learning in the Universities, such Pastors as did never familiarly converse with the poor and vulgar of the flocks, and try the exercise of personal instruction and exhortation upon them, are no more to be regarded in many controversies about the Pastoral work and discipline, than an unexperienced Physician, or Chyrurgeon, or Soldier or Pilot in many cases of their professions: Which maketh many learned self-conceited Doctors, become the plagues; while they think themselves the pillars of the Church.

There are no parents or masters but find it presently in their children, how quickly they will learn a Catechism, and therein the Creed, Lords Prayer and Decalogue, while they scarce understand the sense and matter of any of the plainnest words which they have uttered: And we find it is just so with too many of the aged also. And therefore if by other questions and explications, you put them out of their rode, and

teach

teach them not to fix their thoughts upon the matter, as well as on the words, it will all prove but as the teaching of a Parrot, and not of a true believer.

And what I have sa'd of Catechising, is true also of *Prayer* and Confession & every other part of worship: In which the hypocrites part is easie; even the out-side *form* and *lifeless image*; But it is the *inward Life*, the *spirit* and *truth*, which is the excellent, heavenly and difficult part.

Eighthly, And some make a formality and a snare of the gift of extemporary expression; And by a preposterous care to avoid all forms, they teach them not these Catechism forms, with that diligence as the matter doth require: But leave their minds void of those orderly well-setled second notions, which should help the first: And thus while some neglect the *soul or spirit* of Christianity, and others neglect the *form or body* of it; betwixt them both it is too much neglected by almost all.

Ninthly, Too many are meer worldlings, and ungodly self-seekers, and enter upon the Ministery but as a trade to live by, and never had that humble holy mind themselves, which they expect in the people; But as riches, and preferment and honour and ease, are the things which they most seek, so they do proportion and choose the means accordingly; And when they have thus made themselves contemptible, and alienated the hearts of the people from them, they then call them all that passion can suggest, not for their sin against God, but for crossing their carnal ends and interest.

Tenthly, And under all this ignorance, negligence and vice, pride maketh too many of them to be enemies to repentance, & to all that would bring them to it: so that they are not so much offended with the people for their own faults, as for disliking theirs: scarce a drunkard a swearer in all the parish is so impatient of hearing of their sins, as many of these high minded impenitent Ministers. Nay so far are they from enduring to be accounted of as they are, that they expect applause and great veneration, when they deserve not pardon: And they think they are neglected or treated unreverently, if their ignorance be not called wisdome, and their hypocrisie go not for the only piety, and their carnal discourse & conversation, (for which God threatneth their damnation, *Rom.* 8. 5, 6, 7, 8, 13.) be not cloathed with some fair and honourable names. And when they have thus set the people so pernicious an example, they storm against them for not being more obedient to them, than they themselves will be to God; and for rejecting the precepts and reproofs of that Scripture which they have rejected and despised before their faces.

I humbly propound it therefore to my Brethren, that if they have a people who despise their Ministery, and turn away from them, and speak against them, and seek after other teachers; that they would first impartially ask their consciences, [have we given them no cause or occasion of all this? Is it not long of us? Have we so preached, so privately overseen and taught them, and so lived, as that all this confusion will not be justly laid at our doors?] When we have first truly
cleared

cleared things at home, we are the fitter then to expostulate with our people; And when we have pulled out the beam of selfishness, carnality, negligence, and pride out of our own eyes, we may the better see to cast the motes of childish peevishness, and discontent out of the peoples eyes,

---

DIRECT. II.

It is needful to the peoples edification and concord, that their Pastors much excel them in knowledge and utterance, and also in prudence, holiness and heavenliness of mind and life: that so both the reverence of their calling and persons may be preserved, and the people instructed by their examples.

I Doubt not but the ministrations of a weak and of an ungodly Minister, are *valid* and may be *effectual* to the flock; And that the innocent people forfeit not their priviledges in *acceptable worship* and *effectual Sacraments*, though a *wicked Pastor* may forfeit his *own acceptance* and *reward* with God. But yet because there are none of us *so innocent*, whose consciences may not justly tell us that we have deserved to be afflicted in that kind, and because God useth to work by means, and vary the success according to the quality of the means and instruments, we may well conclude

clude that the *Gifts* and *Holiness* of the Pastors is a very excellent and needful help, to the peoples setled *Piety* and *Peace*: And that where this help is wanting, that ordinary means is wanting, by which God useth to convey this blessing.

I have met with many who are either insufficient or ungodly themselves, or are guilty of bringing such into the Churches, who use to make very light of this, and say, God is not tied to mens goodness or abilities in distributing his graces: which is true, but nothing to the purpose: He is not tied by any *force* or *necessity*; nor is he so tied as that he *cannot* do otherwise: But yet this is his ordinary way of working: which hath made it a maxim, that as to means, *Infused graces are obtained in the same way as acquired gifts*: And let the contrary minded answer me these questions.

First, If it be only the *Office* of the Ministery, and not the *Gifts* and *Graces* that are ordinarily needful to their success, why doth Religion decay and perish in all parts of the world, where the Gifts and Graces of the Ministers decay? Why are almost all the Greek Churches, the Armenians, the Russians, the Abassins, so lamentably ignorant? and most of them as vicious as ignorant; in so much that the notorious wickedness of their lives, and contemptibleness of their understandings, doth keep Christianity out of most of the Heathen and Infidel Nations of the world, that are acquainted with them? and keepeth up the reputation of Mahometanism and Heathenism. Is not the experience of all the Christian world a sufficient proof? The Greeks

and

and other such corrupted Churches, have a truly ordained Ministery as well as we, if that were enough to serve the turn.

Secondly, What is more evident among our selves than that Parishes do much vary in piety and concord as their Pastors vary in ability, piety, diligence and fidelity.

Thirdly, Though Parents have all equal authority to instruct and rule their children and families, is any thing more notorious, than that notorious ignorance and impiety prevaileth in most families where the Rulers are ignorant and impious? Yet they have as true a power from God to do their duty, as the Pastor hath to do his: yea and promises from God for the success.

Fourthly, What is the *Office*, but an *Authority* and *Obligation* to do the Ministerial *work*? And will *work* succeed well that is not *done*? Or will it be done by bare *Authority* and *Obligation* to do it? Will it serve to the building of your house, to the conduct of an Army, to the healing of your sores or sicknesses, that you have an Architect, a Captain, a Chyrurgeon, and Physician, whose office is to do these works?

Fifthly, What need men study or bestow so many years at the University, if *Ordination* and *Office* be enough?

Sixthly, Interpreting the Original Text is one part of the Ministerial work: If the bare *Office* without the Tongues, did never make any of you a good Translator and Expositor, why should the bare office serve turn for other parts of the work, without proportionable abilities?

A a 3　　　　　　　Seventh-

Seventhly, Why do you lay so much blame on the Ministers who dissent from you, or that are the teachers of the dissenting people, as if all the divisions were caused by them, if the difference of teachers make no difference in the work and flocks.

Eighthly, Why is it that in most ages of the world, the Pastors of one mind have desired the silencing or deposing of those that were against them, as being injurious to the flocks, if all Ministers be alike to them, what need there so much silencing, imprisoning and banishing as the world hath seen, if the Office alone do make sufficient Pastors?

Ninthly, Why also is there so much difference between the Pastors reputations and their labours when they are dead? Why is the name and works of an *Augustine*, a *Hierome*, a *Basil*, a *Nazianzen*, more honourable than of any other Pastor, who had as true ordination and office as they?

Tenthly, Why should the Kingdome be at so much cost upon the Ministery? And why should one have more maintainance than another? If the Office alone be all thats necessary, one *Abuna* may serve for ordination in all the Empire of *Abassia*, & a few Priests may be had for ten pounds a year, who have the same ordination as the ablest men. But having sufficiently shamed this errour I dismiss it.

If the reverence due to the *Office* be once lost, the labours of all the Ministery will be obstructed: And if only the *Person* lose the reverence of his place, his own labours will be hindered: The

con-

contempt of the *Office*, and so the *whole* Ministery tendeth to *Infidelity* or Atheism: And the contempt of *particular* Ministers, tendeth to *Schism*, and to the ignorance and corruption of their flocks. And though the contempt of the *person* is bad enough of it self, yet if it fall on *many*, and there remain not a considerable number who preserve their necessary reputation, it turneth to the contempt of the Office it self, and consequently of the Gospel.

And it must be *apparent worth*, that must preserve the *persons* honour. The silver lace did make the Apprentices in *Apelles* shop to reverence a foolish gallant a while; but when he began to *talk*, they all fell on laughing at him. Our grave attire will go but a little way, to keep up our reputation, without some better testimony of our worth. An empty head, a stumbling and hesitant tongue, dry and dull and disorderly preaching; and senseless, cold or confused praying, a vain and frothy kind of talk; a common and carnal conversation; all these or any one of these, will more abate the reverence of our persons, than the title of Doctors, or the length of our clothing, or the enlarging of the philacteries, will advance it. *Math.* 23. 5. *Mark.* 12. 40. *Luk.* 20. 47. It is their double measure of the spirit of wisdome, and Goodness, which must procure a double measure of honour to the Ministery.

And if we excel them never so much in *Learning*, it will not suffice unless we excel them in our proper Ministerial gifts of preaching exhortation and prayer, which are the works of our

in more orderly, clear and congruous expressions than the Pastor can, it tendeth to bring down the honour of the Pastor, in the peoples esteem. Some think to repair this, by casting out all prayer except that which is read out of a book or recited by memory alone; that so there may be no observable difference of mens abilities: But this is so far from curing the peoples disease, that it increaseth it: And they still say, all this is no more than we can do our selves, or than a child of ten years old can do. And if you extend the case to all other parts of the Ministery, where the reason is the same, they will say [what reverence is due to such? or why should we maintain & honour men, for doing no more than our children can do?

And the Popish devise, to make a disparity, by keeping the people in ignorance, is the basest and most pernicious plot of all. When the Pastors instead of excelling the people, would keep down the people from increasing in their knowledge and expression, this is so notorious a discovery of *envy, pride* and *malignity* conjunct, that the people presently fly from such Pastors, as supposing them to be ministers of the Devil, because they see them bear his image. What do we teach them for, if we would not have them learn and profit? What greater honour can a Teacher have, than to make his Schollars as wise and able as himself? Every one who is a child of Light, and believeth in him who is the Light of the world, will suspect that man to be a Minister

ster of the Prince of darkness, who is a malicious adversary of Light. This is that brand of the *Roman* iniquity, the hindering men from the reading of the Scriptures, and magnifying ignorance, which maketh men so commonly think them to be the *Ecclesia malignantium* and the Antichristian brood. Thus Cardinal *Wolsey* declaimed against the Art of Printing, as that which would take down the honour and profit of the Priesthood, by making the people as wise as they. It is not by keeping *them down*, or *envying* their *abilities*, that we must keep our distance from the people; but by *rising higher* our selves, and excelling them in all ministerial gifts. Else why should we be thought any fitter to be their Teachers and Guides, than they to be ours?

Yea though we excel them in all these abilities, it will not serve turn to the ends of our Ministery, unless we also excel them in holiness and every Christian vertue. The Devil *knoweth* more than Ministers: And if he have a tongue to speak he wanteth not utterance. He is the most excellent and honourable, who is likest to God, and hath most of his image. And God hath more proposed himself to mans imitation in *Goodness*, than in *Greatness*: He hath not said, *Be Great, for the Lord your God is Great:* but [*walk in the Light, as he is in the Light,* 1 *John* 1. 7. and *Be holy for the Lord your God is holy,* 1 *Pet.* 1. 16. *Lev.* 10. 7. & 19. 2. & 21. 8. To be *Great* and *Bad* is to be *able* to do mischief: To be Learned ingenious and Bad, is to be *wise* to do *evil*, and a *crafty* and *subtle* instrument of the devil, *Jer.* 4. 22. It was no laudable description
of

of *Elymas*, *Act.* 13. 8. 10. [*O full of subtlety and all mischiefs, thou child of the devil and enemy of all righteousness, wilt thou not cease to pervert the right wayes of the Lord?* Satan would never transform himself into an Angel of *Light*, nor his Ministers into the Ministers of *Righteousness*; nor would Pharisees and Hypocrites cover oppression by *long prayers*, if *Light, Righteousness*, and *long prayers*, were not laudable in themselves, and necessary in the preachers of the word of God, and had not a goodness in them capable of being a cloak to their iniquity. 2 *Cor.* 11.14, 15. *Mat.* 23. 14. *God is Light.* 1 *Joh.* 1. 5. And *God is Holy:* If therefore Satan or any hypocrite would credit their falshood and wickedness, they must pretend to *Light* and *Holiness*: And he that will keep up the true honour of his Ministery, and be accepted with God, and reverenced by good men; must do it by *real Light* and *Holiness.* An ungodly Minister hath a radicated enmity to the the holy doctrine which he preacheth, and to the holy duties and life which he exhorteth the people to: And how well, how sincerely, how readily, how faithfully, they are like to do the work which they are enimies to, you may easily judge. *The carnal mind is enmity to God: for it is not subject to his law, nor indeed can be.* Rom. 8. 6,7,8. I know that they are not enemies to the *honour* nor to the *maintenance:* and therefore may force themselves to do much of the outside of the work: But where there is an inward enmity to the *life* and *ends* of it, we can expect but a formal, unwilling, and unconstant discharge of such unpleasing duty. *Truth* is for *Goodness*: The

Know-

Knowledge which maketh you not *Good* is lost, and hath mist its end. If therefore your Love to God and man, your mortification & unblameableness of life, your heavenly mindedness, be no greater than the peoples (or perhaps much less) do not wonder if you lose your honour with them, and if you grow contemptible in their eyes. *Mal.* 1. 10. 14. *I have no pleasure in you saith the Lord—— Cursed be the deceiver which hath in his flock a male and voweth and sacrificeth to the Lord a corrupt thing.* Mal. 2. *And now O ye Priests, this commandement is for you: If ye will not hear, and if ye will not lay it to heart, to give glory to my name, I will send a curse upon you —— The Law of truth was in* Levi's *mouth, and iniquity was not found in his lips: He walked with me in peace and equity, and did turn away many from iniquity! For the Priests lips should keep knowledge, and they should seek the law at his mouth, for he is the messenger of the Lord of Hosts: But ye are departed out of the way; ye have caused many to stumble at the Law, ye have corrupted the Covenant of* Levi, *saith the Lord of hosts: Therefore also have I made you contemptible and base before all the people, according as ye have not kept my wayes, but have been partial in the Law.*

1 Sam. 2. 17. 24, 30. *The sin of the young men was very great, before the Lord; for men abhorred the offering of the Lord: —— Ye make the Lords people to transgress —— Wherefore kick ye at my sacrifice, and at my offering, which I have commanded —— I said indeed that thy house —— should walk before me for ever: But now the Lord saith, Be it far from me; for them that honour me, I will honour, and they that despise me shall be lightly esteemed.*

If as *Moses* you stand nearer to God than the people do, you must be so much holier than they, and your faces must shine with the beams of God in the peoples eyes. They that *with open face behold in Christ as in a glass the glory of the Lord are changed into the same image from glory to glory, as by the spirit of the Lord*, 2 Cor. 3. 7, 17, 18.

If therefore by your low and common parts, and carnal lives, you make your selves contemptible, instead of exclaiming against the people, cry out against your selves, and lament your sins; and the more you have aggravated the crimes of Schism and other errors in your flock, the more penitently bewail your sin which caused it, and remember that you have aggravated your own transgression. If you are children in parts and goodness your selves, you are unfit either to upbraid the people with their childish weaknesses, or to cure them.

DIRECT. III.

In all your publick Doctrine and private Conference, inculcate still the necessary conjunction of Holiness and Peace; and of the Love of God and Man; And make them understand that Love is their very Holiness, and the sum of their Religion; the end of Faith, the heart of Sanctification, and the fulfilling of the Law: And that as Love to God uniteth us to Him, so Love to man, must unite us to one another; And that all Doctrine or practice is against God and against Christ and against the great work of the Spirit, and is enmity to the Church and to mankind, which is against Love and Unity. Press these things on them all the year, that your hearers may be bred up and nourished with these principles from their youth.

IF ever the Church be recovered of its wounds, it must be by the peaceable *Dispositions* of the Pastors and people. And if ever men come to a *peaceable Disposition*, it must be by *peaceable Doctrine* and principles: And if ever men come to *peaceable Principles*, it must be by the full and frequent explication of the *nature, pre-eminence, necessity* and *power* of *Love*: That they may hear of it *so much,* and *so long,* till love be made their *Religion,* in the infancy and youth of their Religion, and by learning it betimes as the sum of *Godliness* and *Christianity.* And if ever they come to this, the *Aged experienced* ripe and mellow sort of Ministers and private Christians, must instil it into *Schollars* and into the *younger sort of Ministers*, that they may have nothing so common in their ears and in their studies, as *Uniting-Love*: That they may be taught to know that *God is Love, and that he that dwelleth in Love dwelleth in God, and God in him.* 1 *Joh.* 4. 16. And that the love of God, doth ever work towards his image in man: 1 *Joh.* 4. 7, 11, 12, 20. And that *all men as men* have *some* of his Image in their *Nature*, as they are *Intellectual, Free Agents exalted above the bruits.* Gen. 9. 6. And therefore we must Love *men as men*, and Love *Saints* as *Saints*; That it is *Love to God and man*, which is the true state of *Holiness*, and the *New creature*, and which Christ came to recover lapsed man to, and which the Holy Ghost is sent to work, and all the means of grace are intended and fitted for, and must be used for, or they are misused. In a word, that *FAITH WORKING BY LOVE*; or *LOVE* and *THE WORKS OF LOVE KINDLED BY THE SPIRIT BY FAITH IN CHRIRT*; is the sum of all the Christian Religion. *Gal.* 5. 6, 13, 22. 1 *Tim.* 1. 5

He that crieth up *Holiness* and *Zeal*, without a due commemoration of *Love* & *Peace*, doth first deceive

Doctrines of Love and Concord. 235

deceive the hearers about that very *Holiness* and *Zeal* which he commendeth, whilest he lamely and so falsly representeth and describeth it; and doth not make them know how much of Holiness consisteth in *Love*; nor that *true zeal* is *Love it self* in its *fervour* and intense degree: And so people are enticed to think that *Holiness* is nothing but the passions of *fear* and *grief*, and earnest expressions in preaching and praying, or scrupulousness and singularity about some controverted things, or some other thing than indeed it is. And they are tempted to think that Christian *zeal* is rather the violence of partial passions, and the fervor of wrath, and the making things sinful which God forbiddeth not, than the fervors of Love to God and man. And when the mind is thus mocked with a *false Image* of Holiness and Zeal, it is cast into a sinful mold, and engaged in the pursuit of an erroneous dangerous course of life; And at last it cometh to an enmity & contempt of that which is *Holiness* and *Zeal* indeed: For it accounteth *Love* but a *Moral-vertue* (which they ignorantly take for a diminutive title of the great and primitive duties required by the light and law of nature it self.) And *zealous love* is accounted by them but a carnal and selfish compliance and temporizing, and a pleasing of men instead of God; And a *zealous* promoting of *Unity* and *Peace*, is taken but for a cowardly neutrality and betraying of some truth, which should be earnestly contended for.

And on the other side they that preach up *Love* to man, and *Peace* and *Concord* without putting *first* the *Love of God*, and a Holy and Heavenly
mind

mind and life, they will cheat the poor ignorant carnal people, by making them believe that God and Heaven may be forgotten, and good neighbourhood to each other is all that is needful to make them happy.

And they will tempt the more religious sort to sin more against Love and *Peace* than before: Because they will think that it is but a confederacy for Satan against Christ, and a submission to the wills of proud Usurpers, to strengthen their worldly interest against godliness, which these preachers mean when they plead for peace. And thus as I have known ungodly Preachers by crying down *Schism*, bring *Schism* into request, while it was no such thing as real Schism, which they meant in their exclamations (till at last the true eruption of schism with its monstrous effects made good people see that such an odious sin there is;) Even so I have known that a carnal Preacher, contemning Holiness, and crying up *Love* and *Peace*, hath tempted the people to have too light thoughts of *Love* and *Peace*, (because it was but a confederacy in sin with a neglect of godliness, which the preacher seemed to cry up) till riper knowledge better taught good people to perceive, that *Love* and *Peace* are more Divine and excellent things, than carnal preachers or hearers can imagine. The wisdom from above is first *pure* then *peaceable* : Let it therefore be a true *conjunction* of *Holiness* and *Peace* which you commend.

DIRECT.

DIRECT. IV.

If others shew their weakness by any unwarrantable singularities or divisions, shew not your greater weakness, by passions, impatiency or uncharitable censures or usage of them: especially when any self-interest doth provoke you.

NOne usually are so spleenishly impatient at the weakness of Dissenters or Separatists as the Pastors are? And what is the cause? Is it because they abound most in Love to the souls of those who offend, or them who are endangered by them? If so, I have no more to say to such. But when we see that the *Honour* and *Interest* of the Pastors is most deeply concerned in the business, and that they are carried by their *impatiency* into more want of Charity, than the other express by their *separations*: and when we see that they well enough bear with themselves in such sins as this, or in others as great; and that they can bear with as great sins in the people with too much patience, when their own interest concurreth not to raise their passions, in such cases we have reason enough to fear, lest pride and selfishness have too great a part, in much that is said and done against schisms in the world.

Is it a greater shame for *children* to cry and wrangle with the Nurse and one another, or for the *Nurse* or *Parents* to go to law with them for it, or to hate them, or turn them out of doors?

Is it a fault for *Children* to be so impatient as to cry and quarrel? And is it not a greater fault in *Parents* that pretend to greater wisedome, to be impatient with them for it? I know you will say that *Parents must not be so patient with sin, as to leave their children uncorrected*: But, I answer, correction must not be the effect of *impatiency*, but of *Love* and *Wisedome* and dislike of sin, and must be chosen and measured in order to the cure of it. Its one thing to be angry for God against sin, and its another thing to be angry for our selves against the crossing of our wills and interests: And its one thing to correct so as tendeth to a cure; And another thing to be revenged or do mischief, or to cast out of doors. Are not you guilty of *Ministerial weaknesses* in preaching and praying, and of many omissions in your private oversight? And do you think that it is meet for the people therefore to revile you with odious titles, and stir up the Magistrate against you for your infirmities.

Is it seemly for them who are the Fathers of the flock and should excel the people in Love and lowliness, in patience and gentleness and meekness, to be so proud and passionate, as to storm against the most conscientious persons, if they do but *set light by us*, and cast off *our* Ministery, though perhaps they hear and submit to *others* who are as able and as faithful and more profitable to them than we? When we can easilier bear with a swearer or a drunkard or the families that are prayerless and ungodly, than with the most Religious, if they do not choose *our* Ministery, but prefer some others before us as more edifying? When we can bear with them that have no understanding or seriousness in Religion at all, but make the world or their lusts their idols, but cannot bear with the weak irregularities of the most upright and devout? If they were never so irregular in preferring *us* before *others*, and in leaving others to *follow us*, we can easily bear with them, and think their disorders may be well excused: And to shew the height of our pride, we still are confident (whether we are uppermost or undermost, whether we have publick liberty or are forbidden to preach) that we are the persons only that are in the *right*, and therefore that all are in the *right* that follow us, and all are in the wrong that *turn* away from us; That it is *Unity* and *duty* to follow *us* and adhere to *us*, and all are Schismaticks who forsake us and choose *others*. And thus the *Selfishness* and *Pride* of the *Pastors*, making an imprudent and impatient stir against all who dislike them, and applauding all how bad soever, who adhere to them and follow them, is as great a cause of the disorders of the Church, as the weakness and errours of the people.

DIRECT. V.

Distinguish between those who separate from the Universal Church, or from all the Orthodox or purest and Reformed parts of it, and those who only forsake the Ministery of some one person, or sort of persons, without refusing Communion with the rest.

AS many occasions may warrant a removal from a *particular* Church, but nothing can excuse a *separation* from the *Universal Church*, so he that separateth only from some particular *Churches*, and yet is a member of the *Universal Church*, may also be a member of Christ and be saved. He may be a Christian who is no member of *your flock*, yea or of any particular Church: But he is *no Christian* who is no member of the *Universal* Church. *Paul* and *Barnabas* may in the heat of a difference part from *one another*, and yet neither of them part from *Christ* or the *Church Universal*.

I do not excuse the fault of them who sin against any *one Church* or *Pastor*. But I would not have the Pastors therefore sin as much, by making their fault *greater* than it is; nor to suffer their own interest partially to call men Schismaticks or Separatists, in a sense for which they have no ground. If they can learn more by another Minister than by me, what reason have I to be offended at their edification, though perhaps some
infirmity

infirmity of judgement may appear in it. A true mother that knoweth her child is like to thrive better by a Nurses milk than by her own, will be so far from hatred or envy either at the nurse or child, that she will consent and be thankful, and pay the nurse. *Solomon* made it the sign of the *false mother*, that would bear the *dividatur*, the hurt of the child for her own commodity; and of the *true mother*, that she had rather *lose her commodity* than the *child* should suffer. And *Paul* giveth God thanks that *Christ was preached*, though it was by them that did it in *strife*, and *envy*, *to add affliction to his bonds*. Phil. 1. He is not worthy of the name of a Physician, who had rather the patients health were deplorate, than that he should be healed by another who is preferred before him. If I knew that man by whom the salvation of my flock were like to be more happily promoted than by me (what ever infirmity of theirs might be the cause) I should think my self servant of Satan the envious enemy of souls, if I were against it.

DIRECT. VI.

Distinguish between those who deny the Being of the Church or Ministery, from which they separate: and those who remove only for their own edification, as from a weaker or worse Minister, and from a Church more culpable and less pure.

FOR these last are not properly *Separatists* in a full sense: Though they think it *unlawful* to joyn with *you*, as supposing that you impose some sin upon them, or that you deprive them of discipline or some ordinance of God; Whether they be in the right or in the wrong, yet still they hold *inward Communion* with you, in *faith* and *love* and in the *same species* of *worship*. And this is such a communion as we hold with many forreign Churches, with whom we have no local present communion.

DIRECT.

DIRECT. VII.

Distinguish between those who hold it simply unlawful to have communion with you; and those who only hold it unlawful to prefer your Assemblies before those which they judge more pure; but hold it lawful to communicate with you occasionally; yea and statedly when they can have no better.

I Excuse not all such from the guilt of all sin herein. For if they prefer that Church or Ministery which they should not prefer, it is their sin. But it is not *that sin* which of old hath been called *Separation* and *Schism*. While a man is free, if he love himself we cannot wonder if he choose that society and Ministery where he thinketh his salvation may be best furthered and secured: All sober Divines who write of the *Ministery* and of *company*, do declare that the difference between *good* and *bad*, yea *good* and *better*, in both these, is of so great importance, that all wise men should be very careful of their choice. If we may without reproach be allowed to be cautelous what wife we choose, what Master or servants, what house, what neighbourhood. what soil, what air; Much more may we be allowed to be cautelous what *Church* and *Ministers* we joyn with; And if we are allowed to choose what Physician we will commit our health and lives to, and are not constrained to use one that we judge to be ignorant or false, surely it would be no heinous schism, if the like liberty be granted and used for our souls. The very Papists give the people liberty to choose their *Confessours*, without removing their dwellings for it: And surely my conscience would tell me at last that I am very selfish and proud if I thought none so fit to instruct and edifie any of the people as my self? No nor *tollerable* in endeavouring it. Have I not heard many, do I not know many, who preach more convincingly, more plainly and more powerfully than I? And what harm is it then if the people hear them? So Christ be preached, and the people instructed, sanctified and saved, what if it be done by another rather than by me? Have not I liberty to do my best? Shall I be an envier at the Gospel and its success! God forbid that I or any faithful Minister, should ever be guilty of so odious a sin! I speak without respect of persons: It is easie and usual both in publick allowed Churches, and in privater assemblies, to preach *our selves* while we seem to be preaching Christ; and by our *perverse preaching* to *seek disciples* and *esteemers* for *our selves*, when we are preaching up self-denial, and seem to be most zealous for the saving of souls. *Act.* 20. 10, 31.

DIRECT.

DIRECT. VIII.

Remember Christs interest in the weakest of his servants, and do nothing to them which Christ will not take well.

THink well how far he beareth with them, and how far he owneth them, and how tender he is of them in all their weaknesses. If it be a *member* of Christ that you are offended with, though you must never the more love the fault, yet remember how you must *use the person*. It was not for nothing that he setteth *little children* before his disciples, when he would teach them not only humility, but respect and patience towards each other by his example. *Mat.* 18. And how terrible a passage is it *v.* 5, 6. *Whoso shall receive one such little child in my name, receiveth me: But who so shall offend one of these little ones, that believe in me, it were far better for him that a milstone were hanged about his neck and that he were drowned in the depth of the sea.* And *Math.* 25. *What is done to one of the least of his brethren* (for so he calleth them) Christ judgeth as done unto himself. He will not break the bruised Reed, nor quench the smoaking flax, until he bring forth judgement unto victory. Remember but Christs interest in them and affections to them, and imitate his tenderness and pitty.

DIRECT. IX.

Distinguish between weakness of Gifts and of Grace, and remember that many that are weak in the understanding of matters of Church-order, may yet be stronger in grace than you.

HE is the strongest Christian and the most Godly man who hath the greatest *Love to God*, and heavenliness of mind and life: And this may be the case of many a one, who by some errour about the circumstances of discipline and worship, is yet a trouble to the Church. He that offendeth you by his mistake and unwarrantable singularity, though he be weak in judgement in that point, and perhaps in many other controversies, may yet be a far stronger Christian, than I who see his errour: He may have more Love to God and man, more humility and self-denial, more fear of sinning, and more fitness to die, and more heavenly desires, and patience in tribulation. Let us therefore value men according to the Image of God upon them, and not despise them as weak in grace, because they are weak in this point of knowledge: Though still their errours are not to be owned.

DIRECT.

DIRECT. X.

Remember the common calamity of the Church and of all mankind: What strange disparity there is in mens understandings! and how the Church on earth is a Hospital of diseased souls, and no one man perfectly healed in this life.

WHo can say I have made my heart clean? *Prov.* 20. 9. He that is kept from *presumptuous sins*, and heartily prayeth and *striveth* against his *known infirmities*, and is desirous to know his unknown sins that he may avoid them, hath attained so far as to be justified by Christ, and loved of those who love as Christ doth. *Psal.* 19. *Joh.* 3. 19. 20. *Seneca* could say that to carp at that fault which was every mans fault, is not to reprove an offender, but to reproach humane nature and all mankind: Christians indeed must lament even the vices which are common to depraved nature, but it is with a common lamentation, which falleth on one man no more than on another. Even as we lament mortality, which is the common punishment of mankind. But he that would have punishment inflicted for a fault which is common to all, would have all men punished or is partial.

If our infirmities are not all the very same, yet it is certain that we are all infirm. Yea we are all of imperfect, and erroneous understandings, though all err not the same errour. And
we

we are every man certain in general that we have errours, though no man know in particular which be his own errours! (For it is a contradiction to say that while I err in judgment I know my errour) so that other men know our errours when we know them not our selves, as we know theirs which are unknown to them. For as all have their *common defects*, so most men have their *peculiar* defects and errours, and others excel those persons in some particulars, who excel them in almost all the rest. Therefore if no errour were to be tollerated, no man were to be tollerated: And the wisest in the world must be numbered with the intollerable as well as the rest. And every one that punisheth others, must be conscious of the same intollerable evil in *himself*, and that nothing but *power* exempteth him from the same suffering, and therefore none but the King should escape. *In many things we offend all: Therefore be not many Masters* (too *imperious* or too *censorious* towards *dissenters* and the *infirm*) *left ye receive the greater condemnation.* Jam. 3. 1, 2.

GOD who is *One*, hath made the creatures MANY and divers: And the further they go from *Him*, the more they run into *multiplicity* and *diversity*: It is admirable in *Nature* to see that among the millions of persons in the world, there are no two that differ not sufficiently to be discernable from each other: And among the bruits and inanimates it is so too: Among horses and oxen and sheep and all creatures, yea though *non ovum ovo similius* be a proverb, yet there are no two that do not differ: No nor among the millions of stones which lye scattered over the surface

in all things of the same opinions and apprehensions: No nor any one man who is in all things long of the same apprehensions and opinions with himselfe: Nor is there any man whose *thoughts* and *affections* do perfectly consent with themselves in *matter* and *order*, any two hours in all his life. And if *multiplicity* and *diversity* have so much cause in nature, how much more must needs be added by the common *corruption* and *pravity* of nature? When all mankind hath so much *ignorance* of the mysteries of Religion, and so many degrees of enmity and unsuitableness to holy things, a great difference of judgement is an unavoidable consequent of this.

And mens various *educations* and *converse*, and *employments* must needs cause a great variety of apprehensions: As their *nature* so their *education* may agree in some *generals*: But there are no two persons at age in the world, whose *educations* have been the same in all *particulars*. Though they were children of the same parents, and bred in the same *house*, and *time*, yet all that they have *seen* and *heard* and medled with hath not been in all points just the same: the same in matter, and time and order and all circumstances. And we see what great diversity of judgements any one of these doth daily cause. To have parents of several minds and tempers: To be bred in families where there is great diversity of knowledge and practise: To live among company of contrary principles and practise: when one man
heareth

heareth *one thing* talk'd of and maintain'd in his daily converse, and another the contrary: When one hath a teacher of one opinion and another of another: Or one hath a *teacher* that is cold, and another one that is fervent; one a judicious one, another a rash and intemperate one; what diversity of apprehensions may arise from any one of these?

And so there may from variety of *passions* of the mind through a diversity of bodily temperatures: One that is naturally *fearful* is apt to apprehend a thousand things as *terrible*, and consequently to be filled with scruples, and to run away from *doctrines* and practises as *dangerous*, where another doth apprehend no danger. And one that is dark, or incredulous, or rash, or stupid, or hardened by any sinful course, is apt to conceive that he is safe in every dangerous way, and to sleep quietly at the brink of death and hell, and to laugh at them that tell him of his peril: As men sit under the same instructions with variety of affections; of fear or hope, of Love or hatred, of joy or sorrow, so variously are they disposed to apprehend what they hear, seeing *recipitur ad modum recipientis*.

And variety of Gods disposing providences must needs also have some such effect. While one is rich and another is poor; one hath crosses of divers sorts, and another hath prosperity; one is full and another is hungry; one is observed, admired and honoured, and another is taken little notice of, or is vilified and despised; One hath many friends and another many enemies: One hath friends that are kind and constant, and
the

Causes of diversities of judgements. 351

the other such as are unkind and mutable; One is preferred by Rulers, and the other is ruined or oppressed; All these will occasion variety of apprehensions: As it was with the Lady who coming in very cold, in a frosty day, pitied the naked beggars at the door; but when she was well warmed chid them away: We all find that our apprehensions are very apt to vary in sickness from what they were in health; and in poverty from what they were in plenty; and when we are angred, displeased or abused, from what they were when we were pleased: Yea when we have but read a lively book, or heard a lively Sermon, from what they were before our affections were so excited.

Also variety of *Temptations* may occasion great variety of apprehensions: When one mans temptations are all alluring, to lust, or gaming or stage-playes, or Romances, or drunkenness, or gluttony, or pastime, and anothers temptations are all to melancholly, and inordinate austerities and despair; When one man is tempted to errours of one kind, and another to the contrary. Even he that overcometh in the main, yet seldome so far conquereth as to receive no misimpression upon his mind.

Moreover variety of *Callings, studies* and *employments* occasioneth variety of apprehensions; A mans mind is much wrought upon by the business and objects which he is daily conversant about: And therefore we find that usually the Courtier, the Souldier, the Sea-man, the Citizen and the Country-man much differ in their apprehensions. And usually (though not every
indivi-

individual yet) as to the *most part*, all men are *wisest* in their *own professions*: Lawyers are wisest in matters of Law and Divines in matters of Divinity. Opportunities of *study* and *instruction* make exceeding great differences in the world. The Lawyer and Physician perhaps may on the by, have bestowed a few years time in Divinity, in the midst of other interrupting studies: When the Divine hath studied almost all his life, and drawn out his meditations in one uninterrupted thred. And so we discern that Lawyers and Physicians have oft different apprehensions, of matters of doctrine, worship and discipline, from those of the best Divines.

And diversity of *Interests* maketh no small difference of apprehensions. And those that are advantaged by their helps and studies may be disadvantaged by their interests. And therefore we say the *Magistrate* and the *subject*, the *Lawyer* and the *Divine*, the *Prelate* and the *Presbyterian*, the Ppist and the *Protestant* (both *Prince*, *Prelates* and *People*) so strangely differ in their thoughts; that one *seemeth certain* of that which another seemeth *certain* to be false; and one ventureth his salvation on that, which another ventureth his salvation against. *Interest* worketh *secretly*, and too much with the best; but openly and predominantly with the worst.

And then the interest and opinion of the several Kingdomes, Churches, Pastors, parties or Sects which men are related to, or are engaged with, doth strongly tend to different apprehensions in all matters which those interests are concerned in. And many very good men, think, that

that *publick interest* may be allowed much power upon their minds, though *private* and *personal* must be denied. Is it not a wonder to see, not only that almost all *Christians* are incorporated into one sect or party or other, but how easily the inconsiderable reasons of their party can prevail with them, and how hardly the better reasons of their adversaries, seem to them of any weight or worth? Not only the parties of Papists and Protestants, Lutherans and Reformed, &c. shew this; but in the same Church the Regulars and Seculars, the Bishops and the Jesuits, the Dominicans and Jesuits, the Thomists, Scotists, &c. declare it. And the difference made by *natural capacities* is yet more than all this. When one man is born to a duller understanding, and another hath a quick and clear apprehension; All that these men read and hear and meditate on, is like to make different impressions on their minds. And this is the greatest thing of any one, which maketh many controversies endless, and maketh both Divines and people run away from one another as dangerously erroneous: If a few men have clearer understandings than the duller and unstudied sort, they are like to be the minor part: For the dull and slothful (and yet self-conceited) will ever be the greater part, many to one, till the golden age return. And when all the world feeleth the consequents of this difference, can we doubt of it, or so far dote, as to think it possible to cure it.

Yet the various degrees of the *Grace of God*, do certainly also make great variety of apprehensions. When God giveth to some those true illumi-

illuminations, those thirsting desires after truth, those heart-experiences, those delightful relishes, those powerful effects and victories, which he giveth not to others, they are made to differ and must needs have different apprehensions of such things. In which sense Christ saith, that he came not to send *peace but division*, that is, to be such an object, and preach so holy a doctrine, and give such *grace*, as would *occasion divisions*, by making his sanctified ones differ from the world, and occasioning the irritation of the worlds malignity.

And indeed the grand difference between the seed of the woman and of the serpent, the holy and the carnal seed, is that which is the root of the greatest and sorest divisions in the world; which will never be reconciled till Christ at the day of judgement shall say to one part, *Come ye blessed*, and to the other. *Go ye cursed: For the carnal mind is enmity against God, and is not subject to his law, nor indeed can be (in sensu composito)* Rom. 8. 6, 7, 8. It was not for nothing that God permitted that great eruption of it, in the first man that ever was born into the world, against his innocent brothers life, on the bare account of their *religious sacrifices*! And the *Cainites* are still too strong for *Abel's* successors, and too numerous. And why did he *kill his brother?* But *because his own works were evil* and his *brothers righteous*. Gen. 4. 10, 11. 1 Joh. 3. 12. And as *Paul* saith of the two sons of *Abraham, as he that was born of the flesh, persecuted him that was born, after the spirit, even so it is now.* Gal. 4. 29. For the *flesh fighteth against the spirit and the spirit against the flesh,*

flesh, *and these are contrary the one to the other*, Gal. 1.17. And that which is *born of the flesh is flesh, and that which is born of the spirit is spirit.* Joh. 3. 6. And *they that are of the flesh do savour mind or understand the things of the flesh, and they that are after the spirit do mind the things of the spirit.* Rom. 8. 5, 6. Our heavenly teacher told his *disciples*, that if they were of the world the world would love them; but because they are not of the world, but he had chosen them out of the world, the world would hate them (even as it hated him.) *Joh.* 15. 18, 19, 24, 25. *Joh.* 17. 14. And every *one that doth evil hateth the light.* *Joh.* 3. 19, 20. Nothing then can be *surer* or *plainer* to a believer, than that there will be still as great divisions and diversity of apprehensions as radicated enmity can breed.

And (to prevent many objections) let these three things be noted.

First, That this grand difference which lieth in the greatest matters, in head and heart, must needs have influence upon abundance of inferiour controversies; Both as the *Persons* and *main cause* are concerned in them. Reason and experience have put this past controversie.

Secondly, That this doth not concern only the *visible Church* and the *world*, but the *visible Church within it self*: For all the *Hypocrites* and *carnal* worshippers, have still the *Cainish serpentine Nature*: Yea those that by advantages and interest are brought over to the *Orthodox* as well as *Christian* side. And it is a happy Church where the *Hypocrites* are not the greater part: And it is neither great Learning, nor degrees, nor the Pa-

stroll

storal office, nor the profession of the highest zeal, which will serve turn to cure the *carnal enmity*, without the sanctifying spirit of grace. So that when controversies arise, we *ee not* in the *hypocrites* that *carnal mind*, which in the strictest profession, or greatest learning, or most venerable function, will work against the interest of holiness: But we are sure that *there it is*, though we know not the persons in whom, but by the full effects.

Thirdly, And note also that there is a mixture or remnant of this unhappy root and principle even in the *sanctified themselves*. And it is hard in a controversie to *perceive in our selves*, much more in *others*, how much our judgements may be moved by this party; and what influence it may have into our conclusions.

So that all this maketh it but too manifest, what a certainty there is of perpetual differences in the Church, upon all these foresaid accounts.

Add also this great and unavoidable cause, that one *errour leadeth in another*: And no man being without some; and every one being *generative*, and inferring more, what will it come to when all those also shall have their off-spring? and the further they go, the more they will increase and multiply?

And as the judgement by *one* is laid open to another (even as *truth* inferreth *truth*) so the *Will* is engaged, and espouseth mens own opinions as their interest; which maketh them stretch their wits in study to maintain what once they have received and asserted: And alas how often have I heard

Causes of different judgements. 357

heard wise and reverend persons cry out against this pride and partiality in others, who in their next discourse or the same, have shamefully shewed it in themselves, making much of their own inconsiderable reasonings, and vilitying cogent evidence against them; and being so intent on their own inventions and cause, that they could scarce have patience to hear another speak; And when they have heard him, their first words shew, that they never well weighed the strength of his arguments, but were all the while thinking what to say against him, or how to go on as they had begun.

Lastly (not to run into any more causes) there is an universal lamentable cause of differences, that almost all people naturally are apt *to be very confident of all their own apprehensions*, And very few have any *due suspicion* of their *own* opinions; or an understanding submission to wiser men. Yea boyes (that are once past their Tutors dictates) and the weakest women, are usually as confident that they are in the right, as the most learned and experienced persons. Yea none are so apt to be too doubtful and diffident of their own understandings as the Learned who are next the highest form: For they have knowledge enough to know what can be objected against them, and to see an hundred difficulties, which the ignorant never saw. So that the more *weak & worthless* and erroneous any ones judgment is, usually the more furious are they in their prosecution of it, as if all were most *certain truth* which they apprehend: These are the boldest both in *schisms* and *persecutions*; as being so sure that their conceits are right, that they dare *censure* or *separate* or *scorn* or *despise*, or *afflict* dissenters.

It is a common thing to hear religious people *speak* meanly and humbly of their own understandings in the *general*; But when it cometh to *particulars*, it is the rarest part of humility in the world to find: . Very few do shew any competent *modesty* (except the grosly ignorant who have no *pretence* to wisdome:) What abundance of good people of the darker sort, have I been fain to rebuke for their *over-valuing me* and *my understanding*; who when I have but crost *their opinions* about any thing which most groundlesly, they took for a duty or a sin, have held as fast their vain conceits, and made as much of their most senseless reasonings, and as passionately and confidently rejected the most unquestionable proof which I have offered them, as if they had been *infallible*, and had taken me for an errant fool.

And this is not the case of one or two Sects only, but *naturally* of *almost all men*, till God hath taught them that rare part of humility to have *Humble Understandings*, and low thoughts of their own judgements, and a due suspicion of their apprehensions.

And their cure is the harder because they know not how to have a humble suspition of themselves, without running into the contrary extream of scepticism, and being cold and unfaithful to the truth; They know not how to hold fast that which *is good*; and to be constant in religion, without holding fast all which they have once *conceited* to be good, and being constant in their errour:

Especi-

Especially when *good* or *evil* is voted to them by that party whose piety they most esteem and reverence.

Nor is this a *Religious* distemper only, but it is so natural to mankind, that even in *common matters* neighbours and neighbours, masters and servants, husband and wife, and almost all, have a strange diversity of apprehensions: One thinks that this is the best way, and another that the other is best; and let them reason and wrangle it out never so long, usually each party still holdeth his own, and hardly yieldeth to anothers reasons.

And when they *do yield*, they are so unhappy that they are as like to yield to one more *erroneous* than themselves, and to change into a *worse* opinion, as to yield to the truth. For commonly, *Appearance, Advantage, Interest*, and a taking tone and voice, do more with them than solid evidence of truth.

Out of all this, if you infer a necessity of *Government*, so do I. But if a necessity of *force and rigor*, think on it again, and first hear what I shall further say: And consider what I have said already. Distinguish between the *common frailties* of *mankind*, and *special enormities*: And forget not that you are *men* and live among men: And let not men be cast out for *Original sin*; nor punish a few for that which is common to all the world; Nor condemn not your selves in condemning others. Of which I further add:

DIRECT.

DIRECT. XI.

Evermore distinguish between the necessary truths and duties, and those which are not of necessity; and between the Tollerable and the intollerable errours: And never think of a Common Unity or Concord, but upon the terms of necessary points, and of the primitive simplicity of doctrine, discipline and worship; and the forbearance of dissenters in tollerable differences.

IF I were to speak but once to the world whilest I lived, this should be my Theam: And yet (for ought that I can perceive by any visible effects) I never spake of any thing with less success. One party writeth copiously of the mischiefs which will follow *Tolleration*. And they say true, if they mean the tolleration of things *intollerable*: The other write as copiously of the necessity of *Tolleration* and *Liberty* of Conscience; And they say true, if they mean only the Tolleration of *things tollerable*. But neither of them saith true if they mean *universally*, and speak in any other sense: There is nothing more plain and sure, than that the tollerating *of all errours and faults* which conscience may be pretended for, or *of none at all*, are utterly destructive of Christian and humane peace and safety. He is scarce well in his wits that holdeth either part universally and unlimitedly: For the one would have no Government,

ment, and the other would have no subjects to be governed. Seeing therefore *bounds and lim. t* there must be, we may reckon them as the third sort of distracted persons, who think that the bounds are so undiscoverable, that the mention of them is in vain; and therefore either *All* or *None* must be tollerated according as Rulers are disposed, or their interest seemeth to require: And therefore they say, *What points le they that are necessary, and what unnecessary? What errours are tollerable, and what are intollerable? Can you name and number them? Or, who must be the judge?* To which I answer.

First, Let it be first supposed that *God hath given us a Law to judge by*, and then we shall quickly tell you who shall be the Judge (A question which the confused world doth further their confusion by, when they are a thousand times answered past all rational contradiction) *Judgement is private* or *publick:* The *judicium privatum discretionis*, which is but the guide of rational acts, belongeth to every private man (which none that is a man did ever yet deny) The *judicium publicum* is either *in foro civili*, determining in order to *corporal coaction*, and this belongeth only to the Magistrates; Or it is in *foro Ecclesiae* determining in order to *Church-communion* or *Excommunication*; and this belongeth only to the Church; (but under the coactive Government of the Magistrate: the Pastors being the *Governors*, and the people in part the executioners.) He that requireth more, understands not this.

Secondly, And what if there be a difficulty what points are necessary and what errours are
intollera-

intollerable ? Yet as long as it is certain that such a *difference there is*, and that accordingly men *must do*; doth it not rather concern both parties to search after it, and practise as far as they can discern, than to cast away Reason, because there is a difficulty in using it aright? Just thus the Papists do with us about the like notion of *fundamentals* or *essentials* of Christianity; They call to us for a just enumeration of the *fundamentals*, and because they find so much difficulty there as may find words and work for a perverse wrangler, they insult as if they might therefore take either *all things* or *nothing* to be *essentials*, and of necessity; As if Christianity had no constitutive essential parts, and so were nothing. And when they have all done they are forced themselves in their writings to distinguish the *fundamentals*, *essentials*, and *universally necessary* points from the rest [as *Davenport, Costerus, Bellarmine, Holden, &c.* do.) And doth it not then concern them as much as us to know which they be ? What if it be a hard thing to enumerate just how many bits a man may eat and not be a glutton? or how many drops a man may drink and be no drunkard? or just what meats and drinks must be used to avoid excess in quality ? or just what sort of stuffes or silks or cloth or fashions may be used without excess in apparel ? will you thence infer that men may eat and drink any thing in quantity and quality, or else *nothing*? or that he may wear *any thing*, or must go *naked*? What if you cannot justly enumerate what herbs or roots or drugs are wholsome and what are unwholsome? which

purge

purge too much and which too little? Must therefore *all* be used indifferently or *none*? If I am not able to enumerate just how many faults or weaknesses may be tollerable in my servants? Must I therefore have none, till I have those that are *faultless*? or else must I allow them to do *any thing* that they list? Though just at the *verge* of *evil*, even that which is *good* may be matter of doubt, yet God in *Nature* and *Scripture* hath given us sufficient light for an upright, safe and peaceable life.

Thirdly, And if ever Baptism had been well understood, by these objectors, the essentials of Christianity had been understood. Hath not Christ himself determined who they be that shall be *admitted into the Church* and numbered with Christians, in the very tenor of the Baptismal covenant? And did not the Church take the *Creed* to be sufficient for its proper use, which was to be the *matter* of the *Christian profession*, as to the Articles of faith to be believed? And yet are we now to seek in the end of the world, what *Christianity* is, and what are the essentials of our faith, and who is to be received as a professor of Christianity.

But this is a subject more largely to be handled if *Rulers* will permit it: And in the mean time because it is not the Magistrates but the Pastors that I am now speaking to, I shall pretermit the most which is to be said, and only acquaint you in the conclusion, that one of these following wayes must be chosen.

I. Either to tollerate *all men* to do what they will, which they will make a matter of conscience or religion; And then some, may offer their children

dren in sacrifice to the devil, and some may think they do God service in killing his servants; and some may think it their duty to perswade people that there is no God nor life to come, nor duty, nor sin; but all things are left to our own wills as lawless.

Secondly, Or else you must tollerate *no errour* or *fault* in religion; And then you must advise what *measure* of penalty you will inflict. If but a *little*, then you *tollerate* the errour still: For they that err will err still; and they that consciencioufly pray as *Daniel* did, *Dan. 6.* or forbear to obey the King as the three Confessours did. *Dan.* 3. will do *so still*, for all your penalty; And so there is *no cure* but a *tolleration* still.

But if you inflict upon them, banishment, or death, you must resolve that the King shall dwell alone, and have no subjects, and so be no King? nor have any *servant*, and so be no Masters; nor endure so much as a *wife*, and so be no husband; and if he have children must use them as K. *Philip* of *Spain* did his eldest son Prince *Charles*, and so be no Father. It can be no less than this at last.

Or if you will *imprison them*, every *subject* must be in prison, and then who shall be the Jaylor, and who shall find them food?

Thirdly, Or else you must deal *partially* and unjustly, and condemn *one* while you acquit *another*, for the same fault; or condemn one sort of errours, while you allow and tollerate *others as great*: As if all were to be punished who believe not *Christs descent into Hell*, while all are tollerated, who deny the rest of the Articles of the Creed.

Fourth-

What must be tollerated.

Fourthly, Or else you must make sure that all the Kings subjects shall be born under the same Planets, and of the same Parents, and have the same temperament and complexion, and the same teachers, and company, and all hear the same words, and all see the same objects, and all have the same callings, employments, interests, passions, temptations, advantages, and the same degree of natural capacity, and of grace: That so there may be no difference or defect in their apprehensions.

Fifthly, Or else you must distinguish and say, that *some are tollerable and shall be tollerated*, and *some errours are intollerable and shall not be tollerated* (in the *tongue* I mean; for you must tollerate them in the *mind* whether you will or not.) And then you will find a necessity of discerning as well as you can, the *tollerable* from the *intolleraule*.

And if so, for Christs sake and his Churches sake, and your own sake, bethink you whether Christ be not the King of his Church, and whether he hath given his Church no Laws for its *Constitution* and *Administration* ? By which we must try who are to be the members of himself and his Church, and to have Communion with himself and one another? and who are to be rejected and avoided? And whether the Holy Ghost is not the Author of the Church-establishment in the Scriptures? And whether we can expect more infallible deciders of such cases, than Christ, and his Spirit and Apostles ? And whether the Church be not the same thing now as then, and its *universal constitution* and *necessary administration* the same ? And whether the primitive Church

Church or ours be the purer and more exemplary? And whether it would do Kings and Kingdoms and the souls of men any dangerous hurt, to have all Christians hold their *Union* and *Communion* just on the same terms as they did under *Peter* and *Paul* and all the Apostles? Or at least whether it be worthy all the clamarous divisions in Christendome, and the blood of the many hundred thousands that have for conscience sake been shed, and the enduring of the outcries of the imprisoned and banished, and their prayers to heaven for deliverance from mens hands, and the leaving of such a name on record to posterity, as is usually left in History on the Authors of such sufferings; besides the present regret of mind, in the calamities of others, and the sad divisions and destruction of Charity, which cometh hereupon; I say whether it be worth the suffering of all this (and O how small a part is this) and all to keep our Churches from the primitive simplicity, and from the same way and communion which *Peter* and *Paul* and the Churches of their times, established and practised? Shall we speak so highly of Christ and his Apostles, and the sacred Scriptures, and yet think all this blood and misery, division and distraction, worthy to be endured, rather than our Union and Communion should be held on the terms which they did appoint and practise? or rather than such terms should be tolerated among us? I know what is said against all this; But this is no place to answer all that is said by such as cannot see how to answer themselves in so clear a case.

DIRECT.

DIRECT. XII.

Remember that the Pastoral Government is a work of LIGHT and LOVE; and what cannot be done by these is not at all to be done by you: And therefore you must make it your great study and employment, first to Know more than the people, and to Love them more than they Love you or one another; and then to convince them by unresistable evidence of truth, and to cause the warmth of your Love to be felt by them, in every word and act of your Ministration; As the Milk is warm by the natural heat of the Mother, and so is fitted for the nourishment of the Child.

AS the Gospel is the revelation of the Love of God, and it is a message of Love which we have to bring, and a work of Love which we cooperate to effect; so it is a spirit of Love which must be our principle, and it is an office and work of Love which we are called to; and the *manner* must be answerable to the work. *Faith* is the *Head*, and *Love* is the *Heart* of the new *Creature*: And as there is no *Light* in our office and work, if there be no *Faith* and evidence of *Truth*, so there is no *Life* in it, if there be no *Love*, God himself in the great work of our Redemption, and Christ in his Incarnation, life & suffering, hath taught

imitate his Lord in this: That as our office participateth subordinately of his office, both *Ruling*, *Teaching* and *Priestly*, so we may participate of that *Spirit of Love*, which was his *Principle* and must be *ours*. If it be not a work of *Love* which we do, it is not the work of a Minister of Christ, and Preacher of the Gospel. Can you well Preach so great *Love* of Christ to men without *Love*? if you shew not *Love* to them, you can never expect to win their *Love* to your selves. And when you overmuch desire to be loved your selves (as which of you doth not,) you pretend that it is to make your endeavours more successful, when you perswade them to the love of Christ. And doubtless a just Love to the person of the Preacher is a good advantage to this success. And in good sadness, can you believe that any thing is so likely to win Love as Love, or did experience ever teach you, that reproach, or contempt, or hurting men was the effectual way to make them Love you? This way hath been long tried by the Mountebanks in *Italy*, *Spain*, and many other Countries, but alas with what success? Indeed *solitudinem faciunt & pacem vocant*, as *Tertullian* saith; When they have killed those that they had first oppressed, they affrighted the rest to *say they loved them*, and *really* won the Love of their surviving blood-thirsty enemies: but that was all. If the new knack of Transfusion of blood cannot do this feat by letting in the blood of a Spaniel
who

him that beateth him) when you
 own, phlebotomy will never

hen that Sermon, that converse, that
discipline in which Love is not ap-
dominant, to be but a lifeless use
to the winning of a sinners heart to
ugh I deny not but when the case
appeareth desperate, the severity of
casting him off, may express more
ffection as to him: But that is being you must shew greater Love to
which must be saved from the infe-

you'l say, *They despise me, and in-*
How others and admire them, who de-
ll of them as I do.

st, we are most of us too partial to
 Judges of our own deserts. Sel-
ften maketh us think better of our
reaching, and our lives, than there
d it too often filleth men with envy
, whose greater worth and better la-
hem to be preferred by the hearers:
ally breeds detraction. I know that
persons heap up Teachers to them-
low seducers, & condemn the faith-
ts of the Lord. But I know withall,
usually a convincing power in the
able experienced Ministers, which
ound in the cold and formal discou-
ocrite. And that there is a suitable
true spiritual *experienced* Christians,
h them to relish this spiritual expe-

Dd   rimental

rimental preaching much more than the more adorned carkasses of formality: And seriousness is still acceptable to serious Christians: Yea even to common natural men, unless the malicious possess them by slanders with prejudice against it. Now if this should be the cause that others are preferred before you, O how heynous were your sin? As if it were not enough for you to *neglect* your duty, and to do the work of God deceitfully, and injure the souls of men in a cause of such importance, but you must also impenitently justifie such a crime, and also malign those that have more of the grace and gifts of God than you, and that do more to help to save mens souls!

Secondly, But suppose that your deserts be as great as you conceive, and their love to you as little; I would further ask you: First, is it for *their own* sake who thus hinder their own edification by it, that you are troubled at them? or is it for *your selves*, because you have not the respect which is your due. If it be the latter, I need not tell you what it is for Ministers of Christ thus to seek themselves, and overvalue their own esteem: If it be the *former*, 2 Why doth it not please you then that they are edified by *others*, though not by you. Do you think that it is not the *same Gospel* which others preach to them. And may not that Gospel edifie and save them by the Preaching of another as well as by yours. And if their dis-esteem of you, be a *sign* or *means*, that they are not edified by you, is not their great esteem of others who are as faithful, a *sign* and means that they are or may be edified by them.

Third-

Thirdly, And why are you not much more troubled at the state of all those who are not converted or edified by you, though they do not fight you or forsake you. How many be there that seem to love and honour you, and yet do not love and honour God? but despise Religion and their own Salvation? If it be for *their* sakes and not your *own* that you are offended, you will grieve most for them that are most ungodly, though they honour you never so much; and you will be *glad* for them that are *faithful* and *Godly*, whose Ministry soever it be that they most esteem.

Fourthly, But suppose them yet so foolish and faulty, as to run from you to their own perdition; The question is, *What is the way to cure them?* Is *Love* caused by hard words or stripes? Will you say to them, *Love me or you shall be fined or imprisoned?* Christ doth not teach you, to use such arguments when you speak for *him*, but to *beseech men in his name and stead to be reconciled to God*, 2 *Cor.* 5. 19, 20. But your *own work* will be done in your own way.

Obj. But Christ threatneth Hell to the impenitent, and Paul *pronounceth him Anathematized that loveth not the Lord Jesus: and he talketh to his hearers of coming with a rod.*

Answ. No doubt but the corrupted mind of man, hath need not *only of Love* to draw them home to God, and work the cure, but of *Threatnings* to *drive them* and to *help on* the cure! And though it be *Love* that causeth *Love*, which is their *Holiness*, yet *Fear* removeth many impediments: But still remember that it is *Love* which

Dd 2   is

is predominant, and *fear* is but subservient; And that the fear which is contrary to Love is a *vice*, and hindereth their salvation: And remember that *Fear* and *Love* towards God, will better stand together, than *Fear* and *Love to you* will: For men know Gods *Soveraignty* and *Justice*; and know that he is not to be questioned or resisted: But if they suffer by *you*, it will not be so digested, nor will it so consist with love. A patient will not bear to be whipt by his Physician to *force* him to take his medicines, though a child will bear it from his parents, whose Love and Power are more unquestionable to him. I desire you but to mark your *own experience*, and let *your Love* be *predominant* in all your ministrations, and use no *force* or *hurting* course which will really abate their Love to you, and then I shall leave you in the rest to your discretion. Secondly, Yet still we grant that *Christs* threatnings may be preached by you, and must be; Thirdly, And that the rod of discipline must be used: But this must be done only on the scandalous and such as more dishonour Christ than you: And it must be so done, that it may appear to be *Christs own work*, and done by you upon *his interest* and at *his command*, and not either arbitrarily or for your selves.

And I shall be bold with confidence to add that in those cases where violent *restraint* or *coaction* is necessary, the *Pastor* is the unmeetest person to meddle in it. It is the *Magistrates* work to *drive* and *force* (where it must be done) and the *Pastor* to perswade and draw. The flock of

Ch... ...ed by name of the Land of God, and his Ministers must *go before with him*, and attend him in the *conduct*; and the *Magistrate* must *come behind and drive*; and it is the *hindermost*, and not those *before* that must be *driven*. Pastors should be so far from calling out for the help of violence (unless it be to keep the peace) that they should rather shew their love and tenderness, by seeking as far as they may to mitigate it: And they should desire that no such ungrateful work be at all imposed upon them, as to seem the afflicters of their flocks: because when once they have lost their love, they have lost their opportunity and advantage of edifying them.

And it is not *Pilate*'s hypocritical washing of his hands that will excuse him: Nor the Romish Clergies disclaiming to meddle in a judgement of blood, which will reconcile the minds of sufferers to them, as long as they are Masters of the Inquisition, or deliver them up to the secular power, and excommunicate and depose the temporal Lords who will not do such execution as they require.

Though I have some where else mentioned it, I will again request the Reverend Pastors of the Church, to peruse the story of *Idacius* and *Martin* in *Sulpitius Severus*. The sum of it is this. *Priscillian* and many others (some Bishops and some Presbyters and some private persons) were zealous in Religion, but heretical (Gnosticks saith *Sulpitius*:) *Ithacius* and *Idacius* were two Orthodox Bishops who were very hot against these hereticks; Both of them men of rash and haughty spirits, and one of them at least (saith

Sulpitius) an injurious person that scarce cared what he said or did by others (see what persons a good cause may be defended by.) These Bishops drew in the Bishops of the neighboring Churches, & in their Synods first condemned the Priscillianists; and next provoked the Emperour against them. The Priscillianists found that if that were the way, an Emperours Court was not so Orthodox or constant, but there might be as good hopes for them: And therefore they got a powerful friend in Court to undertake their business, and got the better of the Bishops: The Bishops being born down for a time, at last *Maximus* was proclaimed Emperour, and came over with power and victory into *Germany* (such another as *Cromwel*, who by the Bishops was accounted a very Religious Christian, but usurped the Empire, and fought against and killed one of the Emperours, and pretended that the souldiers made him Emperour against his will.) This *Maximus* (whether sincerely or for his own advantage is unknown) did take part with the Orthodox and greatly honour the Bishops and promote Religion, and got a great deal of love and honour. *Ithacius* and *Idacius* & the rest of the Bishops apply themselves to *Maximus* against the *Priscillianists*; who hearkened to them, and to please them put *Priscillian* and some others to death, and punished others, by other ways of violence. The more rude ungodly sort of Christians, so far concurred or over-went the Bishops, that they turned their fury against any that seemed more Religious than their neighbours: so that if any one did but fast and pray more, and read the Scriptures more than others, he was reproached as a Heretick and favourer of the Priscillianists: *Martin* Bishop of *Turen* was at that time a man of no great Learning, but so famous for holiness, Charity, and numerous miracles, as the like is scarce written with credibility of any man since the Apostles (for which he is canonized a Saint.) This *Martin* was grieved, partly to hear strictness brought into reproach, and partly to see Magistrates called to the suppression of heresies by the Bishops; and so every heretick taught how to persecute and suppress the truth, who could but get the Emperour on his side: Therefore he petitioned the Emperour for mercy to the *Priscillianists*, and told him that it was a thing not used by Christians, to propagate sound doctrine or suppress mens errours by the sword: He also avoided the Synods of the Bishops, and refused not only their Councils, but their Communion: Whereupon the Bishops not only despise him as an unlearned man, and one that deceived the people with false miracles; but also suggested to the Emperour that he was a favourer of the hereticks himself: Insomuch that *Martin* hardly escaped suffering with them, through the Bishops calumnies. But the great piety and clemency of the Emperour preserved him; And at last did promise him the saving of the lives of some that were further appointed to suffer, on condition that he himself would communicate with the Bishops. *Martin* saw that there was no other means to save the life of one that else was presently to die, & thinking that Christ who would have mercy and not sacrifice, would in such a case al-

low

low it, he promised to have Communion with the Bishops, and so did communicate with them the next day and saved the mans life. When he had done it he was in great doubt and perplexity about it, whether he had done well or not ? and in this trouble went secretly out of the City homewards: And by the way in a Wood as he was in heaviness and doubt, an Angel appeared to him; and rebuked and chastened him, for communicating with them, and bid him take warning by this, lest the next time he hazarded his salvation it self by it. And *Martin* professed that long after this, the gift of miracles was denyed him; but he communicated with the Synod and Bishops no more.

This History I only recite without determining how far the Reader is to believe it: But I must say that the *reading* of it was a temptation to me, to doubt concerning my Communion, the *Reader* may easily know with whom. For though I know how credulous and fabulous many ancient Writers were, yet I considered, that this Historian is one of the most ancient, one of the most learned; one of the most strictly Religious of all the old *Historians* of the Church; and that he was himself an intimate acquaintance of *Martins*, and had it from his own mouth; and most solemnly protesteth or sweareth that he feigneth nothing, and that the miracles of *Martin* were known to him partly by his own sight, partly by *Martin's* own Relation, and partly by many credible witnesses: And they were so *believed* commonly in that age by good men, that it was the occasion of his Canonizing. And if such History is not to be believed, I will not mention the consequences that will hence follow.

And yet on the other side I considered: First, That it was possible that a holy man might be mistaken by fear and scrupulosity, and take that for an Angels apparition which was but a dream: Secondly, That his avoiding Communion with the B sh ops might be only a prudential act, fitted to that time and place, upon accidental or circumstantial reasons which will not suit with another time and place: Thirdly, It is dangerous making the actions of any men, upon pretense of any Revelations and Miracles, to be instead of Scripture, the rule of our faith or duty; much more to prefer them before the Scripture when there is a contrariety between them. Fourthly, And his separation was but temporary, not from the *Order*, nor from any of the *other Pastors*, or from the *people*; but only from *those individual persons*, whom he supposed to be scandalous. And these considerations I judge sufficient to resist that temptation.

Whoever understandeth what a *man* is, and what a *Christian* is, and what the office and work of a *Pastor* is, will make no doubt, but that his Guidance must be *paternal*, and that as *Love* is the *effect* to be produced in the people, so *Love* in him must be the *means* of causing it; & that he must expect that the success of his preaching & discipline should not exceed the measure of Love, which is manifested therein; further than as *God* may extraordinarily work beyond the aptitude of *the means* And when he hath complained of the people as sharply as he will, he shall find that *whatsoever is*

is

is that *Love cannot do, in order to their conversion and edification, and which Light or evidence cannot do in order to their conviction, is not by him to be done at all.* And if he will be trying with edge tools, he may cut his own fingers sooner than cure an erring mind; And shall find that the people will much worse endure acts of force and corporal penalty, from a Pastor, than from a Magistrate; and will hardly believe by any cloathing that he is a sheep, if they once perceive that he hath bloudy teeth. Our work is to win the *heart* to Christ: And he is unfit to be a Pastor, that knoweth not how hearts are to be won.

DIRECT. XIII.

When you have thought of all the evils that will be uncured, when Love and evidence have done their part; yet reject not this way till you have found out a better; which will do the work that is to be done, and that with fewer inconveniences.

I Am not now about to state the bounds of Liberty in matters of Religion; (It requireth a full Treatise by it self; and many tediously dispute the case before they ever truly stated it.) Much less am I perswading Magistrates, that they must permit every deceiver to do his worst, to draw the people from *God,* or from *Christ Jesus* the Mediator, from *faith* and *godliness,* any more than

than from *Loyalty*, *Peace* and *Honesty*. But I am speaking only against that partial, factious, needless, dividing and pernicious *violence*; which is pretended to be the *chief*, if not the *only* cure of all the errours or disagreements in the Churches, by those that know no part of Chyrurgery but amputation.

Some speak much of the many disorders which will be uncured, if *Violence* do no more than *Teaching* and *Love*: But I humbly ask of them: First, are those disorders such as *are curable* in this life; or such as are the *unavoidable* miseries of our corrupt and imperfect state? Secondly, will *force* cure them better than *evidence* of truth, and *Love* will do? Thirdly, will they be so cured without a greater mischief? God telleth the Sabbath-breakers of *Israel*, that when they were rooted out, the *land should keep her Sabbaths*: Was that a *mercy* or a *judgment*? Would you *so cure* Sabbath-breaking and disorder? and take a *solitude* for *Peace*? Fourthly, is not the work to be done, the saving of mens souls? And shall any be saved against his will? And then should not all force be meerly such as is subservient to the ends of Love? Fifthly? will stripes change the judgment in matters of Religion? Sixthly, is he any better than a Knave or an hypocrite, who will say or swear or do that through *fear*, which he verily thinketh God forbiddeth him, and is displeased for, and feareth it may damn his Soul? Seventhly, Is it the honour and felicity of souls to *be such*? or of Church or Kingdome to be composed of such? Eighthly, is not a conscientious fear of sinning against God, a thing
we'l

well pleasing to him, and necessary to mens salvation, and to the Churces welfare, and to the safety of the lives of Kings, and of the Kingdoms peace? And is there not then great cause to cherish it (though not the errours that abuse it.) And should not all care be used to cure the ungodly world of impiety and searedness of conscience, which makes them make a mock of sin. And if conscience were once debauched and mastered by fear, and the people be brought to prefer their fleshly interest before their spiritual and to fear mens punishment more than Gods, would not such debauched consciences have a great advantage, to make such men the masters of the estates and lives of others? And are the lives of Kings, and the estates of neighbours, and the peace of Kingdoms, competently secured, where God is not feared more than fines or corporal penalties? Ninthly, if force be so far followed till it have changed mens judgments or conquered conscience, or exterminated and destroyed all that will not be thus changed or conquered, who differ from superiors in unnecessary things, will it not (all things well considered) prove a dear *price* for that which might be had at much cheaper rates? Are not the most conscientious, necessary helpers of the Ministery, by their example, to cure the unconscionableness of the rest? And therefore should be countenanced & encourag'd? Tenthly, would not the cessation of unnecessary impositions, cast out the most of the scruples of conscientious people, and cease the saddest divisions of the Churches? If *Rome* could have been content with a religion of no more Articles than

the

he Apostles was, and would on those terms have held Communion with other Churches? O what rends and ruins had it prevented in the Christian world? Are not the old Apostolick rules and terms sufficient to the safety and peace of Christians? Were those worthy persons, B. *Usher*, B. *Hall*, B. *Davenant*, B *Morton*, with the *Bergii*, the *Crocii*, and all the great pacificators deceived, who wrote and preached and cryed out to the world that [*so much as all Christians are agreed in, is sufficient matter for their concord; if they would lay it upon no more*] vid. *Ush. serm.* before King *James* at *Wansted*. Or do you think it was their meaning [*Let all Rulers multiply unnecessary scrupled impositions in their own dominions, and for scrupling them, let them silence, imprison and banish at home; And then let them send to their Neighbour Churches for Unity, Peace and Concord, and tell them that the subscribing to the Scriptures generally, and to the Creed, Lords Prayer, and Decalogue and Sacraments particularly, are terms sufficient to this end.* (*Supposing that good order, decency, & peace be kept up by suitable discipline both Ecclesiastical and Civil.*) And why would not this serve for all the world? Or why should more scrupled things be called necessary to order and decency than indeed are so? My desire of the Churches peace which caused me to write all the rest, provoketh me to touch this subject briefly, which will scarce endure to be touched.

DIRECT.

DIRECT. XIV.

When you reprove those weak Christians, who are subject to errours, disorders or divisions, reflect not any disgrace or contempt upon Religion, and conscientious strictness; but be the more careful to proclaim the innocency and honour of serious Godliness, lest the prophane and ungodly take occasion to despise it, by your opening the faults of such as are taken for the zealous Professours of it.

Honest hearers take most notice, what is the *main scope* which the Preacher aimeth at, and the business which he driveth one. Some men take occasion by the errours and faults of such as have seemed seriously Religious, to make all *seriousness* and diligence for our salvation, to seem to the hearers to be meer hypocrisie, and not only a *needless* but a *hurtful* thing; and to perswade the people that an ignorant carelesness of their souls, with good neigbour-hood, quietness and mirth, is better than all this ado. Which is no more or less than to preach for Atheism and Ungodliness in practise, so it be veiled with the hypocritical profession of the Christian faith. And this unhappy sort of Preachers do seldme miss to fall upon the real and supposed miscarriages of men that are or seem Religious, in some part of their sermons and familiar discourse; which

being

being done to so odious an end, as to bring *serious Religiousness* it self into dislike, it maketh the best of the hearers abhor such reflections, because they abhor the *scope* of them; Believing that Holiness need not to be preached against in the world, till mens hearts are more enclined to it, and till all its enemies abate their opposition! And if it were to be done, yet not by a Minister of Christ: He that preacheth against Holiness (how covertly soever) preacheth against God. Whereas if a mans design be to *promote Religion*, the sober hearers (though partly guilty) will bear his reproof of the faults of professours, with much more patience, when they see it is for God and godliness that he doth it. I speak by experience, and must give them this testimony, that I have many and many a time poured out my soul in earnest reprehensions of the errours and disorders of rash *dividing* zeal; and the hearers have taken all with patience, when the same persons could not bear the tenth part so much, from some preachers whom they imagined to aim in it, at the depressing of the honour of true and serious Religion. Therefore be sure what sort of men soever you are reproving, that you say nothing which tendeth to make the ignorant or ungodly sort of your auditors think, that it is *zeal* or *strictness*, or careful diligence about their souls, which you condemn: But still put in sufficient caution for the necessity of a holy heart and life.

DIRECT.

DIRECT. XV.

Discourage not the Religious from so much of Religious exercises in their families, or with one another, as is meet for them in their private stations.

BY this means many Pastors have been very great causes of schisms and separations. Some of them are so carnal and selfish, that they make the Ministery but a trade for their benefice and honour: And therefore for fear lest the people should encroach upon their advantages, they drive them as far off as they can, and care not how ignorant they are so that thereby they may but lock up the mystery of their trade securely for themselves: and keep the people in a blindfold reverence, dependance and obedience: How ordinarily the Roman Clergy practise this iniquity, the nations that are kept in darkness by them, are doleful testimonies. Like the great Dog that will not endure the little one to come near his carrion or his bone. And some are so excessively fearful of schism, that they dare not endure the people to pray together, or repeat a sermon, or search the scripture, and exhort one another daily, in that manner which God requireth private men to do, for fear least they should go further, and grow proud of their own gifts and doings, and despise their Pastors, and set up for themselves! When as this very inordinate jealousie is the likely and the common

way

way to bring them, to the evil that is so much feared. While peoples care of their salvation is cherished and stirred up, and the Pastors do provoke them to pray and search the scriptures and help each other in the way to heaven, they are honoured & loved by the faithful of their flocks, as men that indeed are true to their great trust, and have a love and care for the peoples souls: And then those Pastors who further the people in such religious exercises, may usually as fathers rule them in it, and keep them from usurping any thing that is proper to the officers of Christ, and from errours, and factions and divisions; and may easily suppress any arrogancy when it appeareth. And that honest desire which religious persons have to do good to others, is thus satisfied by such sober exercises as belong to them: And so Pastor and people do peaceably, lovingly and successfully concur to carry on the work of Christ, whilest each one moveth in his proper place. I speak this, through the great mercy of God, from very great and long experience: having still kept up such lawful meetings and sober exercises as are not unfit for private Christians, and thereby kept out all heresies, factions, schisms and arrogancies from the flock; with the great increase of their knowledge, humility, piety, and just observance of their guides.

Whereas when the foresaid inordinate jealousie doth restrain people, or discourage them from any of that which is their proper work; First, they grow into distaste of such Pastors, and take them for enemies to godliness and to their souls:

Secondly, they grow next as jealous of all the Pastors doctrine, as he is of them; and think it no fault to draw off further from him themselves, and then to disaffect others to him: Thirdly, their appetite to Religious exercises, when it is restrained groweth inordinate, and affecteth that which belongeth not to them. Fourthly, they conceit that there is some necessity of their turning *teachers*, to do that which the Teachers will not do. Fifthly, they next keep their meetings *by themselves*, from under the eye and inspection of their Teachers. Sixthly, then they take liberty to vent what cometh in their minds, whilest there is none to regulate and contradict them. Seventhly, and at last they set up for themselves; and the chief speakers among them become Pastors to the rest, and so too often speak perverse things to draw away disciples after them. *Act.* 20.30.

Wisdome and Love may prevent all this: Envy not the gifts or graces of your people? Is it not the end of all your studies and labours to promote them? Are they not the fruits of Gods mercies and your own endeavours? Will you grudg at your own successes? In stead of restraining them, let none so earnestly drive them on, to such Religious exercises that belong to them, as your selves; and help them and oversee them in the performance; And then you shall have advantage to restrain them from that which belongeth not to them: And you shall have them the great assisters of your Ministery, who will more uphold your honours, than all the prophane and ignorant will do: yea they will be your glory,

ry, crown and joy at the appearing of Jesus Christ, 1 Thes. 2. 19, 20.

DIRECT. XVI.

Be not wanting in abilities, watchfulness, or diligence, to resist seducers by the evidence of truth; that there may be no need of other weapons: And quench such sparks among your people before they break out into flames.

THe clamours and wayes of violence used by many Pastors, are oft but an unhappy means to supply the defect of their own abilities and duties: And those who are conscious of an insufficiency in themselves to do their parts, do most intemperately call out to the Magistrates to help them, and do most unmannerly censure them, if they answer not their expectations: And indeed if the sword of the Magistrate be such an universal remedy, and may serve instead of the ability and labour of the Minister, let it also serve to cure the sick, instead of the skill and labour of the Physician; and let all other callings as needless be put down, and let us have none but Magistrates alone.

First, Some Ministers are so *ignorant*, that if one of their people do but turn Antinomian, Anabaptist or Separatist, they are *not able* to confute them: Much less if one that is *learned* and well-studied introduce these errours: If the

Sect.

Sectary challenge them to dispute, its two to one but errour will triumph, through the insufficiency of him that should defend the truth. And then this insufficient Minister, will turn to railing, or call out to the Magistrate for his help, to declare to all that he is too weak: which will harden and encrease the seduced party, and make them think that it is the *weakness* of his *cause*.

Secondly, And too many Ministers, who seem more able, are Lordly and lazy, and carry themselves strangely and at a distance from the people, and are seldome familiar with them in private: And so they give advantage to such seducers as creep into houses, to sow their tares; and for the weaker sort to vend their errours, when there is none to contradict them: These Pastors take their proper work, to which they are called, for a *slavery* or a *toil*. They are so *proud* and *idle*, that for them to watch over all the flock, and to teach them publickly and from house to house, night and day with tears as *Paul* did, and to watch where any spark appeareth, and presently to quench it, doth seem to them such a drudgery and burden, that God were unmerciful if he should impose it on them: That is, They think God unmerciful if he will not rather let the patient die, than put the Chyrurgeon to the trouble of dressing his sores: If he will not let the people be damned rather than put Ministers to so much labour to instruct and save them. If it were but to take their tythes and honour, and to be reverenced by the people, and to preach once or twice a week, a sermon which tendeth to their applause, they could submit to

this

this much: But *Paul's* exhortation *Act.* 20. seemeth intollerable preciseness. But souls will not be informed or reformed at so cheap a rate. Sin hath corrupted them more than so. If we will sleep, the envious man will not sleep: but when we awake, we shall find that he hath sowed his tares. Sometimes *grievous Wolves will enter, not sparing the flock*: and *sometimes of our own selves will men arise, speaking perverse things, to draw away disciples after them: Therefore watch.* Study hard and *meditate on those things, and give your selves wholly to them, that your profiting may be known to all:* that you may be able *to stop the mouths* of gain-sayers; and to edifie and establish all the flock; that they *be not as children tossed to and fro, and caried up and down by every wind of doctrine, by the cunning slight and subtilty of men, by which they lie in wait to deceive.* For to this end did Christ give offices and gifts: Study therefore to shew your selves workmen that need not be ashamed, rightly dividing, methodizing, opening, and so defending the word of truth, *Act.* 20. 20, 28, 29, 30. *Eph.* 3. 12, 14. 2 *Tim.* 4. 15, 16. 2 *Tim.* 2. 2, 15.

Ee 3   DIRECT.

DIRECT. XVII.

Be not strange to the poor ones of your flock: but impartial to all; and the servants of all, 3. mind not high things, but condescend to men of low estate. Rom. 12.16.

ALL souls are equally precious unto Christ; whether rich or poor. O set the strange example of Christs condescension still before your eyes. Was it the *high* or the *low* that were his *familiars*? Did he live in *fulness* and ride in *pomp*, and associate only with the *rich* and *great*? O see him washing his disciples feet? And hear him teaching them by that example, what they ought to do for one another. He came not to be ministred unto but to minister: How sharply did he rebuke his disciples when they *strove who should be greatest*? And setting a little child before them, hath taught us what must be our ambition: And that he *that will be the greatest must be servant of all*: Our greatness lieth in the greatest of our humility and usefulness: *Math.* 18. 1, 2, 3, 4. & 23. 11. *Luke* 22. 24, 25, 26. *Matth.* 20. 28.

It is lawful and meet that men in power should be honoured by us, and also that the people be taught to honour them: and that you keep such interest in them as is needful to the publick *good*: & therefore all converse with them is not *unlawfull*: But when Ministers *only attend* on the *rich*, and are *strange* and *seldom* among the poor, it makes them accounted carnal worldly men; and

Be not strange to the Poor.

is unsuitable to their Lords example, and to the work of their calling. The poor are far more numerous than the rich; and therefore our work is more among them. And death will quickly level all. And when we have all done, we shall find, that the poor receive the glad tidings of the Gospel; and the poor of the world may be rich in faith, and heirs of the Kingdome, which God hath prepared for them that love him. *Matth.* 11. 5. *Jam.* 2. 5, 6. And that the rich do hardly enter into the Kingdome of heaven. *Jam.* 2. 6, 7. *But ye have despised the poor: Do not the rich men oppress you, and draw you before the judgement seats?* It is the poor that must be the chief crown and comfort of your labors: Therefore be not strangers to them; if you would not have them account you lordly, worldly and self-seeking men: If you will leave them to themselves, and think your selves too good to be their companions, or to come into their smoaky Cottages, and then think that a lordly command or rebuke, should serve the turn to keep them from errour and schisme and disorder, you may find your errour to the Churches cost, when it is too late. And it will be but a pitiful excuse for your pride or laziness, to cry out of seducers for creeping into such houses, which you disdained to come into your selves: what do you by avoiding them, but invite any others thither that will come, and leave them as it were swept and garnished for such evil spirits.

Ee 4   DIRECT.

DIRECT. XVIII.

Spend and be spent for your peoples good; and do all the good that possibly you can for their bodies as well as for their souls: and think nothing that you have too dear to win them: that they may see that you are truly Fathers to them, and that their wel-fare is your chiefest care and business.

ALL men love themselves; and naturally and necessarily love those that they know do greatly love them. And all men are sensible of their bodily concernment, and consequently of that good that is done to their bodies: He that setteth himself to relieve the poor, and to put on others to relieve them, to visit the sick, and help those that are in trouble, and to comfort the afflicted, to do what good he can to all, and hurt to none, shall find that their ears will opened to his doctrine, and that they will follow him towards heaven with much less resistance, than otherwise he must expect. Few such Ministers do ever want success of their labours. And the covetous, close-handed, self-seeking and cruel, are always hated. And let his mony perish with him, who thinketh it better than the souls of men, and the work of God.

DIRECT. XIX.

Keep up the Reverence of the ancient and experienced sort of Christians, and teach the younger what honour they owe to those that are their elders in age and grace: For whilest the elder who are usually sober and peaceable, are duly reverenced, the heat of rash and giddy youth will be kept in order.

Usually where the elder bear the sway, the Church hath peace (Though I know some deceivers grow worse and worse:) And it is where the young and rash are become the predominant most esteemed party, that schism and disorders do prevail. And though some tell the people, what honour they owe their *Elders by office*; yet few acquaint them what honour youths owe both to the Elder in age and in experience and grace. It will therefore be much of the prudence of the Pastors, to keep up the honour of the Elders of the people, and to preserve in the younger a due esteem and reverence towards them.

DIRECT. XX.

The Pastors who will preserve the Churches Peace, must neither neglect to preserve their interest in the Religious persons of their charge; nor yet be so tender of it as to depart from sober principles or ways to please them, nor to make them their rulers, nor follow them into any exorbitancies to avoid their censures.

Both these extreams will tend to confusion. First, they that care not at all what men think of them, do but despise their advantages to do good, whilst they think that they only despise the praise or dispraise of men. We are commanded not to please our selves, but to please all men for their good to edification, Rom. 15. 1, 2, 3. Our power over them is upon their minds and wills, and not like Magistrates upon their bodies or estates: Therefore when we have lost their hearts, we have lost our power to do them good: They will not easily hear him that is despised or abhorred by them. Therefore a prudent care must be taken, that we be not prodigal of our interest in them, lest it prove to be cruelty to their souls.

Secondly, And yet if we give up our selves to their conceits and humours, and forsake the way of truth or peace to keep their favour, it will prove the more dangerous extream. I have before

fore noted the peril of Ministers and the Church by this temptation. The rawest and the rashest professours are commonly the most violent and censorious; And so ready to scorn and vilifie the gravest wisest Pastors, who cross their opinions, that many honest Ministers have been overcome by the temptation; to forsake their own judgements, and to comply with the violent to escape their censures and contempt: But this is not the way to the Churches peace. It may prove a palliate cure for a time, to put by at the present some sudden inconvenience: But it prepareth for after troubles and confusions. First, it will make the rashest and indiscreetest people (which is usually the women and young men) to be the Governours of the Church: Whilest all their Teachers must humour them lest they displease them. Secondly, When you have followed them a little way, and think there to stop, you must follow them still further, and never can foresee the end: For that weakness and passion of theirs which causeth up one errour to day, is pregnant with innumerable more; and may cry up more to morrow, and so on. And one errour commonly draweth on more, and one miscarriage engageth them to another: And the last are usually the worst: And the same ends and reasons which made you go out of the way to please them, will make you still follow them, how far soever they go, unless you repent. Thirdly, And if you repent and leave them, it must cost you dearer then prevention would have done: And you might have at much cheaper rates, forsaken them, just there where they forsook the way

way of truth and peace. Fourthly, And you will by following the conduct of giddiness and passion, disadvantage your Ministry as to all the less zealous, and all the more sober and peaceable of the godly; And you will bring your selves into contempt with these, for your levity injudiciousness and instability: And so you will lose much more than you will get. Fifthly, And in the mean time you will be made but the vulgars instrument to do hurt: you will be used by them but to confirm themselves in their errours, and to further dividing and unpeaceable designs. Sixthly, And when all is done, and your consciences are wounded, and you are made the heads or leaders of factions, at last those of themselves that God sheweth mercy to, will see their errour, and when they repent, they will give you little thanks for your compliance. A sinful humouring of rash professours, is as great a temptation to godly Ministers, as a sinful compliance with the Great ones of the world: I mean it is a sin, which our station and disposition afford us as great temptations to. For though to a worldling, wealth and honour be stronger temptations; yet to a godly man the applause or censure of those whom we account most wise and godly may tempt much stronglier. And alas how ordinarily doth the fire of Church and state, which flameth about our own ears, convince us of our errour, in following those whom we should lead! O how many doleful instances of it doth Church-history afford us! There are not many of the tumults that have cost the lives of thousands about Religion, but were kindled by the young

inju-

injudicious professours, who drew in their Teachers to humour them in countenancing too much of their disorders. Historians tell us that when King *Francis* of France had forbid the reproaching of the Papists way of worship, and silenced the Ministers for not obeying him; many of the hot-brain'd people, took up the way of provoking them by scornful pictures & *libels*; hanging up & down in the streets such ridiculous and reproachful rhimes and images: But this (which was none of the way of God) began that persecution (by provoking the King) which cost many thousands, if not hundred thousand lives before it ended. And the Synod at *Rochel* which refused the grave counsel of *Du Plessis*, *Du Moulin* and many such others, was stirred up by the peoples zeal; and ended in the blood of many score thousands, and the ruine of the power of the Protestants in *France*. Abundance of such sad instances might be given, if *England* need to go any were else for matter of warning than to it self. He that after the experiences of this age, will think it fit to follow the conduct of injudicious zealots, is left as unexcusable as almost any men, that never had a sight of hell. The dreadful ruine of *Jerusalem* according to Christs prediction (such as the world hath scarce seen besides) was just in the like manner brought about by those furious ones whom *Joseph* calleth the zealots.

But if you will do all things *good* and *lawful* to win men, & offend them by no *unnecessary thing*; and yet stand your ground, and stir not an inch from *truth* or *soberness*, *piety* or *peace*, to please any people in the world. This way shall do your

work

work at laſt: Men will at laſt perceive the worth of ſober principles and ways: At leaſt when Mountebanks have killed moſt of their patients, the reſt will repent, and wiſh that they had hearkened to the counſellers of peace. They that run round, when they find themſelves giddy and ready to fall, will lay hold upon ſomewhat which is firm and ſtable. Compliance with one of the contentious parties, may make you cried up by that party for a time: But the contrary faction will as much cry you down; and your eſtimation is but like an Almanack for a year: And they themſelves that needed your ſinful help for ſome preſent job, will be like enough ere long to caſt you off (as is aforeſaid:) And if they do not, you are objects of pity to ſober ſtanders by: And in the next age, the name of a *Melanchthon*, a *Bucer*, a *Bergius*, a *Crocius*, an *Uſher*, and other ſuch Peace-makers, will be precious to poſterity, when the memory of fiery dividers will be diſhonourable. Keep your ſtanding, and ſtick cloſer to truth and juſtice and peace, than to any party, and reſolvedly give up your ſelves to pleaſe God, and you will be no looſers by it; And its two to one but at laſt ſome of the contenders, will deſire you to be the arbitrators of their controverſies, when they are weary of contending, and will give you the honour of healing the wounds, which their raſh injudicious zeal hath made.

DIRECT.

DIRECT. XXI.

The Pastors who will preserve the peace of the people, must not contend among themselves: Especially they must take heed, that they engage not in any needless enmity, against any of those Divines, who for their learning or piety are most highly reverenced in the Church.

First, When Pastors fall into parties, they alwayes draw the people with them: some will take one part and some another. If the Officers divide, the souldiers will certainly be divided. And though one of the dividing parties may get the advantage of the sword, and suppress the other, they are neverthelefs in the way to increase the fchifm, while the people will think never the worse of the party which is afflicted and troden down. Schifmes are most commonly begun or at leaſt formed among the Paſtors: And among them the cure must be begun; and principally performed. And when the wound is made, it muſt not be despised; but the threatned iſſues muſt be foreseen; and the neceſſity of a cure apprehended: and scarce any pains or coſt muſt be thought too great to quench the fire. The proud and carnal person, who thinks all is well, if he can but secure his intereſt, and by spurning at diſſenters, make them ſeem contemptible; doth caſt oil upon the flames, and may
him-

himself feel the greatest near at last. And he that can stand by as unconcerned, and deny his service to Love and Peace, and to the wounded Church, lest it cost him too dear, may soon find that he hath lost, even that which he hath thought to save. O that the Peacemakers would cry aloud, and sound the retreat to contending Pastors, and O that God would rebuke that *pride* and *carnality*, self-conceitedness and love of worldly things, which will not suffer them to hear.

Secondly, And especially when those that are most reverenced and valued by the zealousest Christians, are envied, or afflicted by the rest, it ever tendeth to divisions in the Church. For the sufferings of such will never abate their esteem, with those who honour them. And if fear should stop their mouths for a time, the fire will still burn within, and be too ready to break out into more open schisms when opportunity serveth them. Yea the Churches of old have found great cause to be very tender how they used such reverenced valued Pastors, though they should fall into any errour; and sometimes to connive or bear with much, lest they should occasion a far worse disease, by the imprudent curing of a lesser.

And I dare be bold to proclaim to the contentious Pastors of all the Churches wheresoever, that *True Piety, Love, Humility* and *Prudence*, can happily heal a great many of dissentions, which to the carnal, uncharitable, proud and imprudent, seem uncurable, and by their malignant medicines are still exasperated and made worse.

But

But alas this quarrelsome distemper in Ministers, hath had such pernicious effects upon the Church, and is still going on to more confusion, that it deserveth and calleth for our common lamentation. And if we must lament it with despair, as an uncureable disease, I fear we must with equal despair lament the Churches ruines, and the consumption of Religion. For how can we expect that the people should hear, if the Pastors be obdurate and remediless? And who shall cure them, if their Physicians themselves be they that do infect them?

I speak not against the necessary defence of Truth, so be it that it be truth indeed which we defend, and that the *defence* be *indeed necessary*; and that the *manner* be suited to the *end*, and to the nature and rule of Christianity. But the itch which caused the Churches scab, is of a different description. For first, it proceedeth from a salt acrimonious humour in the blood: Not that there is no blood in our veins which hath better principles and qualities: But alas it is tainted with this corroding salt, which hath bred our leprosie: As if Christ had made us the salt of the earth, not to preserve the world from putrefaction, but to bite and fret all that we have any thing to do with (yea and those that we have nothing to do with) and by the salt Catarrhs of our back-bitings and peevish censures and reproaches, to bring the Church of Christ into a consumption. There is in many of us a love and zeal for Truth in the general (and no wonder if we are but men.) But when we meet it we know it not; but revile it, and scratch it by the face: As the Jews did long

F f   for

for the coming of the Messiah, but when he came, they knew him not, but crucified him as a deceiver and blasphemer; their prejudice fixing them in the dungeon of unbelief. *Mal.* 3.1,2,3. *The Lord whom ye seek shall suddenly come to his temple; even the messenger of the Covenant whom ye delight in—— But who may abide the day of his coming, and who shall stand when he appeareth. For he is like a refiners fire, and like fullers sope: and he shall sit as a refiner, and purifier of silver, and he shall purifie the sons of Levi——* What abundance of the zealous honourers of *Truth* are daily employed in reviling and contradicting it ? As they do by *Peace*, even prosecute it to the death, by the moſtperverſe oppoſitions, and unpeaceable principles and practiſes, while they cry up nothing more than Peace ? And do they deal any better by *Holineſs* it ſelf. He that is for a *Holineſs*, which conſiſteth not in *Love to God and man*, (to *God* for *himſelf* and to *Man for his ſake*) is like the Heathens who are zealous for a God; but he muſt be made of ſomething unlikeſt to him that is God indeed: Or like the Mahometans, who are zealous Muſſelmans or believers; but it is in the moſt groſs deceiver. And he that will promote *Love* by ſnarling and barking at all that are ſtrangers to him, and not of his own houſe, ſhall at laſt partake of the fruits of ſuch Love as he promoted: And he may as wiſely hope at laſt to bring the Church to *Peace* alſo, by worrying it, by ſplenetick cenſures & diviſions, in deſpight of the experience of our preſent age, and of all the world. What ever is done againſt LOVE is done againſt *Holineſs* and againſt God, and againſt the *Life* of the Church: And therefore if any Love-killer do call himself, a servant of Christ and a friend to *Holiness* or to the *Church*, he must first prove that *murdering* it is an act of *friendship*, and a service acceptable to Christ: One would think by their practise, that some men took *Abrahams trial* for their *Law*, and accounted it the *work* of *justifying faith*, to *kill the Church*, and offer it up in sacrifice to Christ: But before they bring us to believe that such a sacrifice is acceptable to him, who offered himself a sacrifice for the Church, and who calleth for a *living acceptable sacrifice, Rom.* 12. 1. They have need to make a better proof of their authority, than *Kelley* did of his Revelation, when he brought Doctor *Dee* to consent to adultery by the same pretended warrant: God who is Love accepteth not such a sacrifice at the hands of Love-killers and Church-destroyers.

But especially when besides this acrimony of mind, there shall other more pernicious diseases be contracted, & foment these *censures* & *reproaches* of their brethren; the malignity of the disease is a sad prognostick. Two such *causes* of it *Paul* layeth open, one *Act.* 20. 30. the other *Rom.* 16. 17, 18. One is the devillish sin of pride; & a desire to have many disciples to be our applauders [*They shall speak perverse things to draw away disciples after them.*] The other *selfishness, carnality and covetousness* [*They serve not the Lord Jesus, but their own bellies.*] And so 2 *Pet.* 2. 3. *through covetousness they shall with feign'd words make merchandise of you:* They buy and sell mens souls for gain: These are *gainsayers* in a double sense: Their *craft bringeth*

Ff2   *them in no small gain*, and lest it *should be set at nought*, for *gain* they do *gain say* the truth, and raise up tumults against the best of the servants of Christ; as *Act.* 19. 24, 27. It is for gain and worldly glory, that they *say* what they say against those that are *wiser* and *sincerer* than themselves.

The sum of all this (and most that followeth) is in 1 *Tim.* 6. 3, 4, 5. *If any man teach otherwise, and consent not to the wholesome words, the words of our Lord Jesus Christ* (mark, it is not to the words of any new *faith-makers* devising, *and to the doctrine which is according to Godliness, he is proud* (though he may cry down pride) *knowing nothing* (though he may cry down ignorance) *but doting about questions* (though he may seem to be wise and of high attainments) *and strifes of words* (while he seemeth to plead for the life of Religion) *whereof cometh envy, strife, railings, evil surmisings* (while they pretend to no less necessary a work, than the saving of Truth and the peoples souls:) *Perverse disputings of men of corrupt minds* (the impatient scratchings of those whose corrupt bloud must needs have vent, and therefore causeth this itch of quarrelling) *and destitute of the truth* (whilest they think they are saving the life of truth) *supposing that gain is godliness* (being so blinded by the love of gain that they make themselves believe, that is the cause of *truth* and *Godliness* which maketh for their gain; and that the raising of them, is the raising of the Church; and that all tendeth to the interest of Religion, which tendeth to make them great and rich). *From such turn away* (that is, own them not in hypocritical wranglings, but turn your backs

backs upon them, as men unworthy to be disputed within their way. Answer not the fool according to his folly, *i. e.* word it not with him in his foolish way; lest you make him think himself worthy to be disputed with. Talk not with him at his rates; And yet answer him according to his folly; by such conviction and rebukes as is meet for fools, and as may make him understand his folly, lest he be wise in his own eyes, and think that none can stand before him.

Secondly, And it is commonly the most *ignorant* sort of Ministers, who are the liberallest of their supercilious contempt of those, whose understandings and worth are above their censures. If a controversie be started, which they either never studied, or have only turned over the pages of a few books, to number the sheets, and never spent one year in the deep and serious search of the truth which is in question; Or if they have clumsie wits, that cannot feel so fine a thred, nor are capable of mastering the difficulties; None then are (usually) so ready to shoot their bolt, and pass a Magisterial sentence, and gravely and ignorantly tell the ignorant, what errours such or such a one maintaineth, as these that talk of that which they never understood. For as I have known many unlearned sorts, that had no artifice to keep up the reputation of their learning, than in all companies to cry down such and such (who were wiser than themselves) for no schollars, but unlearned men; so many that are or should be conscious of the dulness and ignorance of their fumbling and unfurnished brains, have no way to keep up the reputation of their wisdome with their simple followers, but to tell them, O such a one hath dangerous errours, and such a book is a dangerous book; and they hold this, and they hold that; and so to make odious the opinions or practises of others, which they understand not: And this doth their businefs with these silly souls, who hear not what can be said against them, as well as if they were the words of truth and sobernefs.

As for the younger and emptier sort of Ministers, it is no wonder, if they understand not that which they had never opportunity to study, or have taken but a superficial taste of: But it were to be wished that they were so humble as to confefs that they are yet but beardlefs; and that time and long study is needful to make them as wife as those (who with equal wit and grace) have had many more years of serious study, and greater opportunities to know the truth: and that they have not their wisdome by special inspiration or revelation; nor so far excel the rest of mankind in a miraculous wit, as to know that by a few years lazy study, which others know not by the laborious humble searches of a far longer time. One would think that a little humility might serve the turn for thus much.

But if ignorance get poffeffion of the ancient and gray-headed, it triumpheth then, and defieth little *David*, and faith, Give me a man that I may difpute with him? Or rather, Away with

derstand. Much time and study is necessary to great wisdome: But much *time* and *study* may consist with very mean attainments; and doth not alwayes reach the wisdome which is sought. And in such a case, the ancient and grey-headed think that veneration is their due; and that if they gravely sentence such or such to be erroneous, they are injured if they are not believed. They have not wisdome enough to make their age honourable; and therefore they expect that their age should make their wisdome honourable.

Thirdly, and because they are not able to endure the light, nor to stand before the power of open truth, they find it necessary to do almost all their work by *back biting*: When they are out of the hearing of those whom they back-bite, among such as are as little sensible of this hateful sin as they; then they have this man and that man, this party and that party to reproach.

Fourthly, And (as Mr. *Robert Bolton* well noteth) to hide the malignity of their sin, and to cheat the hearers and their own consciences) they will first seem to praise him, and to confess that he is in other respects a very worthy, a learned or a pious man, and then bring in their back-biting with a [but.] And that which must sanctifie all this sin, and turn it into a work of zeal, is the seeming interest of God, and of Religion. They do all out of a *zeal of God* (I cannot say, *A zeal for God*) though it be not according to knowledge. If it was an untruth which they spake it was for Religion: If they did *back-bite*, it was to preserve the hearers from errour and danger: If they reviled *that* which they never understood it was to keep the Church from the infection: If they tear the Church, and use their reputation to murder Love, and to make others odious who are wiser than they, all this is but for the defence of truth: And if it be non-sense or envy which they vent, they never repent of it (that's the mischief) because they think that the *Lord* and *the Church*, and *the hearers have need of it* And so all those Texts are to them *Apocripha*, which condemn their sin. *Psal.* 15. 3. 2 *Cor.* 12. 20. *Rom.* 1. 30. *Prov.* 25. 23. And sin is so befriended in mans corrupted nature, that they meet but with few *angry countenances to drive away* such reverend *back-biting tongues*.

Nay that they may abuse Gods word and name, against God, to the devils service, they arm themselves (as the Tempter did *Math.* 4.) with Gods authority and scripture, and will charge those with sin who would reprove their sin, and bring them to repentance: And as Master *Herbert* noteth, how the Pope under the reverend garb of Christs Vicar, doth do the like things to the suppressing of the Church and Truth, as Turks and Heathens do under the name of open enemies: so these men find that the names of *Ministers* and *Christians*, with the *words of God abused*, are among the well-meaning, a more effectual means to do that work which God abhorreth. I have long used to resist this sin of *back-biting*; and (not to justifie the faults of any, but) to convince the *back-biter* of his sin. And I seldome do it, but they report of me that I am a

defen-

defender of such and such corruptions: One back-biteth men as Prelatists and formalists; another the Presbyterians; another the Independents; and another the Anabaptists; and say *such a one is of such sect*, and ever with epithetes of reproach: And when I tell them that the way to do them good, is to convince them of their errour to their faces, and not to talk of them behind their backs, they report me presently to be a patron of the sect, because I was a reprover of their unchristian vice.

And many of them having not so far digested their Religion, as to see the evidences of it in themselves, are fain to take it upon trust from others: And they choose that party to cast this great trust upon, which they think to be most venerable. The Papist chooseth for number and worldly pomp and order: The carnal self-seeker chooseth the party, which may most further his preferment and honour in the world: The honester sectaries do choose the party, which seemeth to them to be the most *illuminated* or most *strict*: And some have the wit, to look most at those, that set as many of these together as may be hoped for. But among whomsoever they cast their lot, their way to preserve the reputation of Orthodoxness and the peace of that conscience which made the choice, is to be liberal in reproaching those that differ in any thing from the sect which they have chosen. (For how much of the Christian world is now in sects, is a thing which requireth more lamentation, than proof.) As the Dominicans when they have written far much more than *Calvin* about predetermination, they have

have no way to keep their honour with their sect (the Papists) but to rail at the Calvinists and belye them, and charge them with that which they abhor, that so they may seem sufficiently to differ from them.

But the greatest reason of this contentious back-biting quarrelling humour, is Ignorance it self; which will not give them leave so much as to see the *difficulty* of the points which they oppose; much less the truth of that which they have not been used to. The way which is *spoken against*, they think they may also boldly speak aginst.

2 And hypocrisie (though mixed with sincerity) hath too great a hand in this with many. The less men are *taken* up in that true religion which consisteth in Heaven-work and Heart-work, in the Love of God and man, and the mortification of their selfishness and pride; the more they are addicted to make it up with a contentious zeal for their several wayes, opinions and modes of worship, that they may not seem to be cold or natral in Religion. They never understood the third Chapter of *James*, nor many other such texts of scripture.

O that the Ministers of Christ were once sensible, not here only but through all the Christian world, what a plague the conjunction of their ignorance and contentiousness, and their dividing selfish zeal hath been to the Churches of Christ? And what they have done against the souls of men, by *violence*, and by *heading parties*, and by laying Heaven and Hell upon the opinions, which they never understood; and by departing from
the

thodoxness or *piety*, by the secret *back-bitings* and reproaches of others, whose persons perhaps they never saw; or whom they never once soberly discoursed with face to face; or whose writings perhaps they never read, or thought it not worth their time and labour to understand them; and yet take it to be their piety to revile by hear say and blind surmises, and judge in a cause which they never impartially heard and understood.

There is none of those Ministers of Christ whom you reproach, but is to be serviceable to his master for the saving of mens souls: And you are satans instruments to block up their way, and to turn away the hearts of people from their doctrine. If every Minister (especially your selves) who hath as great an errour, should be made odious for it to their hearers; you might all put up your pipes, and find that your artifice hath first silenced your selves, by the righteous law, — *Nec enim lex justior ulla est : Quam necis artifices arte perire sua.* Or in the words of Christ; *With what measure you mete, it shall be measured to you again.*

Did you see the ugliness of ignorant peevish contentious zeal, as contrary to holy *Light* and *Love*, you would think you saw a devil, spitting out fire and brimstone, and would never more take it for your honour, nor for a mark of a child of God.

And if you knew how every word of obloquy especially by *back-biting* against your brethren,
doth

doth tend to infect the hearers with the same vices and kill their Love, and lead them into divisions, you would take heed for the sake of others. (Unless you are of those who are foolisher than the devil, and would build Chrifts house and Kingdome by dividing it. *Math*. 12.) One raileth at *Luther*, and another at *Calvin*, and another at *Arminius*, and another at this man, and another at that; for matters which are above their reach; and the people are taught to rail at all; and to make it also their talk behind mens backs, to prate against this man and that man and the other; and in time to shew it, by breaking into sects: In a word such carnal courses of their Teachers; do make or harden carnal professors, to be one for *Paul*, and another for *Apollo*, and another for *Cephas*, but few sincerely and prudently for Christ: so that instead of Holiness, Love and Concord, we have in almost all company little but ignorant censorious wrangling, at the opinions of those that they never were acquainted with, or at the controverted practises, or circumstances of worship, which are not suitable to their prejudice and custome, and of which they never desired to be the impartial hearers of a just account.

If ever God will shew mercy to his Church, he will give them Pastors after his heart, who shall abound in *Light* and *Love*, and lead the people into Concord upon the ancient terms; and make it their work, to bring this Love-killing spirit into hatred; whether it work by the way of striving-disputes, or dividing principles or practises, or by reproaching others; by corporal

ral cruelty, or by a Religious censorious cruelty, which doth not *strike men*, but *unchurch* and *damn them*, and *separate* from them as men unfit for Christian communion. And whilest the Pastors take another course, we must patiently wait and pity the Church, and fore-see our further misery in this prognostick; though the guilty being puffed up with the conceits of their preciousness to God, do promise themselves the desires of their hearts.

Are not the sons of *Levi* yet refined? when they have been in so many furnaces and so long! When wisedom, holiness and humility are their nature, and selfish pride and worldliness are cured, this wrinkled malignant ENVY will then cease; and an honest emulation to excel one another in wisdom and Love and all good works, will then take place. And then we shall not like drunken men, one day fight and wound each other; and the next day cry out of our wounds; and yet go on in our drunken fits, to make them wider.

DIRECT.

DIRECT. XXII.

Lastly, Let all the *Ministers of Christ*, so deeply study their wonderful pattern of Love and tenderness, meekness and patience, and all those passages of holy Scripture, which still commend those vertues to his servants, till their souls are cast into this sacred mould, and habituated to this Image and imitation of their Lord: And then Vertue will go from them, and they will be healing among all where-ever they shall come; As fire goeth out from the flinty contenders by their collisions, which maketh them still incendiaries and consumers of the Churches Peace.

I Will therefore end these Directions with the bare repetitions of some more of those sacred words, (besides those fore-recited which may be fit to breed such a gracious habit, in those that will faithfully study and receive them.

Isa. 9. 6, 7. The government shall be laid upon his shoulder, and his name shall be called Wonderful, Counsellor, the mighty God, the everlasting father, the Prince of Peace: Of the increase of his Government and Peace there shall be no end.

Isa. 40. 11. He shall feed his flock like a
shep-

shepherd; he shall gather the lambs with his arm, and carry them in his bosome, and shall gently lead those that are with young.

Isa. 42. 1, 2, 3, 4. Behold my servant whom I uphold: mine elect in whom my soul delighteth: I have put my spirit upon him; he shall bring forth judgement to the Gentiles: He shall not cry, nor lift up, nor cause his voice to be heard in the street: A bruised reed shall he not break; and the smoaking flax shall he not quench, he shall bring forth judgment unto truth: He shall not fail nor be discouraged, till he have set judgement in the earth; and the isles shall wait for his law.

Isa. 44. 3, 4, 5. I will pour water upon him that is thirsty, and floods upon the dry ground: I will pour my spirit on thy seed and my blessing on thy off-spring: And they shall spring up among the grass, as willows by the water-courses: One shall say, I am the *Lords*, and another shall call himself by the name of *Jacob*: and another shall subscribe with his hand unto the Lord, and surname himself by the name of *Israel*.

Psal. 110. 2, 3. Rule thou in the midst of thine enemies: Thy people shall be willing in the day of thy power, in the beauties of holiness.

Ezek. 34. 2, 3, 4, 5. Wo to the shepherds of *Israel* that feed themselves; should not the shepherds feed the flocks? Ye eate the fat and cloath you with the wool, ye kill them that are fed, but ye feed not the flock: The diseased have ye not strengthened; neither have ye healed that which was sick; neither have ye bound up that which was boken; neither have ye brought again that which

which was driven away, neither have ye sought that which was lost; But with *Force* and with *Cruelty* have ye ruled them; and they were scattered because there is no shepherd — Read the rest of that Chapter.

Isa. 11. And there shall come forth a rod out of the stem of *Jesse*, and a branch shall grow out of his roots: And the spirit of the Lord shall rest upon him, the spirit of wisdome and understanding, the spirit of counsel and might, the spirit of knowledge, and of the fear of the Lord: and shall make him of quick understanding, in the fear of the Lord, and he shall not judge after the sight of his eyes, nor reprove after the hearing of his ears; but with righteousness shall he judge the poor, and reprove with equity for the meek of the earth: and he shall smite the earth with the rod of his mouth, and with the breath of his lips shall he slay the wicked — The wolf shall dwell with the lamb, and the leopard shall lie down with the kid: and the calf and the young lion and the fatling together; and a little child shall lead them: And the cow and the bear shall feed; their young ones shall lie down together: and the lion shall eat straw like the oxe; and the sucking child shall play on the hole of the asp, and the weaned child shall put his hand on the cockatrice den. They shall *not hurt, nor destroy* in all my holy mountain: for the earth shall be full of the knowledge of the Lord as the waters cover the sea. See also *cap.* 65. 25.

Isa. 2. 2, 3, 4, 5. And it shall come to pass in the last days, that the mountain of the Lords house shall be established in the top of the mountains,

tains, and shall be exalted above the hills, and all nations shall flow unto it: And many people shall go and say, Come ye and let us go up to the Mountain of the Lord, to the house of the God of *Jacob*, and he will teach us of his ways, and we will walk in his paths: For out *Zion* shall go forth the Law, and the word of the Lord from *Jerusalem*: And he shall judge among the nations, and shall rebuke many people: And they shall beat their swords into plow-shares, and their spears into pruning-hooks: Nation shall not lift up sword against nation, neither shall they learn wars any more. O house of *Jacob*, come ye and let us walk in the light of the Lord.

Mal. 2. 5, 6, 7 8, 9, 10. My covenant was with *(Levi)* of *life* and *peace*; and I gave them to him for the fear wherewith he feared me,—— The law of truth was in his mouth, and iniquity was not found in his lips: He walked with me in Peace and Equity; and did turn many from iniquity: For the Priests lips should keep knowledge: and they shall seek the Law at his mouth: for he is the Messenger of the Lord of hosts. But ye are departed out of the way: ye have caused many to stumble at the Law: ye have corrupted the Covenant of *Levi*;—Therefore have I also made you contemptible and base before all the people, according as ye have not kept my ways, but have been partial in the Law.

Zech. 9. 9. Behold thy King cometh unto thee: he is just, and having salvation; lowly and riding on an ass.—He shall speak peace to the heathen, and his dominion shall be from sea to sea——

Math. 11.29. Learn of me, for I am meek and lowly in heart; and ye shall find rest unto your souls.

Luke 4. 18. He hath anointed me to preach the Gospel to the poor, he hath sent me to heal the broken-hearted —43 I must preach the Kingdome of God to other Cities also, for therefore am I sent.

Mark 3. 20, 21. The multitude cometh together again, so that they could not so much as eat bread. And when his friends heard of it, they went out to lay hold on him; for they said, He is beside himself.

John 4. 32, 34. I have meat to eat that ye know not of—My meat is to do the will of him that sent me and to finish his work.

John 9. 4. I must work the works of him that sent me while it is day: the night cometh when no man can work.

Luk. 22. 24. And there was a strife among them, which of them should be accounted the greatest. *Math.* 20. 25, 26, 27. But Jesus called them him and said, ye know that the Princes of the Gentiles exercise dominion over them, and they that are great exercise authority upon them. But it shall not be so among you: but whosoever will be great among you let him be your Minister; and whosoever will be chief among you let him be your servant: Even as the son of man came not to be ministred to, but to minister and to give his life a ransome for many.

Job. 18. 36. My Kingdom is not of this world—Else would my servants fight.

Luke

Luke 12. 14. Who made me a judge or a divider over you?

1 *Pet.* 5. 2, 3, 4. Feed the flock of God which is among you, taking the oversight thereof; not by constraint but willingly; not for filthy lucre, but of a ready mind. Neither as being Lords over (or, Over-ruling) Gods heritage, but being ensamples to the flock: And when the chief shepheard shall appear, ye shall receive a crown of Glory.

2 *Cor.* 1. 24. Not for that we have dominion over your faith, but are helpers of your joy.

Math. 23. 8. Be not ye called Rabbi; for one is your Master Christ: and all ye are brethren.

1 *Cor.* 4. 1, 2. Let a man so account of us as of the Ministers of Christ, and Stewards of the mysteries of God.

2 *Cor.* 10. 8. & 13. 8, 10. For we can do nothing against the truth, but for the truth; according to the power, which the Lord hath given me to edification, and not to destruction.

Act. 20. 18, 19. Ye know after what manner I have been with you at all seasons: serving the Lord with all humility of mind, and with many tears,—20 And have taught you publickly and from house to house—In every City bonds and afflictions abide me; but none of these things move me, neither count I my life dear unto my self, that I might finish my course with joy; and the ministery which I have received of the Lord Jesus, to testifie to you the grace of God.———
29, 30, 31. Grievous wolves shall enter—And

of your own selves men shall arise, speaking perverse things to draw away disciples after them: Therefore watch, & remember that by the space of three years I ceased not to warn every one night and day with tears.

33, 34. I have coveted no mans silver or gold or apparel: yea your selves know that these hands have ministred to my necessities, and to them that were with me: I have shewed you all things, how that so labouring ye ought to support the weak——

2 *Cor.* 12. 5. Of my self I will not glory but in my infirmities. So 9, 10. I take pleasure in infirmities, in reproaches, in necessities, in persecutions, in distresses for Christs sake: for when I am weak, then am I strong.

2 *Tim.* 2. 23, 24, 25. But foolish and unlearned questions avoid, knowing that they do gender strifes: And the servant of the Lord must not strive but be gentle to all men; apt to teach, patient in meeknefs instructing those that oppose themselves, if God peradventure will give them repentance to the acknowledging of the truth.

1 *Tim.* 3. 2, 3. A Bishop must be blamelefs, apt to teach——no striker, nor greedy of filthy lucre, but patient——

Tit. 1. 7 8, 9, 10. A Bishop must be blamelefs as the Steward of God, not *self-willed* (or self-pleasing, or stiffe in his own conceit) not soon angry, not given to wine, no striker, not given to filthy lucre, but a lover of hospitality, a lover of good men, sober, just, holy, temperate, holding fast the faithful word, as he hath been taught, that he may be able by sound Doctrine, both

both to exhort and to convince the gainsayers, for there are many unruly and vain talkers and deceivers, whose mouths must be stopped—

2 Cor. 10. 3, 4, 5. For though we walk in the flesh, we do not war after the flesh: For the weapons of our warfare are not carnal but mighty through God, to the pulling down of strong holds, casting down imaginations, and every high thing that exalteth it self against the knowledge of God, and bringing into captivity every thought to the obedience of Christ.

Rom. 14. 1. Him that is weak in the faith receive ye, but not to doubtful disputations—Let not him that eateth despise him that eateth not; nor him that eateth not judge him that eateth: for God hath received him—To him that esteemeth any thing unclean, to him it is unclean. But if thy brother be grieved with thy meat, now walkest thou not charitably: destroy not him with thy meat for whom Christ died—For the kingdome of God is not meat and drink, but righteousness, and peace and joy in the Holy Ghost: For he that in these things serveth Christ, is acceptable to God, and approved of men. Let us therefore follow after the things which make for peace, and things wherewith one may edifie another—He that doubteth is damned if he eat—

Rom. 15. 1, 2, 3. We then that are strong ought to bear the infirmities of the weak, and not to please our selves. Let every one of us please his neighbour for his good to edification: For even Christ pleaseth not himself. Now the God of patience and consolation grant you to be like minded one towards another, according to Christ

Gg 3   Jesus,

Jesus, that ye may with one mind and one mouth glorifie God—Wherefore receive ye one another, as Christ received us to the glory of God.

Phil. 3. 15, 16. Let us as many as be perfect be thus minded, and if in any thing ye be otherwise minded, God shall reveal even this unto you. Nevertheless whereto we have already attained, let us walk by the same rule, let us mind the same things.

Eph. 4. 2, 3. With all lowliness and meekness, with long suffering forbearing one another in love: endeavouring to keep the unity of the Spirit in the bond of peace—15. Speaking the truth in love—16. Edifying in Love.

Phil. 2. 3. Let nothing be done through strife or vain-glory, but in lowliness of mind, let each esteem other better than themselves. Look not every man on his own things, but every man also on the things of others. Let this mind be in you which was in Jesus Christ—that made himself of no reputation—14. Do all things without murmurings and disputings.

Jam. 3. 17. The wisdom from above is first pure, then peaceable, gentle, easie to be intreated, full of mercy, &c.

1 *Thes.* 2. 5, 6, 7. Neither at any time used we flattering words, as ye know, nor a cloak of covetousness, God is witness: Nor of men sought we glory, neither of you nor yet of others, when we might have been burthensome (or used authority) as the Apostles of Christ: But we were gentle among you, even as a nurse cherisheth her children. So being affectionately desirous

rous of you, we were willing to have imparted to you, not the Gospel of God only, but also our own souls, because ye were dear unto us.

Gal. 5. 22. The fruit of the spirit is love, joy, peace, long-suffering, gentleness, goodness, faith, meekness—

2 *Cor.* 10. 1. I *Paul* beseech you by the meekness and gentleness of Christ—

Gal. 6. 1. Brethren if a man be overtaken in a a fault, ye that are spiritual restore such a one in the spirit of meekness—Bear ye one anothers burdens and so fulfil the law of Christ.

Col. 3. 12, 13. Put on as the elect of God, holy and beloved, bowels of mercy, kindness, humbleness of mind, meekness, long-suffering, forbearing one another, and forgiving one another, &c.

1 *Tim.* 6. 11. Follow after righteousness, godliness, faith, love, patience, meekness.

Tit. 3. 2. To speak evil of no man, to be no brawlers, but gentle, shewing all meekness to all men—

1 *Pet.* 3. 4. The ornament of a meek and quiet spirit, in the sight of God is of great price.

Lev. 19. 18. Thou shalt love thy neighbour as thy self.

Rom. 12. 9, 10. Be kindly affectioned one to another with brotherly love, in honour preferring one another.

Rom. 13. 10. Owe nothing to any man but Love—Love worketh no ill to his neighbour—Love is the fulfilling of the Law.

Joh. 13. 35. By this shall all men know that ye are my disciples, if ye have love to one another

John 13. 34. & 15. 12, 17. This is my commandement that ye love one another—As I have loved you—A new commandement—

Gal. 5. 14. The Law is fulfilled in this, Thou shalt love thy neighbour as thy self.

1 *Thess.* 4. 9. Ye are taught of God to love one another.

1 *Pet.* 1. 22. Love one another with a pure heart fervently.

1 *Pet.* 3. 8, 9. Be all of one minde; having compassion one on another; love as brethren; be pitiful be courteous: Not rendring evil for evil, or railing for railing; but contrariwise blessing, knowing that ye are thereunto called, that ye should inherit a blessing.

1 *Pet.* 2. 23. Who when he was reviled, reviled not again: when he suffered he threatned not.

Matth. 5. 44 45. Love your enemies; bless them that curse you, do good to them that hate you; and pray for them which despitefully use you and persecute you; that ye may be the children of your father, which is in heaven—For if ye love them that love you, what reward have you? do not even the publicans the same? And if ye salute your brethren only, what do ye more than others? do not even the publicans the same?

Math. 6. 14. For if ye forgive men their trespasses, your heavenly father will also forgive you. But if ye forgive not men their trespasses, neither will your father forgive your trespasses.

Math. 5. 39, 40, 41. I say unto you that ye resist not evil: but whosoever shall smite thee on thy right cheek, turn to him the other also:

And

And if any man will fue thee at Law, and take a-way thy coat, let him have thy cloak also—

1 *Thef.*5.12,13,14. We befeech you brethren to know them which *LABOUR AMONG YOU*, and are over you in the Lord, and admonifh you, and to efteem them very highly in love for *THEIR WORK SAKE*, and be at peace among your felves: Now we exhort you brethren warn them that are unruly, comfort the feeble minded, fupport the weak, be patient toward all men: fee that none render evil for evil to any man; but ever follow that which is good, both among your felves and to all men.

1 *Cor.*9.19. Though I be free from all men, yet have I made my felf fervant unto all, that I might gain the more. And unto the Jews I became as a Jew that I might gain the Jews: to them that are under the Law, as under the Law, that I might gain them that are under the Law: To them that are without law as without law (being not without law to God, but under the law to Chrift) that I might gain them that are without law: To the weak became I as weak, that I might gain the weak: I am made all things to all men, that I might by all means fave fome: and this I do for the Gofpels fake.

1 *Cor.*8.1. Knowledge puffeth up, but charity edifieth: and if any man think he knoweth any thing he knoweth nothing yet as he ought to know: but if any man love God, the fame is known of him, *v.*4. But take heed left by any means this liberty of yours becom a ftumbling block to thofe that are weak: 12. But when ye fin againft the brethren and wound their weak confcience, ye fi
againft

against Christ. 13. Wherefore if meat make my brother to offend, I will eat no flesh while the world standeth, lest I make my brother to offend.

Joh. 13. 3. Jesus knowing that the father had given all things into his hands, and that he was come from God and went to God, he riseth from supper and laid aside his garments, and took a towel and girded himself; After that he poureth water into a Bason, and began to wash the disciples feet, and to wipe them with the towel wherewith he was girded. 12, 13. So after he had wash'd their feet and had taken his garments, and was set down again, he said unto them, Know ye what I have done to you? Ye call me *Master* and *Lord*, and ye say well, for so I am: If I then your Lord and Master have washed your feet, ye also ought to wash one anothers feet:
"For I have given you an example, that ye should
"do as I have done to you. Verily, verily, I
"say unto you that the servant is not greater than
"his Lord, neither he that is sent greater than he
"that sent him. If ye know these things, happy
"are ye if ye do them.

Qu. *To what purpose do you set together all these words of Scripture, without any exposition, or telling us what you conclude from them.*

Answ. I purposely avoid glosses and collections, that you may not say that I obtrude any thing on you of my own, which is not the mind of your Lord himself. And I set them together that they that overlook them, may have a deeper apprehension than they have had. First, What is the true spirit of a Christian, and nature of Christianity?

stianity? Secondly, What is the office and work of the Ministery, and which way they are to win souls, and convince or silence gain-sayers and extirpate errours, and prevent or cure schisms, and secure the Churches peace? And as for them that can seriously persue all these words of the spirit of God, and yet can find in them no matter of correction or instruction without a Commentary and argumentation, I have no more to say to them at this time; but to add Christs next words *Joh.* 13. 18. *I speak not of you all! I know whom I have chosen.*] And I shall annex a few texts which characterize the contrary spirit; Contrary I say, to *CHRISTIANITY* and the faithful *MINISTERY*, and with them I shall conclude.

1 *Joh.* 3. 12, 13. Not as *Cain* who was of that *Wicked One*, and slew his brother. And wherefore slew he him? Because his own works were evil and his brothers righteous (*Heb.* 11. 4. By faith *Abel* offered to God a more excellent sacrifice than *Cain*) *v.* 13. Marvel not my brethren if the world hate you——Whosoever hateth his brother is a murderer: And ye know that no murderer hath eternal life abiding in him. (We ought to lay down our lives for the brethren.)

Joh. 8. 44. Ye are of your father the devil, and the lusts of your father ye will do: he was a murderer from the beginning——

1 *Sam.* 25. 25, 27. As his name is, so is he: *Nabal* is his name, and folly is with him——He is such a son of *Belial* that a man cannot speak to him.

Read the story of *Doeg*, 1 *Sam.* 22.

Read

Read also *Ezra* 4. 13, 14, 15, 17.

Esth. 3. 8. *Haman* said to the King—There is a certain people scattered abroad, and dispersed among the people, in all the Provinces of thy Kingdom; and their Laws are divers from all people, neither keep they the Kings laws: therefore it is not for the Kings profit to suffer them.

Dan. 3. 12. There are certain Jews—that O King have not regarded thee; they serve not thy Gods, nor worship the golden Image which thou hast set up—

Dan. 6. 5. We shall not find any occasion against this *Daniel*, except we find it against him concerning the Law of his God—7. All the Presidents of the Kingdom, the Governours and Princes, the Counsellors and Captains have consulted together to establish a royal statute, and to make a firm decree, that whosoever shall ask a petition of any God or man for 30 dayes, save of thee O King he shall be cast into the den of Lions, *v.* 11. These men assembled and found *Daniel* praying and making supplication before his God (which he did three times a day as aforetime)—13 They said, that *Daniel* that is of the captivity, regardeth not thee O King, nor the Decree that thou hast signed, but maketh his prayers three times a day—

Amos 7. 12, 13. *Amaziah* said to *Amos*, O thou Seer, go flee thee away into the Land of *Juda*, and there eat bread and prophesie there: But prophesie not again any more at Bethel: for it is the Kings Chappel, and it is the Kings Court.

Math. 23. 29, 30, 31. Wo unto you Scribes, Pharisees, Hypocrites, because ye build the tombs of the Prophets, & garnish the sepulchres
of

of the righteous, and say, If we had been in the dayes of our fathers, we would not have been partakers with them in the blood of the Prophets. Wherefore ye be witnesses to your selves that ye are the children of them which killed the Prophets, Fill ye up then the measure of your fathers—

*Joh.*11.48. If ye let him thus alone, all men will believe on him, and the Romans shall come and take away both our place and nation.

*Act.*4.1,2. And as they speak to the people, the Priests and the Captain of the Temple, and the Sadduces came upon them, being grieved that they taught the people—And they laid hands on them and put them in hold—*v.*17. That it spread no further among the people, let us straitly threaten them that they speak henceforth no more in this name. 18. And they called them and commanded them not to speak at all, nor teach in the name of Jesus.

*Gal.*4.29. But as then he that was born after the flesh, persecuted him that was born after the spirit, even so it is now—

3 *Joh.*9.10,11. I wrote to the Church, but *Diotrephes* who loveth to have the pre-eminence among them receiveth us not—and not content therewith neither doth he himself receive the Brethren, and forbiddeth them that would, and casteth them out of the Church. Beloved follow not that which is evil, but that which is good. He that *DOTH GOOD*, is of God ; but he that doth evil hath not seen God.

1 *Thes.*2.14,15. For ye also have suffered like things of your own Countrymen, even as they have

have of the Jews: who both killed the Lord Jesus and their own Prophets; and have persecuted us: and they please not God, and are contrary to all men; forbidding us to speak to the Gentiles that they might be saved; to fill up their sin alway: for the wrath is come upon them to the uttermost. ☞

Luke 9. 54, 55. Lord wilt thou that we command fire to come down from heaven, and consume them, even as *Elias* did? But he turned and rebuked them and said, ye know not what manner of spirit ye are of: for the son of man is not come to destroy mens lives, but to save them.

I conclude as I began: that the consciousness of our own ordinary and lamentable infirmities, and the greatness of the Churches sufferings thereby, in all fore-going ages, & in this, will condemn us of impudent self-ignorance, if Ministers be not compassionate and tender towards the weaknesses of the people, who cannot be expected to equal them in knowledge. Alas, brethren, what are we (even after so many years study & preparation) that we should be supercilious & cruel to the infirm! what difficulties puzzle us? what a loss are we at in our ordinary studies? How weakly do we preach and pray and write? How easily do we see this in one another, as our mutual censures & severities shew? Who troubled *Paul* and the first Churches, but erroneous Teachers? Who prated maliciously against *John*, and cast out the brethren, but a *Diotrephes*? Who brought in the errours of the *Millenaries*, the corporeity of Angels, the errours of the *Arians, Eunomians, Nestorians, Eutichians,*
Mace-

Macedonians, and almost all the rabble in *Epiphanius, Augustine* and *Philastrius,* but Bishops or Presbyters? Who have caused and kept open the wounds of the Churches of the East and West so long? Who introduced all the errours (about praying for & to the dead, *&c.*) that are in most of the Liturgies of the Churches in East and West? And all the errours that are found in so many Councils and Confessions of Churches; and in so many Volumes of Controversie as are extant? Who set up the *Roman* Usurpation and Tyranny? Who set up the Papal power above Princes; & determined in the *Laterane* Council for their power to depose them and alienate their dominions? Who set up Usurpers & raised wars against Emperours and Kings upon these grounds? Who brought in Transubstantion with the rest of the *Roman* absurdities? who have been the Masters of the bloody Inquisitions? And who hindereth the preaching of the pure doctrine of the Gospel in all the *Romanists* dominions? Is it not an erroneous Clergy?

You'l say, *Those are Papists and so are not we?*

Ans. No, God forbid we should! But they are a mistaken *Clergy*; which sheweth us that the *Clergy* are as liable to be dividers & troublers of the Church as the Laity are; and have done much more.

If any hence would infer, that the Pastors must be vilified or deprived of their just liberties and power, I would more largely tell such a one, that it is also the Clergy that have opposed all these Heresies and sins; and that have maintained obedience to Princes; and that have preserved the
Scrip-

Scriptures and the Christian faith; and that have been the salt and lights of the world, without whom Christianity never long continued in any nation; And that have been the chief instruments of bringing all the souls to Heaven that have passed thither from the militant Church. (But I have done this in two sheets for the Ministry long ago.) So that our faults consist with the honour of our function, and of our necessary labours, and with the praise of the more blameless.

And even so, though the peoples weakness, and inclinableness to unwarrantable separations and schisms, be blameworthy, as a fruit of their infirmity and injudiciousness: Yet must we remember that they are the Members of Christ, and we must not deny his interest in them: nor judge or use them hardlier than Christ himself hath done, or alloweth us to do: But study his Love and tenderness and forbearance, that we may follow him in serving him; and not follow our uncharitable passions, and call it, a serving of him; who liketh no such hurtful service. He that loveth Christ in none of his Infants or weaker members, but in the strong & more prudent sort alone doth love him in so few, that he may question whether he loveth him indeed at all; And whether ever he shall hear, *Inasmuch as ye did it to the least of these my brethren, ye did it unto me.*

April 14. 1668

The

The way of Division by Violence.	*The way of Peace by Love and Humility.*	*The way of Division by Separation.*
I.	**I.**	**I.**
Depart from the Apostolical primitive simplicity; and make things un-necessary, seem necessary in Doctrine, Worship, Discipline, and Conversation.	Adhere to the ancient simple Christianity and make nothing necessary to your Concord and Communion, which is not necessary.	Depart from the Apostolical Primitive Simplicity; on pretence of strict observing it; And make new Duties and new sins, which Scripture makes not such.
II.	**II.**	**II.**
Endure no man that is not of your mind and way; But force all to concord upon these terms of yours, what ever it cost.	Love your neighbors as your selves; Receive those that Christ receiveth, and that *hold the necessaries of Communion*; be they Episcopal, Presbyterian, Independants, Anabaptists, Arminians, Calvinists, &c. so they be not proved *Heretical or wicked.*	Account all those ungodly that use set prayers, or worship not God in the same manner as you do.

III.

By Violence.	*By Love.*	*By Separation.*

By Violence

III. Brand all Dissenters with the odious names of Schismaticks, Hereticks, or seditious Rebels; that they may become hateful to high and low.

IV. When this hath greatly increased their disaffection to you, accuse bless them that curse their *Religion* you, do good to them of all the expressions of that disaffection, to make it and persecute you odious also.

V. Take those for your enemies that are their friends, & not those

By Love

III. Speak evil of no man, and especially of Dignities & Rulers: Revile not when you are reviled: speak most of the good that is in Dissenters; and do them all the Good you can.

IV. If any wrong you, be the *more* watchful over your *passions*, & *opinions*, and *tongues*; left Passion carry you into extreams: and Love your enemies; them that hate you; and pray for them that despightfully use you. And do not evil, that good may come by it.

V. Impartially judge of men by Gods interest in them, and not your own or your parties.

By Separation

III. Brand all *Dissen-*ers with the odious names of *graceless*, &c: That you may make them all seem unlovely to others.

IV. When this hath stirr'd them up to wrath, call them *wicked persecutors*, and have no communion with them.

V. · Backbite and reproach all those as *Compliers* with sin, or such as strengthen the hands of · · the *wicked* and the *persecutors*, who would recal you to Love and Humility: And cherish all sects be

By Violence.	*By Love.*	*By Separation.*

| those for your friends which are their enemies: And cherish those be they never so bad, that wil be against them, and help you to root them out. | parties. Reprove the wayes of *Love-killers* and *Backbiters*, and let not the fear of their *Wrath* or *Censures* carry you into a compliance with them, or cause you by silence to encourage them: But rejoyce if you should be Martyrs for *Love* and *Peace*: For — | be they never so erroneous or Passionate that will take your part, and speak against them : But First, When the Wrath which you thus kindled hath consumed you ; Secondly, or your Divisions crumbled you all to dust : Thirdly, and your scandals hardened men to scorn Religion to their damnation ; remember, *Wo to the World because of offences*, and wo to him by whom offence cometh. |

But remember that for all this you must come to judgement.

And reade these following words of Mr. R. Hookers, which he useth of some part of the History, which out of *Sulpitius* I before mentioned ; *Ecclef. Pol. Epist. Ded.*

Blessed are the Meek, for they shall inherit the earth.

Blessed are the Peacemakers, for they shall be called the children of God.

Blessed are they which are persecuted for Righteousness sake; for theirs is the Kingdome of heaven.

Read *Act.* 20.30. 1 *Cor.* 1. 10, 13. & 3.3. *Rom.* 16. 17, 18. *Jam.* 3. 13, 14, 15, 16, 17. Study these on your knees.

"I deny not but that our Antagonists in these Controversies, may peradventure have met with some not unlike to *Ithacius*, who mightily bending himself by all means against the Heresie of *Priscillian*, (the hatred of which *one evil* was *all the vertue he had*) became so wise in the end, that every man careful of vertuous conversation, studious of the Scripture, and given to any abstinence in diet, was set down in his Kalender for suspected *Priscillianists:* "For whom it should be expedient to approve their soundness of faith, by a more licentious and loose behaviour. Such Proctors and Patrons the truth might spare. Yet is not their grosnesse so intollerable as on the contrary side, the scurrilous and more than satyrical immodesty of *Martinism*; The first published schedules whereof being brought to the hands of a grave and very honourable Knight, with signification given, that the Book would refresh his spirits, he took it, saw what the title was, read over an unsavoury sentence or two, and delivered back the Libel with this answer; *I am sorry you are of the mind to be solaced with these sports, and sorrier you have herein thought my affection like your own.*

www.ingramcontent.com/pod-product-compliance
Lightning Source LLC
Chambersburg PA
CBHW051844300426
44117CB00006B/258